LAST CALL FOR BUD LIGHT

The Fall and Future of America's Favorite Beer

ANSON FRERICKS

THRESHOLD EDITIONS

New York Amsterdam/Antwerp London Toronto Sydney New Delhi

Threshold Editions
An Imprint of Simon & Schuster, LLC
1230 Avenue of the Americas
New York, NY 10020

First Threshold Editions hardcover edition February 2025

THRESHOLD EDITIONS and colophon are trademarks
of Simon & Schuster, LLC

For information about special discounts for bulk purchases,
please contact Simon & Schuster Special Sales at 1-866-506-1949
or business@simonandschuster.com.

The Simon & Schuster Speakers Bureau can bring authors
to your live event. For more information or to book an event,
contact the Simon & Schuster Speakers Bureau at 1-866-248-3049
or visit our website at www.simonspeakers.com.

Interior design by Jaime Putorti

Manufactured in the United States of America

1   3   5   7   9   10   8   6   4   2

Library of Congress Cataloging-in-Publication Data has been applied for.

ISBN 978-1-6680-7090-1
ISBN 978-1-6680-7092-5 (ebook)

To everyone I've ever shared a Bud Light with—
especially my wife, who always keeps my beer half full—
and to those I will hopefully share one with in the future—
including my mom, who never cared much for beer—
I look forward to making more memories, telling more stories,
and having more laughs.
Here's to keeping the good times flowing,
and to always bringing out your best.

Contents

Prologue

The wait for the seven-floor elevator ride was taking longer than usual. Anheuser-Busch had recently moved its sales and marketing team from St. Louis to New York City, and more and more people were crammed into the glitzy new office. One of the elevators was broken, and a mob was waiting in the lobby. I decided to take the stairs.

I was on my way to meet Brendan Whitworth, the North American CEO of Anheuser-Busch. The meeting was critical. We had an opportunity for a partnership that could breathe new life into a company that had entered something of a midlife crisis. I'd crunched the numbers. The capital outlay would be negligible, but the profits could be immense. Anheuser-Busch, where I was President of U.S. Sales & Distribution, could make millions.

As I rounded the corner from the stairwell to Brendan's desk, the office décor suddenly struck me with new meaning. A turn-of-the-century advertisement hawking Anheuser-Busch's 10-cent Faust beers hung on an iron-textured wall. The rare visual indulgence among what was otherwise an efficient, modern, glass-walled space. Nearby, an oil painting of a bottle of Budweiser rested in an oversized gilded frame, just barely missing the exposed pipes in the ceiling above. It was the perfect juxtaposition of the old and new. The vintage and modern. Even the lighting was marked by contrast. Naked industrial Edison bulbs hung from the ceiling aside sculptures made from dangling Bud Light bottles that looked like they might have been enjoyed at a backyard barbecue the weekend before. The ways of the old guard and the new.

The company had gone through many big transitions. From generations of ownership by the famed Busch family to the takeover by the unstoppable global beer conglomerate InBev. From opulence and Clydesdales to efficiency and zero-based budgeting. From Saint Louis to New York. Somehow, all of it was captured on my way to Brendan's desk. This could be a turning point, too: Anheuser-Busch could go from a storied brewery whose brands were getting a little flat to something modern, something of-the-moment, something more.

The partnership wasn't without its risks, of course. The proposed partner was controversial—polarizing even—in some quarters. Some of our customers might be turned off. There might even be boycotts, though I thought the risk was extremely low.

But the upside was huge. It was an expansion opportunity, a chance to introduce ourselves to a new community. To make an impact, in a way that aligned with our mission to create a future with more cheers. We could start out small, see how it went, and hopefully grow our relationship over time. Our partner's existing fans would grow to become our fans, and vice versa. A partnership to expand our audience, to appeal to a younger, more contemporary crowd.

I made my pitch. The CEO wasn't convinced. Neither was Legal.

"Denied," Anheuser-Busch's Legal & External Affairs Chief, Cesar Vargas, decried. "The reputational risks are simply too high." Brendan didn't push back. The partnership was killed on the spot.

You might think I'm describing a conversation in which Bud Light decided not to pursue its ill-fated marketing partnership with transgender activist Dylan Mulvaney. But I'm not. I'm describing a very real conversation about a different partnership: a proposed distribution partnership with Black Rifle Coffee Company in 2022.

If you haven't heard, Black Rifle Coffee's mission is to serve coffee and culture to people who love America. For many customers, it's the American heartland alternative to Starbucks. Its founder, a former U.S. Army Green Beret, was fed up with the way that Starbucks seemingly caters to the coastal, latte-loving elites. How it pledges to hire refugees over American citizens and promotes progressive politics. Black Rifle would be different. It would be pro-veteran, pro–first responder, pro-America. Its name is a reference to the black training rifle issued to troops at boot camp. It hires veterans and military spouses. It hosts archery tournaments for disabled vets. For a time, the founder let one of his down-on-his-luck former military colleagues crash in a trailer on the office grounds. It is a brand for someone who wants a drink that respects freedom and the people who fight for it, that doesn't hold rural and blue-collar workers in contempt.

The company's coffee, by the way, is also quite good.

The combination of strong product and targeted marketing was proving explosive. In 2019, Black Rifle sold $82 million worth of coffee. By year end 2021, that figure had ballooned to $233 million. The company had opened a handful of brick-and-mortar coffee shops where baristas slung handcrafted drinks with colorful names like a "camo latte" with Irish cream and mint and what I presume must be a highly caffeinated beverage called only "jet fuel." But the real growth potential was in selling ready-to-drink cans and bagged coffee through retail channels. In certain markets, Black Rifle was already on the shelves at Walmart, Publix, 7-Eleven, Sam's Club, and more. But it wanted to expand.

That's where Anheuser-Busch could come in. Since the end of Prohibition, Anheuser-Busch has invested hundreds of millions of dollars building out a world-class distribution network. Hundreds of wholesalers already managed routes to deliver Budweiser, Bud Light, Busch, Michelob Ultra, Stella Artois, and other Anheuser-Busch brands to these very same grocers, convenience stores, and retail outlets. They also distributed non–Anheuser-Busch brands like energy drinks, waters, and teas.

It would be a match made in heaven: Anheuser-Busch could distribute Black Rifle Coffee's coffee cans on the same trucks that carried Bud Light. Black Rifle Coffee wouldn't have to set up its own logistics chain, and Anheuser-Busch could grow its revenue.

But in January 2022, Anheuser-Busch's top brass didn't see it that way. Black Rifle Coffee may have been beloved by veterans and the Fox News crowd, but what would the New York City illuminati think of Brendan when news of the partnership spread at cocktail hours and dinner parties? Of course, they didn't frame it that way. Instead, they invoked the mantra of "reputational risk" as though Anheuser-Busch's customers would suddenly revolt if they knew that the truck that carried their beer to the store had also carried Black Rifle Coffee.

If that proposition doesn't seem unlikely enough, consider for a moment the fact that Walmart, Publix, Sam's Club, 7-Eleven, Circle K, and many, many other retailers were *already selling* Black Rifle Coffee at their stores. No one cared. Literally no one. No one was protesting outside Walmart because a helicopter mom with toddlers in tow noticed that Black Rifle Coffee was selling bagged coffee called "silencer smooth"; peace-loving dads weren't avoiding Slurpees with their kids after softball practice because 7-Eleven also sold "vanilla bomb" coffee in a can. It was a nonissue. People understand that big companies—Walmart and 7-Eleven and, yes, even Anheuser-Busch—sell lots of different products under many different brands to many different customers.

But I was supposed to believe that our consumers were suddenly going to switch to Chardonnay (or, more realistically, Coors Light) if someone took to Instagram with a Change.org petition armed with photos of Black Rifle Coffee being unloaded from an Anheuser-Busch truck. Come on.

At that moment, I knew that the company where I had spent eleven years had changed. And not for the better. Anheuser-Busch's executives weren't evaluating a partnership that could reach new customers and increase shareholder value, they were concerned because Black Rifle Coffee didn't jive with *their personal* values and those held by their progressive stakeholders. They had lost touch with Anheuser-Busch's brand. With its mission. With its consumers. And *that's* what set the company up for a much bigger, much more public failure nearly a year later.

That's the one you've heard about: Where the world's largest beer brand, Bud Light, teamed up with a controversial transgender activist, Dylan Mulvaney, to celebrate Dylan's first 100 days of "girlhood," alienating customers everywhere and leading to the company's precipitous decline. Billions of dollars in shareholder value were erased. Overnight. All because the company's executives were blinded by their own biases and lost sight of Bud Light's historic branding of being "easy to drink, easy to enjoy."

That part you know. But there's so much more to tell. About a humble, nineteenth-century brewery with grand ambitions and charisma to spare. About an equally ambitious Brazilian trio, who did the unthinkable: mount a successful hostile takeover of the largest beer company in the world, using American shareholder capitalism as its spear. About the subsequent missteps of foreign executives trying to understand American consumers. About many companies, including Anheuser-Busch, adopting European Stakeholder Capitalism and its increasingly controversial tenants of Environmental, Social, and Governance (ESG) and Diversity, Equity, and Inclusion (DEI) as guiding principles. About a company getting lost in a culture war that was, and remains, bigger than even Anheuser-Busch itself. And about competing visions for the future. One that says corporate America should focus on delivering value to shareholders and consumers, the other that says companies should be judged by political activism on behalf of "stakeholders." And finally, about a possible redemption arc that both Anheuser-Busch and corporate America as a whole have the power to write, if only they're willing to pick up the pen.

This is that story.

CHAPTER 1

From Beer Fan to Beer Financier

I have been a fan of Anheuser-Busch almost as long as I can remember. One of my earliest memories of the company is from the 1989 Super Bowl, when I was five years old. My hometown Cincinnati Bengals played the San Francisco 49ers in Miami. This wasn't the only game being played that night, though. Anheuser-Busch's two largest brands, Bud and Bud Light, were also playing in the first-ever Bud Bowl.

The Bud Bowl was a breakthrough in Super Bowl advertising. It marked the first time that a company produced an ad for the Super Bowl, about the Super Bowl, that would not run after the Super Bowl. Five Bud Bowl commercials would run as a game within a game. It started with a pregame commercial, and then a Bud Bowl commercial would run each quarter. Bottles of Bud Light competed against bottles of Budweiser while "can fans" cheered from the crowd. It was one of the most expensive Super Bowl ads ever produced. In a predigital world, it cost $3 million to do the stop-motion shots. It cost an additional $3 million to buy the beer category advertising exclusivity that effectively shut out MillerCoors, Anheuser-Busch's largest rival, from any presence during the game.

And it was interactive. In the months leading up to the Super Bowl, every twelve-pack of Bud and Bud Light included an "unofficial" scorecard. Fans used this scoreboard to record the score of the

Bud Bowl at the end of each quarter and then mailed it in for a chance to win $100,000. Sales exploded.

My parents hosted a big Bengals Super Bowl party for our neighbors and friends. There was a ton of excitement. Bengals fans were hoping to see Ickey Woods do the Ickey Shuffle after touchdowns. Boomer Esiason was hoping to avenge the Bengals' 1984 Super Bowl loss to Joe Montana. I remember everyone eating Little Caesar's pizza and all of the adults drinking Bud and Bud Light. Although 100 percent of the people at our party were disappointed when the Bengals lost in the last twenty-six seconds of the game, 50 percent of the party was cheering when Team Budweiser kicked a field goal as time expired to win Bud Bowl 1.

The rest of the country was cheering for Bud and Bud Light as well. Budweiser was already the number-1 beer brand in the country. Miller Lite, introduced in 1975, was number 2, and Bud Light, introduced in 1982, was number 3. After a few more Bud Bowls, Bud Light passed Miller Lite in 1994 for the number-2 beer brand in America. Throughout the rest of the 1990s, Budweiser and Bud Light dominated pop culture. The Budweiser Frogs ad was introduced at the 1995 Super Bowl. Bud Light debuted its Real Men of Genius ads in 1998, and Budweiser closed out the decade with its famous "Wassup" ads in 1999.

Although I was not legally able to drink, I knew Budweiser and Bud Light were "cool." Knowing the latest commercials and catchphrases bought social currency at the lunch table. Since I couldn't legally buy beer, I bought the next-best thing—Bud & Bud Light neon signs, commemorative steins, and vintage team cans on eBay. I also asked my local grocery store for leftover displays. I decorated my room like a sports bar. In between posters of Ken Griffey Jr. and Michael Jordan, I had Bud and Bud Light neons, pin tackers, coasters, and NASCAR inflatables. On my bookshelves, I had Spuds MacKenzie glasses, Bud Light bottle openers, and Budweiser frog figurines. My parents, bless them, never objected (they probably assumed it was better than getting drunk).

By the end of high school, Anheuser-Busch became more than just a personal icon. It became a national icon. In 2002, during my senior year, Anheuser-Busch produced arguably their greatest Super Bowl commercial. With the country still reeling from the terror attacks of September 11th, Anheuser-Busch produced an ad showing Clydesdales galloping across America and ending up across from where the World Trade Center Towers once stood. The horses then honor the memory of those lost with a memorable and awe-inspiring bow. The ad aired only one time. That was all it needed to convince me that Anheuser-Busch was the epitome of America in a bottle. Brave. Resilient. Principled. Honorable. Reverent. Unafraid.

Bud Light became the number-1-selling beer in America that same year, right as I was heading to Yale.

In college, I brought a lot of my neon signs with me to decorate the house that I lived in with ten other guys. More signs were acquired from the local liquor store as we converted our living room into an actual sports bar, complete with a custom bar, multiple TVs, and beer on tap.

As a broke college kid, I mainly purchased Natural Light, Anheuser-Busch's value beer, when we had parties. Bud and Bud Light were "premium" beers and reserved for smaller gatherings where the budget didn't need to stretch as far. Their ad campaigns in the mid-2000s made it worth paying a few extra bucks for good times with good friends.

All eleven people in our house were college athletes. Budweiser was running a slew of ads featuring an athlete named Leon. Leon was a satire on spoiled and selfish athletes, but he spoke "truth." He was probably inspired by a mix of Alan Iverson's infamous "talkin' 'bout practice" rant and Randy Moss's statement to a reporter, when asked how he was going to pay a fine, that "When you're rich, you don't write checks," you pay with "straight cash, homie." Every team, even in college, tends to have a person with this personality, so all of the athletes in our house could relate. And a cold Bud was often the reward after a tough game.

At the same time, Bud Light was also running ads featuring everyman Ted Ferguson, Bud Light daredevil. Ted was famous for irreverent stunts that would reward him with a Bud Light. His feats included staying at work for two minutes past 5 p.m. on a Friday and "listening to his girlfriend." As college kids making our first forays into the working world with internships and navigating our first serious coed relationships, we could easily relate. It seemed like Bud Light was practically made for us. It was an easy call to say "make it a Bud Light" when we were at the bars. The brand tracked our college experience.

Upon graduation in 2006, I moved to Boston and took a job in finance at a private equity firm. This job gave me the ability to regularly purchase Bud and Bud Light. I shared a large, open loft apartment with two other guys. We had a kegerator that exclusively served Bud Light. We had the largest apartment of all of our Boston friends, so by default, we usually threw most of the parties. It was typical to go through multiple kegs in a weekend while hosting fifty of our closest friends and whoever else showed up.

I was living in that apartment when Bud Light sales peaked in 2008. That was the same year Bud Light won an Emmy for the first time with its "Swear Jar" ad. The ad shows what happens in an office when a swear jar is introduced and workers have to pay a cash fine to the jar each time they swear. Comedy and swear words immediately break out when workers are told a case of Bud Light will be bought with the proceeds from the jar. I have no doubt the financial firm where I worked would have played out exactly like the commercial: everyone would be swearing for Bud Light. This commercial was banned from the Super Bowl because it was too risqué. Instead, it became one of the first viral internet ads, racking up more than 12 million views in YouTube's infancy. Even when banned from the biggest advertising event of the year, Bud Light found a novel way to connect.

At the end of 2008, Anheuser-Busch's chapter as an American company came to an end. It was purchased in a hostile takeover by a smaller (but more aggressive) Belgium-based company called InBev. InBev was a roll-up of breweries in South America, Europe, and Canada and brands they owned like Stella Artois, Beck's, and Labatt. It was more financially disciplined than Anheuser-Busch and had more global ambitions. Anheuser-Busch shareholders were offered $70 per share, which was a 40 percent premium to the approximately $50 per share the company had traded at for the past five years. The $52 billion transaction was the largest all-cash deal in history at the time and created the world's largest brewery, which was renamed Anheuser-Busch InBev, or AB InBev for short.

In 2011, after finishing business school, I joined AB InBev. I witnessed the stock's ascent to its 2016 peak price of $135 per share, to its descent—sometimes slow, sometimes rapid—to its 2023 $50-per-share price. I witnessed the brand evolve as well, from one synonymous with Americana to one facing an identity crisis of its own making. Twelve years after I joined, in 2023, Bud Light would lose its title as the most popular beer in America. A failed marketing partnership with controversial transgender influencer Dylan Mulvaney was the immediate cause for the brand's abrupt decline.

I am writing this book to show that the decline of AB InBev and Bud Light is not as sudden as everyone thinks. Thousands of decisions and choices over fifteen years led to the ill-advised partnership with Mulvaney. Anheuser-Busch was not a perfect company when it was purchased by InBev, and it especially lacked financial discipline, but it knew how to build brand loyalty and inspire passionate customers.

InBev knew how to run businesses more efficiently, but lacked the ability to create new brands and connect with the consumer. In theory, the combination would build on the strengths of each. In reality, the InBev culture won and the brands ultimately lost.

I am also writing this book because I believe that a broken Anheuser-Busch is bad for the country. It can and should be rebuilt, and the lessons from its downfall applied across the business world. Historically, Anheuser-Busch brought folks together with Super Bowl ads, humor, and thousands of local sports sponsorships. They also donate millions of cans of drinking water to the Red Cross each year to aid in disaster relief and donate millions of dollars to Responsible Drinking initiatives.

They partner with more than five hundred predominantly family-owned distribution businesses to make these marketing and relief efforts happen. These family businesses have the right to distribute Anheuser-Busch products in their cities and are some of the most generous organizations in their communities. They have been hit hard by the sales decline at Anheuser-Busch because they do not have global divisions that can offset U.S. losses. They have had to lay off employees and cancel many of the traditional sponsorships and donations their communities depend on.

By addressing what went wrong, I hope to share lessons that can help AB InBev return to its throne as "The King of Beers." I hope these lessons inspire executives at other great American brands to focus their attention on their most important asset, the consumer. That will be good for the company, and it will be good for millions of fans like me who count on the company and its distribution partners to provide cold beer, good times, help when needed, and a "beer half full" outlook on life.

CHAPTER 2

The World's Largest Private Equity Firm That Happens to Sell Beer

I wasn't really supposed to work at Anheuser-Busch. Did I love drinking their beers with friends? Yes. Did I love slinging around phrases like "Wassup" from their Bud and Bud Light commercials? Of course. But I saw working at a beer company as totally different. I'd just worked my way through Harvard Business School (HBS), and didn't exactly consider beer a serious profession. It seemed more like working at Willy Wonka's Chocolate Factory. Substitute a chocolate river for beer fountains and Oompa-Loompas for Clydesdales and Dalmatians, and you have what most people imagine working at Anheuser-Busch is like. It sounds great in theory, and it's fun to discuss over a couple of beers, but once sobriety kicks in, other jobs tend to be more appealing. Besides, I never saw myself as a big corporate guy. I especially didn't view myself as a corporate Consumer Packaged Goods, or CPG, guy. Large CPG companies are slow-moving. They are hierarchical. They are boring. And they'd be especially boring when there aren't really beer fountains or Clydesdales and Dalmatians at the office.

I always saw myself as a finance guy. I traded my own stock portfolio as a teenager. I interned on Wall Street in college. After graduating in 2006, I worked in private equity during its peak years. In 2009,

I went to HBS to advance my career as a *master of the universe*—the popular term at the time for major figures on Wall Street. While there, I was on track to ascend to the highest levels of the financial world. In the summer of 2010, I interned in New York City for Citadel, the legendary firm founded by Ken Griffin. As of 2024, it is the most successful hedge fund of all time. It has gained more than $74 billion for investors since inception, topping even Ray Dalio's Bridgewater.

I was working on Citadel's Global Equities Long/Short Hedge Fund that summer. I was on the healthcare team, tasked with figuring out which orthopedic companies were going to sell more hip and knee replacements in the coming year. To do this, I had to figure out weather forecasts for the coming winter. More snow meant more people would fall and bust their hips and knees. Less snow meant less bodily damage. Then I had to figure out which companies were most likely to gain share of the replacement market with new innovations and techniques. It wasn't necessarily the most meaningful work, but the money was good.

One day that summer, a fellow HBS classmate invited me to a Thursday happy hour at Anheuser-Busch's Global Headquarters. The Global Headquarters was in Midtown Manhattan, three blocks from where I worked at Citadel. My friend was interning there for the summer, and Anheuser-Busch asked her to invite other NYC-based interns to learn more about the company. I didn't know much about Anheuser-Busch as I headed out. Of course, I knew about their beers, and the promise of free beer was the main reason I attended the event. I was also a massive fan of their Super Bowl commercials and sports team sponsorships, but I didn't know much else. I remembered that Anheuser-Busch was sold to a European competitor called InBev in 2008, but I didn't know who ran the company, what the culture was like, or what Anheuser-Busch InBev's (AB InBev) long-term goals entailed.

Upon arrival, I was pleasantly surprised to see an office that resembled the trading floors I was used to on Wall Street. AB InBev used an open-office concept, where executives sat in close proximity to their teams. No one had an office, not even the CEO. The one big difference was that Anheuser-Busch had a big bar, stocked with many of their beers, prominently carved into a section of the trading floor. It wasn't exactly Willy Wonka's Beer Factory, but it was an upgrade from most banks where I had worked.

A bunch of Anheuser-Busch executives attended the happy hour and used it as a recruiting opportunity. I struck up a conversation with Tony Milikin, AB's Global Chief Procurement Officer. Tony had recently been hired by the company to start a Global Procurement Organization in Belgium for tax-efficiency purposes. His organization worked closely with the finance department, and he was in charge of purchasing the billions of dollars' worth of barley, hops, aluminum, cardboard packaging, transportation, and other input and logistics materials that went into producing beer. Tony also played college baseball, and his son was one of the top-ranked lacrosse recruits in the country. I played college lacrosse, so we had a lot to discuss and we immediately hit it off over a few beers.

After talking about sports and my summer at Citadel, Tony asked me point-blank if I wanted to come work for him in Belgium. I promptly told him that I am not a corporate CPG guy. My brother worked at Procter & Gamble, and based on his experience, I knew that CPG salaries were average and bonuses were small (at least relative to finance). Plus it took forever to ascend to a senior level in the organization due to bureaucracy and hierarchy—two things I despise. Generally speaking, the only time my brother could get promoted was when his boss got promoted, and that could take years.

I explained to Tony that I was a finance guy. I was twenty-six years old and had already been involved in deals where hundreds of millions of dollars were on the line. Finance was the ultimate meritocratic industry. Finance folks worked long hours and delivered on insane time lines. It was eat what you kill. Get bonused and rewarded for the capital you put to work and the returns that you generate. Age and experience didn't matter. Results did.

Tony immediately disarmed my concerns. "Anheuser-Busch is the world's largest private equity firm that happens to sell beer," he said. I was intrigued, but not convinced. He then explained how a group of Brazilian investment bankers first consolidated the South American beer market and created a company called AmBev. They then bought a European beer maker known as InBev, which owned Stella Artois, Hoegaarden, and Leffe. From there, they purchased Anheuser-Busch in 2008 and renamed the company Anheuser-Busch InBev. These purchases created incredible shareholder value and made the Brazilian founders billionaires. They weren't done yet, though. Tony predicted that the company would shortly pay down the debt from the Anheuser-Busch transaction, and then they would go on to purchase Grupo Modelo (Mexican brewer of Corona and Modelo), SABMiller (South African Brewer of Castel), and eventually Coke or Pepsi. The goal was to create the world's largest CPG company. I thought Tony was drunk.

I especially thought he had one too many beers when he mentioned that executives at AB InBev were compensated like private equity (PE) professionals. I figured he had no idea how, or how much, private equity professionals made. Generally, private equity professionals make a salary, a bonus, and then they get "carry" in a fund. The "carry" in the fund is where most of the money is made. Most PE funds receive a "carry" of 20 percent of the fund's profits. For example, let's assume a PE firm raises $100 million from investors. The firm then invests that fund into a number of businesses over a five-year time period, and then has another five years to realize their investments. Let's assume that the fund makes a 2x return on its investments and is able to return a total of $200 million to investors (the $100 million initial investment plus the $100 million in gains). For their work, the PE firm will take 20 percent of the gains, or $20 million of the $100 million gain. That $20 million "carry" is then split among the partners of the firm. Incentives are aligned because the PE firm makes money only when it generates returns for investors.

Surprisingly, Tony explained that AB's model was similar, and in many cases, superior to this model. There was a salary, a bonus, a bonus-matching program (where an employee could reinvest a portion of their bonus into company stock and AB would match it 3:1), and option grants that functioned like "carry." It was not unheard of for top employees to receive annual option grants in the 7–8 figure range, even a few years out of business school. These option grants worked like "carry." They were granted at a specific stock price and they vested in five years. After five years, if AB generated shareholder value and the stock was above the "strike price," or the price at which the options were granted, they were known as "in the money." If they were below the strike price, they were worthless. For example, let's assume an executive received 10,000 options at a stock price of $100, or a $1 million option grant. If that stock doubled to $200 in five years, those 10,000 shares would be worth $1,000,000 (($200-$100)*10,000). If the stock declined to $99, they were worthless. Unlike carry in a fund, which generally occurs during the back half of the ten-year life span of the fund, new options would vest every year once I had been at the firm for five years.

All of this sounded great. I was definitely more interested in AB than when I arrived, but not convinced to leave the prestige of finance after a few beers with Tony. AB was still a massive global company, run by a bunch of Brazilians whom I hadn't met, and I was being asked to leave the U.S. and take a job in a country that I had never stepped foot in. I thanked Tony for his time and said that I would be happy to stay in touch. We exchanged contact information, and Tony mentioned that he would follow up.

I finished my summer internship at Citadel a few weeks later and returned to HBS for my second year. I was focused on returning to private equity after school. I enjoyed my summer at Citadel, but I found the hedge fund world to be too solitary and too disconnected from operating a business. Private equity investing was more team oriented, and I enjoyed working directly with company management to drive business strategy and results.

Within a few weeks of school starting, Tony Milikin reached back out. He said that he was going to be in Boston for a conference with AB's CEO, Carlos Brito. The two of them wanted to grab dinner with me. This seemed odd. Many CEOs stopped by Boston for conferences or to attend classes and events at HBS. But none had ever had dinner with me, nor did I know any of my classmates who received an opportunity like this.

The three of us went to dinner at a local pub near campus. Other companies recruiting at HBS often took students to fancy steak houses or high-end restaurants. This wasn't AB InBev's style. The pub had a variety of Anheuser-Busch beers on tap and burgers and wings on the menu. This fit with the low-key, blue-collar culture AB InBev executives liked to project. The first thing we started talking about was my disdain for large corporations, bureaucracy, and hierarchy. Brito couldn't agree more. He told me a story about a dinner party he attended a few years back when he was living in Belgium. The CEO of another large CPG company was also there. Brito and the other CEO started to compare company cultures. The other CEO spoke about formal rules and processes for promoting employees. Most employees got promoted after a prescribed period of time in a role and based on how long they had been at the company. This contrasted greatly with Brito's approach, which was to promote based on merit. AB was a meritocracy. It didn't matter how old you were, how long you had been at the company, or what you had done previously. What mattered was the results that you got in your current role and your capacity to dream big about future transformational opportunities. He gave me multiple examples of people at the organization who rose quickly, including himself. Brito was CEO of the company by the age of forty-five (and had just recently turned fifty). He dreamed of creating the world's largest and most admired CPG company by the time he retired. That was a cool dream. Much cooler than the hedge fund and PE folks who I spoke with who just dreamed about doing the next deal.

Brito's dream was ambitious. It made sense to me. Massive value, in the hundreds of billions of dollars, would be created if he could pull it off. Meritocracy made sense to me. The world's largest private equity firm that happened to sell beer also started making sense to me. Beer was tangible. Consumable. Everybody liked talking about it and had a good beer story to tell. Most of my best days and nights involved a cold beer. Private equity compensation also made sense to me. Having the CEO know my name was also a plus.

As I finished a Budweiser with Tony and Brito, they asked me again to join the company. They wanted me to join in a financial role that would help them realize their dream. Specifically, I would be in charge of using financial instruments to hedge the purchase of $5 billion in commodity spend. Every ingredient that goes into beer is a commodity—barley, hops, aluminum for the cans, paper for the packaging, and more. I would be responsible for the policy and purchasing of these commodities at budgeted prices. Eventually, I could move into other parts of the organization, like sales and marketing, and run large business units. They even threw in an expat offer to sweeten the deal, whereby they paid for all of my housing and vehicle expenses while living in Belgium.

I thanked them for the evening, but I told them that I had more work to do. I really wanted to learn more about the company and think through the opportunity. They left disappointed but offered to put me in contact with additional executives while I was thinking through their offer.

||||||||||||||

I also had to run the opportunity of moving to Belgium by my long-time girlfriend, Tori. She and I got engaged a week after my dinner with Brito and Tony. I figured the night you agree to spend the rest of your life with someone is as good a time as any to discuss where we wanted to live after both finishing our master's degrees the following spring. In retrospect, I could have asked my fiancée that evening if she wanted to live on the moon with me after graduation, and she probably would have said yes. That is not a reflection on me as a person, but the night you get engaged, anything seems possible and exciting.

After discussing the opportunity with my now fiancée that evening, Tori said, "What's the worst that could happen if you take this opportunity? We move to Europe. We basically have an extended honeymoon for a few years as we get to travel every weekend. If you don't like the job, we move back to the States and you take a finance job at a private equity firm or a hedge fund." That didn't sound like much downside.

Then she went on: "And what's the best that could happen? Instead of hating the job, you love it. You get to be part of building a cool company, launching great brands, and getting experience running large business units. And everything that these guys are telling you about the company being a meritocracy and rewarding people who get results with promotions and option packages comes true." That sounded like a pretty good risk-adjusted return opportunity.

I still needed to learn more about the history of AB InBev, though, and why Brito was so confident that he could create a company worth hundreds of billions of dollars by selling beer.

Chapter 3

"Making Friends Is Our Business": The Rise of Anheuser-Busch

The more I learned, the more I realized that my initial assumptions of Anheuser-Busch as the "Willy Wonka" of beer weren't accurate. Working at Anheuser-Busch, especially in the decades before the InBev acquisition, was WAY better than anything Willy Wonka could have ever imagined. It was the ultimate work hard, play hard corporate environment. Jets. Amusement parks. Celebrities. Sporting events. Exotic animals. Helicopters. All paid for by beer. Lots and lots of beer.

It wasn't always that way, of course. The company started out humbly enough. Anheuser-Busch traces its roots to the 1850s, when German soap maker Eberhard Anheuser became a part owner of a failing St. Louis brewery called the Bavarian. He may have been skilled at making soap, but his brewing skills were nonexistent. The beer was so bad, in fact, William Knoedelseder, a journalist and author of the book *Bitter Brew*, claims that patrons "would spit it back across the bar at bartenders."[1]*

Fortunately, he soon teamed up with Adolphus Busch, a young,

For readers interested in a more in-depth, and quite colorful, accounting of Anheuser-Busch's early years and enduring family drama, Knoedelseder's book Bitter Brew *is an entertaining read.*

recent immigrant to St. Louis from Germany. Busch—the second youngest of twenty-two children—spent his meager inheritance on a brewing supply business. He supplied ingredients to Anheuser and served a short stint in the Union Army during the Civil War. In 1861, Busch married Anheuser's daughter Lilly and went to work with his father-in-law. He bought half the company and, over time, changed the company's name, beer recipe, and history.

Today, we think of "locally brewed" beer as a modern thing, but in the 1870s, that's basically all there was. Beer spoils quickly, especially in heat. Transportation was lacking. None of it was refrigerated. People drank beer that was produced in their own communities.

Adolphus Busch sought to change that. He envisioned a beer with national appeal. And he made it happen. To do so, he traveled back to Europe, to learn new brewing techniques that had yet to reach the New World. He learned a new brewing method called Krausening, through which beer is fermented in cool, underground caves a second time, allowing for natural carbonation to occur. The result is a light, frothy beer. One beer caught his eye: a pilsner called Budweiser, named for a brewery in the town of Budweis. Upon his return to the States, Busch worked to replicate the recipe, using the highest quality ingredients they could source. Busch would later purchase the rights to the Budweiser trademark and marketed it as an upscale product, packaging bottles with foil-wrapped corks to evoke fine champagne.

Busch was a pioneer in other ways as well. Budweiser was the first beer to undergo pasteurization before bottling to lengthen its shelf life.[2] Busch also launched the industry's first refrigerated freight cars as well as a network of rail-side icehouses to keep beer cold during transport.

"He was vertically integrated before there was a name for it," Knoedelseder has explained. Anheuser-Busch owned the railcars that shipped the beer. And the company that built the railcars. And the company that made the wooden beer barrels. And the beer bottles. And even the coal company that powered the plant.

He also spearheaded Anheuser-Busch's long legacy of marketing genius. He introduced the company's logo. He sponsored beer give-aways in saloons. He saturated the media of the day with print advertising in magazines, playbills, and billboards. He created giveaways, including a pocketknife with a small hole that featured an image of Adolphus himself. In the 1880s he turned the Anheuser-Busch brewery into a tourist destination by offering tours to the public.

"Our business is not just making beer," Adolphus was fond of saying. "Making friends is our business."

But even then, Anheuser-Busch was a company prone to excess. Adolphus himself lived extravagantly. He owned several mansions, from California to St. Louis to New York, that housed his collection of furniture and fine art. He owned a personal railcar, the Adolphus, which chauffeured Busch and his family across the nation. A private spur line was built to transport the coach virtually to the doorstep of One Busch Place, the family's primary residence.

When it came to the brewery, he similarly spared no expense. According to one 1878 account, the brewery's offices were among "the finest and most tastefully appointed of any in the city" bearing "the characteristics of the president's office of a large bank." The floor was "tessellated marble, and the furniture is of the most exquisite workmanship, and elegantly veneered." Ornamented French plate glass and Axminister carpets adorned the room. Even the toilet rooms were remarkable, per the report.

Perhaps too remarkable, by some accounts. In Anheuser-Busch's early years, Busch was denied a loan from prominent French bankers in St. Louis, who believed that Busch's office "possessed a level of opulence out of keeping with his businesses' limited success" and so was deemed a poor risk for the financiers. But Busch was able to secure funding from others, and went on to grow the business exponentially.

By 1901, Anheuser-Busch surpassed the million-barrels-brewed mark—a virtually unimaginable amount of beer for the time. The Busch family was living large. In 1911, Adolphus threw a party with 13,000 guests to celebrate his fiftieth wedding anniversary and gave each of his nine kids a million dollars to build their dream homes, according to *Under the Influence: The Unauthorized Story of the Anheuser-Busch Dynasty* by Peter Hernon and Terry Ganey.[3]

And the brewery was just getting started. When Adolphus died at seventy-five in 1913, his eldest son, August A. Busch Sr., inherited the most popular beer brand in America. And it continued to grow.

Until Prohibition hit. The Busch family had seen the movement coming. For years it had been lobbying against the temperance movement. But it was still hit hard. To survive, it had to pivot to other products.

One was a beverage called "Bevo" that tasted almost identical to beer, but with a legal .5 percent alcohol content. Anheuser-Busch launched the nonintoxicating near beer in 1916, four years before Prohibition took effect nationwide. It was an immediate success, selling more than two million cases in the first six months. The company was so bullish on Bevo that it spent $10 million—about $280 million in today's dollars—to construct the world's biggest bottling plant, which opened in 1918.

But that success didn't last long. By the mid-1920s, sales cratered along with the rest of the near-beer market. "The company hadn't anticipated that people would be so willing to break the law to buy bootlegged beer," says Tracy Lauer, a former Anheuser-Busch archives director.[4]

But there were other opportunities. It was illegal to sell beer, but not its ingredients. So Anheuser-Busch began to sell Budweiser-brand barley malt syrup and yeast. They were labeled as baking ingredients, but no one was fooled. One supermarket display featured an apron-clad grocer knowingly winking at customers.

Anheuser-Busch was also more creative. Over the course of Prohibition—which lasted from 1920 to 1933, far longer than many predicted—the company branched out into twenty-five different product categories. It sold thirty-pound drums of frozen eggs and ice cream, to take advantage of its fleet of cold storage cars. It developed a recreational vehicle called the Lampsteed Kampkar. It even sold infant formula.

But beer was always at the heart of the company. It celebrated the day that Prohibition was repealed. More than twenty-five-thousand people gathered outside the brewery on the night of April 6, 1933. When the clock struck midnight, sirens and steam whistles sounded as fifty-five trucks carrying Budweiser burst through the wooden doors of the brewery for the first time in more than a decade.[5]

The following day, August Busch Jr. and Adolphus Busch III surprised their father with a gift. They told him they had purchased him a new car. When he went outside to inspect it, he was greeted by a horse-drawn beer wagon, with six Clydesdales hitched to the carriage, meant to evoke the nostalgia of an earlier, simpler time.

A second horse-drawn beer wagon was sent by rail to New York City, where it delivered beer to former governor Alfred E. Smith, an ardent fighter for Prohibition's repeal, before heading to Washington, D.C., to deliver Budweiser to President Franklin Delano Roosevelt at the White House. The pomp and circumstance surrounding the horse-drawn carriage proved hugely popular, as the Clydesdales drew crowds who gathered to watch their tour along the East Coast and celebrate repeal.[6]

Over time, the company changed hands in the way the British monarchy thrones kings: from August Busch Sr. to his eldest son

Adolphus III, to his brother August A. Busch Jr., nicknamed "Gussie,"
who took the helm after Adolphus III's death in 1946. Each ushered
in a new era of prosperity, but Gussie oversaw the true nationwide expansion of Anheuser-Busch. Under his reign, Anheuser-Busch went
from a single brewery outpost in St. Louis in 1933 to twelve breweries across the country in 1980.[7] He oversaw the company's first foray
into television advertising, spurring tremendous growth. And he expanded the business into amusement parks, including Busch Gardens
in Tampa Bay, Florida.

Gussie was also an avid fan of baseball, and purchased the St. Louis
Cardinals in 1953. Per an account by Sanford Wexler in the journal
Financial History,* Gussie was outraged that the Brooklyn Dodgers,
led by Jackie Robinson, were crushing the Cardinals, and asked the
team's management how many black players they had hired for the
team. When they answered none, Gussie screamed: "We sell beer to
everyone!" The following season, the St. Louis Cardinals had their first
black player, Tom Alston, to play first base.

"Gussie was the alpha Busch. He was unbridled in his appetites,"
Knoedelseder, the *Bitter Brew* author, said.[8] "A notorious Lothario, a
barroom brawler, a f—k-you kind of guy. When he took over the company, they were concerned: 'Holy Jesus, now we've got Gussie!' He was
vindictive. But he was also amazingly charismatic and wonderful good
fun, and probably the best beer salesman that ever lived. He ate life up
by giant spoonfuls."

The family's reputation gained notoriety during Gussie's reign.
"There is a history of family food fights," Knoedelseder reported. "At
the Ritz, during a food fight after the Cardinals had lost a baseball

---

* *The full article, which chronicles Anheuser-Busch's storied history through 2002, is well
worth reading in full, not only for his captivating retelling but also for the archived images
of Budweiser's early advertising.*

game, a lawyer standing next to Gussie said, 'I'm just wondering, Mr. Busch, what you do when you win.' Well, when they win, they take the fire extinguishers off the wall and blast people as they come off the elevator."

Their St. Louis castle was more alive than ever. Quite literally. The family lived on a 281-acre property outside of St. Louis known as Grant's Farm, as the property was once owned by Ulysses S. Grant. The family lived in a mansion known as "The Big House." In Gus's time, the property was populated with monkeys, llamas, grizzly bears, peacocks, and even a baby elephant. The glitterati also drank in the "The Big House's" hospitality. Frank Sinatra, Ed McMahon, and President Truman all visited the estate.

Gussie also led the company's annual sales convention—the most elaborate event of the year, bringing together executives, wholesalers, wives, and the marketing team for a multiday, celebrity-studded affair. The Carpenters performed. So did Tony Bennett. And Paul Newman. Anheuser-Busch sold more than one of every two beers consumed in America. It was printing money.[9]

But while revenue was up, profitability was down. In 1973, the company's profits had fallen by $11 million over the prior year, making competitor Schlitz the more profitable of the two. Cost-cutting was constantly discussed, but never taken seriously. For one, Gussie couldn't stomach the thought of making even a single change to the company's brewing process. "I could cut production costs by 50 percent, but where quality is concerned, the subject is verboten," longtime Anheuser-Busch consultant Russell Ackoff said. Even *Forbes* began to question the company's expenses, asking, "Will Gus Busch's pride yield to economics?" The answer appeared to be no.

Expenses were trimmed only at the margins. Gussie would now pay for his own helicopter; but the company would pay for his four cars and two private drivers. The company's executives would still keep their car privileges as well, but the company would try to transition to more fuel-efficient vehicles to save on gas.

Gussie's time at the helm came to an end in 1974, after the death of his daughter Christina in a car accident threw the family patriarch into despair. He drank heavily and began acting erratically. His son, August III, was forced to step in. The public story was that Gussie had voluntarily resigned; in truth, it was a coup. August III secretly worked with the board to oust his father from the company.

During August III's tenure, the family was often in the headlines for the controversies caused by the next generation—August IV—who earned a reputation as something of a playboy. But it wasn't all parties and good times. In 1983, nineteen-year-old August IV totaled his Corvette on a tight curve in Arizona, killing the passenger, twenty-two-year-old Michele Frederick. August IV had left the scene in a daze, and was later found in his bed, naked, blood caked on his face. By then, any alcohol had left his system. Without any physical evidence that he was drunk at the time of the crash, no charges were filed.

||||||||||||||||

Two years later, August IV again made headlines after he led police on a high-speed chase following a night out in St. Louis. He wasn't stopped until his Mercedes took a bullet to a tire.

In the corporate offices, the beer wars waged on. Miller had been bought by tobacco giant R.J. Reynolds in 1970, which quickly went to work out-advertising, out-competing, and out-suing Anheuser-Busch. Miller's introduction of Miller Lite in 1975 was another battleground. The move was initially dismissed by Anheuser-Busch leadership as a gimmick. "We think our beer is light enough," said vice president of brewing Andrew Steinhubl. August III himself predicted Miller Lite would flop.

But it was a resounding success. The brand avoided the "diet" angle and marketed directly to men as a "less filling" beer. Two years later, Miller Lite owned 10 percent of the entire beer market in the United States. Anheuser-Busch initially responded with Natural Lite and Michelob Light, but both were seen as late and desperate moves.[10]

Anheuser-Busch was beginning to realize that its old ways of doing business were no longer working. Its core customers were no longer primarily drinking beer at bars; they were now mostly bringing it home to drink while watching sporting events. Anheuser-Busch needed to go where its customers were. By the time it looked into it, its archenemies were already there: Other beer brands, including Miller, had already bought rights to the World Series, the Super Bowl, Monday Night Football, the NBA playoffs, and more.

So August III dug deeper. He instructed the company's almost one thousand wholesalers to list every sporting event in their market, and then tried to sponsor them. From Alabama football to Notre Dame basketball to hydroplane racing to hot-air ballooning, no event was too local or too obscure. "If there was a three-legged sack race being cheered on somewhere, then, by God, there had better be a Budweiser sign at the finish line," Knoedelseder writes. In parallel, the company waited for rights to major events to expire, and then outbid and outspent its competitors on nearly every sport.

Then, in 1982, seven years after the launch of Miller Light, August III finally relented and decided to lend the Budweiser name to a light beer. The team spent months tinkering with the recipe to ensure it would retain a full flavor profile, while reducing calories. Not too bitter, not too sweet. Lower the alcohol content, but not too much. When testing was complete, August insisted on personally flying to Los Angeles, where the new beer was brewed, to taste the first commercial pack that came off the line. The result was Bud Light.

It proved to be a turning point in the beer wars, with Miller never again presenting a serious threat to Anheuser-Busch's dominance.

To be sure, Bud Light did not rise to prominence based on taste alone. Marketing had a lot to do with it. From the beginning, the goal was to associate Bud Light with sports, music, and fun. "Bring out your best," its original slogan implored.

The latter half of the 1980s saw Spuds MacKenzie—the "original party animal"—debut as Bud Light's first spokesdog, surrounded by beautiful beach babes and glamour icons. Spuds was an immediate hit, appearing on the *Late Show with David Letterman*, giving interviews to Joan Rivers, and even hiring his own PR rep to squash rumors of his untimely death in an airline crash in Texas, or a limo accident in New York, or a hot tub incident in California.

In the 1980s and 1990s, Bud and Bud Light were synonymous with sports. There was no bigger beer than Budweiser, and no bigger stage than the Super Bowl. The Clydesdales first appeared in 1986 and made repeat performances throughout the 1990s.[11] The 1989 Super Bowl debuted the Bud Bowl, while 1995 brought the Budweiser Frogs—a trio soon parodied on *The Simpsons*, which showed the three "Bud," "Weis," and "Er" frogs devoured by an alligator screaming "Cooooooors."[12] Back then, Anheuser-Busch understood that being lampooned by *The Simpsons* was a far greater honor than earning a global marketing award in Cannes, France (though the frogs won that, too).

By the late 1990s, Bud Light had finally surpassed Miller Lite as the number-1 light beer in America. That gave Anheuser-Busch a lock on the number-1 and -2 spots. It appeared unstoppable.

Everywhere you looked, Anheuser-Busch was there. Bud Light was the official beer of the NFL, sure, but it also sponsored the Bud Light Professional Frisbee Team and the Professional Bowlers Association and aerobatic planes and team roping events. In the 1990s, Anheuser-Busch understood its customers, and developed those relationships by meeting and celebrating with customers wherever they were. Making friends, after all, was the company's business.[13]

Making friends was also a big part of August IV's life. He joined Anheuser-Busch after college and was working his way through the company ranks. His weekend parties at the company's lakefront compound in the Ozarks were legendary. The luxury compound boasted four homes, six boats, a tennis court, a dock with its own kitchen, and a helicopter landing pad—a big plus since it was just a forty-five-minute flight from company headquarters.

The property had been purchased by August III in 1982, but he had used it mainly as a high-end getaway for executive retreats. The strategy committee, and sometimes their wives, would be flown by company aircraft to the compound for several days to meet and relax. There were also Busch family gatherings, birthday parties, and the like. Close friends, major distributors, and even some Cardinals players could reserve the compound. But the soirees they held were nothing like the kinds of parties August IV threw.

During the day, August IV, then the vice president of marketing, would take his entourage of Anheuser-Busch colleagues out on the lake to "Party Cove," where, according to *The New York Times*, "boaters, drinkers and exhibitionists gather for weekends of sun-drenched, alcohol-fueled, sometimes X-rated revelry."[14] Sometimes more than a thousand boats would gather, tethering themselves to each other like a massive, floating frat party. At night, the group would hit the clubs, where beer and drugs and women could be enjoyed until the early hours of the morning. Then it was back to the compound for more. The compound's staff would dread learning that August IV was coming for the weekend, as they'd have to stay up and work late to clean up after the revelers eventually went to bed.

In 2002, August III retired at the age of sixty-five. But the family patriarch didn't feel August IV was ready to lead. He was still too immature, not yet ready to give up his partying ways. So in a break from company practice, the board appointed longtime Anheuser-Busch executive Patrick Stokes to lead the company.

August IV still had something to prove. For the next few years, he ran the U.S. beer division, which was by far the company's most important, while he tried to convince his father, and the board, that he should be the next CEO.

But he had trouble shaking his party-boy image. His father wanted him to settle down. So he tried. In 2001, forty-one-year-old August IV wed Kathryn Thatcher, a pretty, twenty-five-year-old blonde he had met at the company's VIP suite at a Cardinals game. Just before the nuptials, August IV sent a video message to Anheuser-Busch colleagues attending a conference in Vail: "Sorry I couldn't be with you, but I'm getting married. I've got a lot of wedding activities I have to attend to. Including a bachelor party—an event I've been preparing for all my life."[15]

The following year, Stokes retired and August IV was appointed CEO of Anheuser-Busch. In a lot of ways, the reascension of a Busch to the AB throne was historic. In 2002, there were no Vanderbilts who ran railroads or Carnegies making steel. But there were still Busches brewing beer. An American dynasty. A testament to the power of American capitalism and companies that stay true to their missions, their customers, and their brands.

But it was also a mistake. By all accounts, August IV was good-looking, well-humored, and cared deeply about Anheuser-Busch. The company was his life. But he found it difficult to walk in his father's shoes. He probably shouldn't have been asked to wear them at all.

His new perspective was nonetheless welcome at Anheuser-Busch, although his reign was ultimately cut short. He recognized the company's extravagances were a weakness and began cutting some of its most obscene costs. He canceled a $40 million order for a new company jet and closed the executive dining hall, where August III had eaten breakfast each morning. He also cut less glamorous programs, like slashing the budget for promoting Budweiser products on restaurant menus by 50 percent.

He understood that consumer tastes were changing. Craft beer was coming onto the scene. People were drinking more wine and liquor. He launched a few new products to try to exploit these market opportunities, but they were spectacular flops. August IV introduced a new product called Spykes, for instance, that were two-ounce airplane-sized bottles of sugary, neon-colored 12-percent-alcohol-by-volume malt beverages that came in flavors like mango, lime, melon, and hot chocolate. The bottles could be consumed as a shot, or added as a flavor enhancer to beer. No self-respecting Bud Light drinker, of course, was going to be caught dead pouring melted skittle juice into their beer bottle. But you know who might? Twelve-year-olds. The outrage was swift; the recall was swifter.

Anheuser-Busch was beginning to feel the pain. Per one *Business-Week* article, in 2005, the company's net income dropped 17.9 percent year over year, to $1.8 billion, its first loss in a decade. 2006 proved worse, with U.S. beer sale shares dropping from 55.5 percent in 2000 to just over 50 percent.

And in 2007, SABMiller and Molson Coors merged, further threatening Anheuser-Busch's dominance.

Meanwhile, August IV continued partying, later and later into the nights. There was an unspoken rule at the company not to schedule meetings before noon—at least not if you expected August IV to show up. August IV was losing control of a company he only ever had a tenuous grip on in the first place.

Yet despite these challenges, Anheuser-Busch still seemed invincible. The Busch family had always thought the company was simply too large to be a target for a takeover. It was the number-1 beer company in the U.S., the world's largest market. Its market capitalization was more than $20 billion. It could be a predator, sure, but not the prey.

And as the events of 2005 through 2007 came into sharper view, it was clear that the vultures were swarming the lumbering giant.

Chapter 4

The Birth of AB InBev

Just as you can't really understand Anheuser-Busch without understanding the Busch family, you can't understand InBev without understanding Jorge Paulo Lemann.

Jorge Paulo Lemann, "The World's Most Interesting Billionaire," Bloomberg once claimed. "Part Warren Buffet, part Sam Walton, part Roger Federer."[1]

The Brazilian was born in Rio de Janeiro in 1939 to a Swiss father and Brazilian mom. He was a tennis player. And a good one. It's what got him into Harvard, where he studied economics. He graduated in three years. Not because he was a genius—he once claimed his "grades were the worst possible"—but because, even then, he was ruthlessly efficient. He figured out that old exams were archived in the library, and that they changed little from year to year. If he crammed hard enough, he could shave a year off his degree and leave the cold Boston winters behind for good. So he did.

After graduating, he played in Wimbledon and twice in the Davis Cup. His dual citizenship allowed him to play once for Switzerland and once for Brazil. But he knew he would never be the best tennis player in the world. So he turned his attention to a career where he could dominate: finance.

He trained at Credit Suisse in Geneva and went to work in a few short-term roles. Then, in 1971, he founded Banco Garantia, which became one of Brazil's most elite investment banks, what *Forbes* called "a Brazilian version of Goldman Sachs."[2] It was there he first joined forces with two men who would become his longtime business partners: Marcel Hermann Telles and Carlos Alberto Sicupira, affectionately called "The Three Musketeers" in Brazil.

Banco Garanita was founded on extreme meritocracy. Lemann personally hired employees, seeking candidates who were "PSD": poor, smart, and deeply desiring to get rich. Seniority didn't matter. High-achieving newcomers could earn bonuses that far exceeded lagging old-timers'.

"Garantia was a place where the words *fanático* and *obsessivo* were considered compliments," per Bloomberg. "The first person to go home for the day often received ironic applause."[3]

In 1982, Sicupira led the group's takeover of Lojas Americanas, the fourth-largest Brazilian retail chain.[4] One of Lemann's business mantras immediately came to mind: "Innovations that create value are useful, but copying what works well is more practical." So he reached out to the CEOs of dozens of retailers, asking to meet and learn more about their businesses. One responded personally: Sam Walton, founder of Walmart.

Lemann and Sicupira flew out to Bentonville, Arkansas. They witnessed how Walmart was able to offer its everyday low prices by obsessively cutting costs at every turn.

The pair returned inspired. They decided to slash base salaries for Lojas Americanas executives, drop perks, and grant target-based stock incentives instead. Lojas Americanas executives did not take it well. They revolted at the idea of trading in their cushy jobs for high-risk, high-reward positions. They told Lemann and Sicupira as much. Then they went to lunch. When they returned, they found that Lemann and Sicupira had locked them out of the building. The executives now had no jobs at all. But the company thrived, going from $300 million in sales to $2.3 billion by 1995. According to the book *Dream Big* by Correa Cristiane, Sicupira soon had a favorite phrase of his own: "Costs are like fingernails: You have to cut them constantly."

The 1980s also saw the Three Musketeers first dip their toe into the beer business, acquiring Brazil's largest brewery, Cervejaria Brahma, in 1989.[5] That, too, proved prescient. The Brazilian beer market was the fastest growing in the world in the 1990s, enjoying 15 percent year-over-year growth.

That kind of growth draws attention. Including from the King of Beers. Back in America, August III was interested in expanding the Anheuser-Busch empire globally, but only at the right price. He was cautious in his acquisitions. In retrospect, probably overly so. But in 1995, August III hosted Lemann and Telles at Busch Gardens in Williamsburg, Virginia, guiding them on a personal tour. Nothing came of the meeting, though, as the price Lemann sought was more than Anheuser-Busch was willing to pay.

Instead, AB bought a 10 percent stake in Brazil's number-2 brewery, Antarctica, and a 51 percent stake in a new joint venture with Antarctica to distribute Budweiser in Brazil.[6]

A few years later, Lemann and Busch met again. But this time, the tables had turned. Lemann had an ambitious proposal—merge Brahma, Antarctica, and Anheuser-Busch into a single company. It would be the Coca-Cola of beer, Lemann professed. For August III, it was a laughable proposition. Anheuser-Busch was an American company. Not a Brazilian one. And an American one it would remain.

But Lemann refused to let his global appetite go unsated. He fired his first shot in what would become a decades-long beer war. He bought Antarctica outright—a move Anheuser-Busch likely could have joined if it so chose, given that its joint venture contract gave it the option to purchase up to 30 percent of Antarctica's shares and appoint a member to its board. But again, the price was just too high. The newly merged company was "Ambev." It proved to be just the beginning of the buying spree.

In 2004, Ambev gobbled up Belgian-based Interbrew to form InBev. Interbrew owned predominantly European beer brands like Stella Artois, Beck's, Bass, and Hoegaarden. They also owned Labatt, which was one of the largest brands in Canada. The new board would have four Brazilians from Ambev, four Belgians from Interbrew, and six independent members, making the newly formed Ambev a truly Belgian-Brazilian company.[7] And from there, the company went on a tear. As *Bitter Brew* author Knoedelseder describes, "InBev was not so much a brewer as it was an investment portfolio of beer brands—more than two hundred of them—that its owners had amassed by gulping down six-hundred-year-old European breweries for breakfast."

The playbook was the same: Use debt to buy a company, slash costs to get the debt ratio down, take out more debt to purchase the next acquisition. It was a variation on the standard private equity playbook, as InBev wasn't interested in quickly gutting or flipping companies for a profit; it tended to hold on to them for the long term.

Soon, it sets its sights on the ultimate brass ring: Anheuser-Busch. For decades, Anheuser-Busch considered itself immune from a takeover. It was too big, too expensive to buy. And its storied history acted as a protective shield. What was Anheuser-Busch without the Busch family? Without St. Louis? Or One Busch Place?

InBev started its pursuit with just a toehold: It negotiated a deal with the newly appointed CEO, August IV, to have Anheuser-Busch distribute InBev's most popular European brands—Stella Artois, Bass, and Beck's—in the United States. On paper, the deal made sense. Budweiser was losing market share to import brands and microbrews popular with young drinkers, and its well-oiled beer distribution network was already in place.

August III didn't like the idea. He recalled his earlier run-ins with the Brazilians, and didn't find them trustworthy. Takeover rumors were already swirling. A partnership would give 3G Capital—the new investment group the Three Musketeers had formed—a front-row seat into Anheuser-Busch's operations.

But August IV disagreed. The new CEO ultimately prevailed, and InBev soon moved into an office right across the street from One Busch Place.

Lemann struck deals, but he didn't run companies. He left that to his deputies, including Carlos Brito—a Brazilian businessman with a Stanford MBA who joined Brahma in 1989 and had been CEO of Ambev (and later InBev) since its inception in 2004. He grew up under Lemann and adopted much of his business philosophy.

Brito adopted zero-based budgeting at InBev, where every line item has to be justified anew each year, rather than using last year's budget as a starting point. Hundreds of middle management roles are often eliminated, along with far smaller policies like allowing employees to make photocopies without permission. While Brito didn't invent the strategy—known as ZBB (zero-based budgeting) in business circles—he became one of its most faithful adherents, earning a reputation as a ruthless cost-cutter.

He also led by example, flying economy and eschewing all the trappings of a prominent CEO. He didn't even have a desk, preferring to work in an open office space alongside colleagues. At times, he's pushed back on his reputation as the grim reaper of corporate costs: "If you think about efficiency, the most efficient decision is to close down the company," he once told an interviewer. "Then costs go to zero. But that's not really why we're here."[8]

For a cost-cutter, the peek into Anheuser-Busch was more tantalizing than Brito could ever have imagined.

It was only a matter of time before InBev made its move.

Anheuser-Busch's defenses were not as strong as they had once been. In recent years, as the share price failed to impress, the company dropped its "poison pill" defense—a provision in the corporate bylaws that would have allowed Anheuser-Busch to buy up shares at a highly discounted price in the event of a hostile takeover, making it prohibitively expensive for InBev to proceed without the board's consent. It also dropped its practice of holding "staggered" elections, in which only a third of the board is up for election in any given year. Now every board member was up for reelection at every annual meeting, making it much easier for an aggressive suitor to install his candidates and wrest control.

But August IV knew something had to be done. So, as detailed in Julie MacIntosh's *Dethroning the King*, August IV flew Wall Street investment bankers to the Ritz-Carlton in Cancún for a strategy session on how Anheuser-Busch could stay competitive. The Wall Street bankers expected there to be one or two firms in attendance; August IV had invited nearly every major firm.

His father thought the meeting was a strategic mistake. He was furious. "All you did by bringing those bankers in there was send a telegraph wire out to InBev that you're ready to be taken over," he shouted at August IV.

August III was right. The meeting was leaked to the press, adding fuel to the claims that Anheuser-Busch was the target of InBev's next merger.

In October 2007, August IV met with Lemann in New York. Lemann mentioned joining forces once again. August IV took the comment as an off-the-cuff remark; it was not.

By early 2008, InBev was working to line up financing for the deal. The gossip intensified. In April, August IV spoke at the annual wholesale convention, promising distributors that a sale would not happen "on my watch."[9] But that wasn't his decision to make. By then, the

Busch family owned fewer than 4 percent of the shares; Warren Buffet owned more stock in Anheuser-Busch than all of the family members combined.

In May, August IV spoke at another large company distributor event in Washington, D.C. August was slurring his words, stumbling onstage. He dropped the microphone. The company said strong cold medicine was to blame, but everyone knew he wasn't okay.

Nine days later, InBev's board of directors met to finalize their planned merger offer to Anheuser-Busch shareholders. But the media beat them to the punch. The day after the meeting, the *Financial Times* ran a story that InBev had offered Anheuser-Busch $65 per share, far above the mid-$50s per share the stock had been trading at.[10] The article named names. The investment banks involved. The advisors. It was credible.[11]

Anheuser-Busch's board told August IV to send an email to Lemann, asking him what was going on. Lemann played it cool, taking days to respond. He agreed to meet. The two met in Tampa on June 2. August was prepped to get clarification on the media reports and some idea of InBev's intent. Lemann stayed mum. The meeting lasted all of ten minutes.

A little over a week later, the formal offer came through. InBev CEO Carlos Brito sent a letter to August IV thanking him for his meeting with Lemann the previous week and cementing the $65-per-share offer that had been reported in the *Financial Times*. It would be an all-cash offer, $46.35 billion in total.

The letter—which was addressed to August IV but written for public consumption—lauded Anheuser-Busch's storied history, and promised to maintain tradition and keep the company headquarters in St. Louis. "We would seek to rename our combined company to evoke the heritage of your key brands," he wrote, and "continue your strong commitment to the communities in which you operate."

The letter might as well have been written to the people of St. Louis themselves.

Not everyone, of course, was convinced. Politicians spoke out about saving Anheuser-Busch from the takeover, including then–presidential candidate Barack Obama, who was questioned about the takeover during a stopover at the St. Louis airport. "I think we should be able to find an American company that is interested in purchasing Anheuser-Busch, if in fact Anheuser-Busch feels that it is necessary to sell." Savebudweiser.com launched a campaign to save the company from its European-Brazilian takeover; SaveAB.com did the same.

Fifteen days later, Anheuser-Busch rejected the offer as inadequate. August IV argued that Anheuser-Busch could drive more value for shareholders on its own. August had floated a plan, called Blue Ocean, to cut more than a half-billion dollars of costs over two years to keep Anheuser-Busch lean and competitive. But it was clear that wasn't going to be enough to satisfy shareholders, many of whom were salivating at the possibility of a $65-per-share buyout. The only real option was for Anheuser-Busch to do a merger of its own, to make itself even larger, so that it would be too expensive even for InBev to buy.

After InBev's Pac-Man–style acquisitions and Miller's recent merger with Coors, there was only one real target left: Modelo, the brewers of Corona and Modelo Especial. Anheuser-Busch already had a 50 percent stake from an earlier venture, and buying the rest of the company would add $10 to $15 in company value, making it too pricey for InBev.

August IV rushed to hammer out a deal with the Mexican brewers, but negotiations often don't go well when one side has a gun to their head, particularly when that gun is in plain view of the other side. Modelo was willing to do a deal, but only at a premium price, and only if Modelo's leadership retained operational control. Anheuser-Busch's board didn't go for it. They knew shareholders would revolt, and the deal would likely be tied up in lawsuits for years.

InBev, however, viewed the possibility of an Anheuser-Busch merger with Modelo as a very real threat. So Brito upped his offer to $70 per share. The $52 billion acquisition price made it the highest all-cash corporate merger in history. It was too good to pass up.

In November 2008, shareholders approved the merger. The corporate keys were handed to InBev.

The cost-cutting began immediately. Hogs get slaughtered, and Anheuser-Busch had allowed itself to grow quite fat. Two days after the merger was finalized, InBev announced 1,400 layoffs. It informed suppliers that the company was revising its pay practices to match In-Bev's, which gave the company 120 days to pay its invoices, rather than thirty. And it sold off more than $7 billion in assets. Busch Gardens was gone. So was SeaWorld. Charitable donations would be slashed. The company that had given $10 million a year to the City of St. Louis and its civic institutions would now be giving very little. The company's retiree group that had met in the brewery and drank free beer was now required to pay for both the beer and the room.

Employees that remained saw the company change before their eyes in ways both big and small. Salaries were slashed to 20 percent below market rate. Trash cans were emptied only three days a week. Office plants would not be watered at all. Brito bulldozed the executive offices on the ninth floor, which had been ornately decorated by Gussie himself, in favor of an austere open-floor plan more reminiscent of a bare-bones startup than a 150-year-old institution.

"The message from InBev," one company veteran told the *St. Louis Post-Dispatch*, "is, 'If you don't think we are serious, then just look at what we are willing to destroy.'"[12]

From a human perspective, this reaction is understandable. Change was happening rapidly, and no one likes losing cushy perks, plush offices, or, for some, their very livelihoods.

But from a business perspective, the cuts were born not of cruelty or callousness, but necessity. Anheuser-Busch had been falling behind in recent years. While its executives traveled the world in private jets and held strategy sessions at the Ozarks compound, its competitors were consolidating, innovating, and becoming more efficient. In business, companies eat or get eaten.

Jorge Lemann wasn't trying to destroy Anheuser-Busch. Just the opposite. "In the end, we're running things for the long run and building companies that will last forever if possible," Mr. Lemann has said.[13] Lemann may be Brazilian, but he saw the culture he infused into his companies as something else: American.[14] Specifically, the culture embodied by the Milton Friedman ideal of American capitalism: that companies should compete with one another to drive value for shareholders, that rewarding shareholders will lead to the most profitable, thriving private sector, and that a thriving private sector will create jobs, drive economic growth, and create prosperity for society as a whole.

AB InBev's ten principles captured this philosophy well. The ten principles fell under "Dream," "People," and "Culture"—the three things that set AB InBev apart. They included dreaming big, having big aspirations for the company that everyone could focus on achieving. The people factors were focused on merit, hiring the best talent, and compensating employees based on success. Culturally, AB InBev wanted everyone to have an ownership mindset, feeling that they had a stake in the success of the enterprise, and were never satisfied or complacent. "We tried to keep this idea of an eternal, forever startup even in a large company like ours and I think that together with meritocracy, it attracts the young, talented people," Brito explained shortly after the merger. These principles drove the company and everyone who worked there.[15]

They also drove the combined company's growth. It wasn't easy. The merger took place on the cusp of the financial crash of 2008 and the Great Recession. In the first year, sales fell 10 percent as customers pulled back and fluctuating currencies weakened the Brazilian real against the U.S. dollar. In the first several months post-merger, the stock price plunged along with the rest of the S&P 500. But by November 2009, the company reported that it was still on track to deliver $2.25 billion on cost cuts from the merger, and announced a $1.55 billion third-quarter net profit.[16] The stock had already recovered from its dip and was positioned for growth. Overall, the stock had risen about 61 percent from late 2008 to late 2009. It steadily climbed from there. By late 2010, AB InBev announced it had achieved another $140 million in cost savings and was making up on the sluggish U.S. beer market by expanding in places like Russia and China. The stock climbed another 20 percent.[17] The trajectory was promising.

To make an omelet, you've got to crack a few eggs. Neither Brito nor the Three Musketeers grew businesses by walking on eggshells; the takeover of Anheuser-Busch would be no different. In 2010, the question for me was whether I wanted to walk with them.

Chapter 5

Welcome to Belgium

Reading up on both parties to the recent merger, I had a pretty good understanding of the company I could join after school. Anheuser-Busch created great iconic American brands. InBev cared about meritocracy and increasing shareholder value. If they could bring out the best in each other, the growth potential was limitless.

Tony Milikin and Carlos Brito sensed I was close to accepting an offer. To close the deal, they set up a VIP meeting for me to attend. Board members would be there. The Three Musketeers would be there, too. I'd be able to meet Jorge Paulo himself.

I was pumped, but I wanted to burn off some adrenaline. The night before the meeting, I decided to play racquetball with my business school roommate. During the match, my roommate hit a hard backhand shot. As he followed through, the edge of his racquet made perfect contact with my two front teeth. Both were knocked to the back of my mouth.

Very few dentists were open in the evening. Luckily, my fiancée found one in downtown Boston who happened to be doing paperwork in his office. She explained the situation: I had an important meeting in New York the following day where it would be helpful to have my teeth. The dentist agreed to see me, on one condition: My fiancée would need to provide assistance, since no one else was in the office.

I rushed to the office, my fiancée-turned-dental-assistant in tow. The dentist delivered the diagnosis: My teeth could be put back into my mouth, but only temporarily. The roots were severed and my teeth would eventually turn black. I also could not bite or chew anything with my front teeth as nothing was anchoring them in place. There was a chance that they would fall out. Eventually, I would need to get both teeth removed again and have implants installed. But for my meeting, I at least had teeth.

The next morning, I flew to New York. I greeted the Three Musketeers with a warning: My words might be slurred, but it wasn't the Budweiser speaking. It was my teeth. Or, more specifically, my lack thereof. Jorge Paulo cracked a knowing smile. "Switch to tennis," the Wimbledon contestant advised. "You should never be so close to a competitor swinging a racquet." My broken teeth had broken the ice.

The meeting went smoothly, and the board members invited me to Belgium over the upcoming Christmas break. I agreed, but only if my former dental assistant could come with me. Ten days later, we were Belgium-bound.

Immediately after takeoff, my two front teeth turned black. Jet black. From a distance, they looked completely missing.

Perhaps I should have taken it as a sign. But Belgium was enchanting. Leuven is a charming medieval town anchored by one of the nation's largest universities. Small chocolate stores and restaurants dot the landscape. But home would never be too far away, as the McDonald's in the city's main thoroughfare proved.

The corporate headquarters was a stately five-story building, clad in brick, right next to a picturesque canal and across the street from the actual brewery where beers like Stella Artois, Jupiler, and Leffe were brewed. Legend has it that many of the bars surrounding the headquarters and the brewery had a direct tap line to the brewery and that is why the beer was always so fresh in Leuven.

Tony Milikin, who originally recruited me to AB InBev at the New York event, offered to give me the tour.

As we stepped inside, I couldn't help but notice that the interior was not nearly as charming as the surrounding city. It was spartan. Efficient. It mimicked the New York City office but on a much larger scale.

Each floor had gray carpets and rows of gray desks. The company practiced a cleanliness habit across all departments called "5S." The 5 *S*'s were Sort, Set in Order, Shine, Standardize, Sustain. Each desktop was barren and there were minimal visuals in a room outside of the paint on the wall. Efficiency and standardization were not only preached, but clearly practiced.

The team Tony was creating was brand-new. It was a startup within a larger organization. There were maybe five people on the team when I first arrived; it would grow to more than forty in the next two years. The new team was based in Belgium for one reason: tax savings. AB InBev is technically headquartered there, although the vast majority of its executives live in New York. But to claim the tax breaks, you have to do *something* in the country. For AB InBev, that was managing global procurement contracts for things like aluminum cans, barley, shipping costs, etc. By doing so, AB InBev could pay a tiny fraction of 1 percent on the profit that it reported in Belgium, compared to the 34 percent corporate tax rate it paid overall.[1]

After a full morning of touring the facility and shaking hands, I had lunch with Tony at the office café. The menu was very Belgian. There were options like Stoemp (mashed potatoes with vegetables and served with sausage), Waterzooi soup (a rich and creamy stew made from egg yolk, cream, butter, and vegetable broth), shrimp and tomatoes, and gratin with chicory. Unfortunately, waffles and chocolates weren't on offer, so I went with the Waterzooi soup. It wasn't bad.

Tony asked where my classmates were working after school. HBS

students had a bad habit of "going with the herd" and almost predict-
ing when bubbles would pop. In the late 1990s, for example, HBS
students fled to Silicon Valley to participate in the first internet bubble.
In the early 2000s, Enron topped the list. In the mid-2000s, investment banking and private equity were the most popular professions,
right before the financial crisis of 2007–08 hit. History showed that
the right thing to do after HBS was exactly the opposite of what your
classmates were doing.

2010 was an interesting time to be recruited by companies. The
corporate scars from the Great Recession were still very real. The banking sector was still grappling with the failures of Bear Sterns and Leh-
man Brothers. Capitalism was on shaky grounds. Investment banks
and finance firms were still recruiting, but it was no longer the "must
have" job.

The real estate market remained depressed. Many people were still
underwater on their mortgages and reluctant to move. Glitzy cities
like Las Vegas and Miami, which buzzed with new developments and
soaring prices during the mid-2000s, now saw a glut of inventory driving prices down. The pain was spreading to more stable cities as well.
Seattle, which is home to Microsoft, Amazon, Costco, and Starbucks,
saw home prices decline by 31 percent in 2010, more than the drop in
Las Vegas.[2] Rents for commercial buildings in prime New York City
locations fell by 50 percent since their 2007 peak. HBS grads were
wary.

What about Big Tech? Apple and Amazon must have been sure
bets in 2010. Not exactly. In 2010, BlackBerry was king. BlackBerry
controlled 43 percent of the smartphone market, after steadily gaining
share from the number-2 player: Nokia. Apple, which had introduced
the iPhone only three years earlier, was still refining its technology.[3]
Remember "Antennagate"? As iPhone 4 users quickly noticed, you
couldn't really hold the phone in your left hand. If you tried, wireless

bars disappeared; sometimes, calls dropped entirely. Apple was slow to respond. When it did, Steve Jobs helpfully advised customers to "just avoid holding it in this way." The comment went viral as proof of an out-of-touch CEO. Apple may have attracted a lot of attention, but not the kind that job seekers like.

For all of Apple's woes, Amazon was worse. In 2010, Amazon was essentially a "poor man's" Apple. Apple, at least, had revolutionary products. They had iPods and iPads. They had an iTunes store. Their commercials featured Coldplay, Bob Dylan, and U2. Even in 2010, Apple was a vibe. Amazon, by contrast, was a bookstore on a screen. Its only real product, the Kindle, was a book on a screen. It was starting to dip its toe into other business lines—it had recently acquired Zappos, for example—but its trajectory wasn't entirely clear. I didn't know anyone who joined Amazon out of HBS, but it would have been a good contrarian play.

Since the Big Tech companies were seemingly in a state of flux, the HBS herd decided to go small, gravitating toward a handful of technology startups. And the most exciting among them? The one with all the buzz? Groupon. The coupon-clipping website that was going to revolutionize business.

The idea was simple, but radical: Groupon would work with local businesses to offer deep discounts on activities like massage parlors, golf courses, trampoline parks, skydiving companies. The fallout from the 2008 Great Recession left consumers looking for deals. But the deals would go live only if a certain number of people purchased them. And they were available for one day only. Groupon capitalized on FOMO before FOMO was an acronym.

The concept was brilliant. Retailers reached new consumers. Consumers got great deals. Groupon got a cut. It was the first social shopping site. Virality was built in: people were desperate to make deals go "live," so they'd often urge friends and family to buy the deals, too.

Growth was explosive. In December 2010, *The Wall Street Journal* reported that Groupon was on track to reach $1 billion in sales faster than any other company in history. At that point, it had 35 million users. And it looked like the company might go public soon.

Many of my classmates bought into the hype. Some joined Groupon. Others went to competitors like LivingSocial. Some even launched Groupon knockoff companies of their own. One classmate was raising venture capital to create "Groupon for military members." Another founded a "Groupon in South Korea." (The Groupon knock-off, by the way, didn't work. But he didn't give up. He pivoted to the "Amazon" of South Korea. That did. The company, Coupang, went public at a valuation of $100 billion in 2021. Which is all to say that following the herd can work out, I suppose, as long as you're willing to switch herds.)

As I was talking to Tony, he asked me how long I thought the Groupon "craze" would last. I wasn't very bullish. There are only so many merchants in a city that will offer a deep discount once, let alone multiple times. And once consumers do something like skydive, they aren't very likely to do it again. I therefore wasn't interested in participating in the Groupon "craze." That would be the right choice as well. Groupon did famously rebuff a $6 billion acquisition offer from Google in 2011 before going public later that year. It did achieve a $17 billion valuation when the company went public, but it was all downhill from there.[4] In 2023, Groupon has lost over 99 percent of its value and reports fewer than 14 million customers (down from 83 million when it went public). Most of its competitors have also gone out of business. The HBS herd once again famously predicted the "peak" of an industry.

After Tony and I discussed all the different industries my friends were considering, we came back to what I was considering—working for Anheuser-Busch InBev. AB InBev was a contrarian play, sure, but one with minimal downside and a lot of upside. Unlike the financial industry at the time, beer was a lot more stable (and, of course, Anheuser-Busch was the world's largest private equity firm that happened to sell beer!). Unlike the technology industry that did not have a clear winner among firms like Apple, BlackBerry, and Amazon, AB InBev was the clear market leader with a lot of room for further consolidation and growth. Unlike the startup world, which had a high likelihood of failure, beer had been around for thousands of years. It was a good bet that people would be drinking it for thousands more.

I told Tony I was in. I was excited to join a startup within a much larger organization. I was excited to work closely with senior executives like Tony and Carlos Brito to manage billions of dollars of commodity spend across the world. I was excited about the potential to work on future blockbuster acquisitions that could create the world's largest consumer packaged goods company. I was excited that one day I might lead large business units for the organization, market and sell some of the world's most recognizable brands, and be part of its storied history. No other firms compared.

I left Leuven that December very optimistic about the future. Tori and I now knew where we were headed after our wedding the upcoming summer. We celebrated in Brussels that evening and in Paris over the next few days. We then returned to the U.S. to finish school and finalize wedding plans. I got my teeth fixed just in time for our wedding—and for our move to Belgium the following day.

Chapter 6

Beat the Monkey

One of my favorite wedding pictures is of me and my wife at dinner. We're both laughing and enjoying the evening. Between us is a bottle of Budweiser. For the next eleven years of our lives, the three of us were a team. For now, at least, I was the family beer-winner. My wife, Tori, would be there to manage and support us through five moves, three kids, and many ups and (some) downs with the company. Budweiser would pay our bills.

I was AB's first Global Commodity Director. This meant that I was responsible for the price and cost of everything that went into a Budweiser, or any other beer in AB's portfolio. Without a brand, beer is one of the most commoditized consumer products. It's barley, water, hops, and yeast. Sometimes ingredients like corn, rice, or wheat are added to alter the flavor. In blind taste tests, most consumers can't tell the difference between a Budweiser, Miller, or Coors. It's branding that makes the difference.

Anheuser-Busch was a master at marketing to consumers. InBev was a master at optimizing for the lowest cost, most efficient path to producing and delivering beer, while maintaining high-quality standards. As Global Commodity Director, I quickly learned why InBev was one of the best operating companies in the world and was able to drive significant value after acquiring businesses.

When I officially joined the company in August 2011, AB had established a strong three-year and five-year track record of delivering excess shareholder value compared to many of their peers. These track records are important for investors because they look at returns over longer business cycles. Long periods of outperformance can attract more shareholders willing to bet that the trend will continue.

Also, when stock analysts at large banks compare corporate performance, they generally group companies among their industry peers. Technology companies get compared to technology companies. Energy companies against energy companies. Consumer product companies against consumer product companies, etc. This is because companies in the same industry can all benefit from, or be hurt by, the same macroeconomic conditions like commodity costs, regulatory shifts, market conditions, and so on. When this happens, it is better to compare the relative performance of companies in the same industry against one another to see who best captures market opportunities.

Relative to a group of consumer industry staples like Proctor & Gamble, Nestle, and Unilever, AB InBev stood out. In the three years prior to 2011, AB InBev's stock increased by 32 percent, while its consumer peers increased their stock by 20 percent. Going back five years, AB InBev increased its value by 84 percent relative to 34 percent for its peers. Impressive numbers, especially with a transformational acquisition and recession mixed in.

Driving shareholder value started from the top. Anheuser-Busch's board of directors and CEO set the mission, or dream, of the company to be the "Best Beer Company Bringing People Together for a Better World." If that mission was continuously pursued, shareholder value should follow. The ten principles mentioned previously underpinned how the company would achieve the mission. These principles, bucketed into categories of Dream, People, and Culture,[1] were cascaded throughout the organization and posted in every company location. They were painted on the wall of my first office.

The message was simple. Everyone pursues the same DREAM. Find the best PEOPLE, who recruit even better people to build quality teams. Do it in a CULTURE that is never satisfied and delivers a great customer experience. Most companies have similar aspirations. The key is to do them, not just have them painted on a wall. AB InBev excelled at executing.

Here's how: The company set clear business and financial objectives, and then tied bonuses and stock compensation to meeting them. You can say your company culture is ambitious and driven, but nothing lights a fire under employees more than having your own paycheck on the line.

In 2011, AB InBev had three strategic financial initiatives to deliver on being the "Best Beer Company in a Better World":

1. Grow revenue ahead of inflation
2. Drive higher profitability and cash generation
3. Strengthen the financial foundation of the business through reductions in leverage (i.e., pay down debt from the $52 billion acquisition of Anheuser-Busch)

Inflation was around 3 percent, so growing revenue ahead of inflation meant revenue had to grow by about 4 percent or more. Straightforward enough.[2]

Driving profitability was clear, too. EBITDA margins, or Earnings Before Interest Taxes Depreciation & Amortization, which is a measure of profitability, had to increase from a record 38 percent in 2010.

Finally, the company aimed to generate more than $10 billion of free cash flow. This cash flow would be used to reduce leverage on the business below a targeted debt/EBITDA ratio of 2.5x.

The entire organization had bonuses tied to these metrics. Bonuses were 25 percent of the total compensation for lower-ranking employees. They could be greater than 300 percent of the salary, including matching stock grants, for higher-ranking employees.

The sales and marketing teams were responsible for growing revenue. They had to sell a certain amount of each brand, at a certain price, to achieve these top-line results. The logistics, supply, and procurement organizations had to drive higher profitability and cash generation. They did this by being more efficient in the brewing process, sourcing lower-cost materials, and optimizing freight with more product on the same trucks. The finance team focused on paying down debt.

It was no coincidence that two of the three financial metrics were tied to bottom-line results, rather than top-line growth. Cost saving was in AB InBev's DNA. Over the previous five years, AB InBev's total volume of beer sold was relatively flat. It vacillated between 2 percent growth or 2 percent declines depending on the year. Revenue growth was therefore achieved through price increases ahead of the rate of inflation, or by selling more high-end beer (i.e., Stella Artois) compared to value beer (i.e., Busch Light). Large jumps in revenue were achieved via acquisition, not via organic growth. Large jumps in profits and cash flow, by contrast, were achieved organically. With beer volumes relatively flat, AB increased its EBITDA margins from 28.6 percent to 38.2 percent from 2006 to 2011. Over this same time period, it tripled its cash flow from $4 billion to more than $12 billion. $3 billion of the increase came directly from acquiring Anheuser-Busch. The rest came from operating the business more efficiently.

2011 continued AB InBev's history of modest revenue growth and strong profit growth. The sales and marketing team achieved its 2011 revenue target. Despite beer volume declining by 0.1 percent globally, revenue increased by 4.6 percent, using the typical playbook of raising prices and focusing on higher-end brands.

Marketing also helped. That year, Bud Light won its sixth and final Super Bowl Ad Meter award for the most popular Super Bowl ad. The ad featured a guy dogsitting "intelligent" dogs and a fridge full of Bud Light. He throws a party while the dogs serve everyone beer and food. The last shot shows the guy cleaning up while the dogs are playing poker, evoking the famous paintings by Cassius Marcelles Coolidge. This ad helped Bud Light grow market share in the United States for the last time.

But this marketing wasn't really an InBev accomplishment. It was a last hurrah for Anheuser-Busch. Many of the sales and marketing execs from the old Anheuser-Busch days were still around in 2011. InBev implemented a three-year retention agreement with top personnel in 2008 to keep them and ensure a smooth transition. Predominantly Brazilian InBev employees would learn from their American AB counterparts during this time period. AB execs stomached the cost cuts and new InBev culture because they had significant compensation packages that vested at the end of 2011. They did an admiral job maintaining the high Anheuser-Busch marketing standards while InBev significantly reduced costs. At the end of 2011, though, many of these execs bolted. But InBev was happy to take credit for their Super Bowl Ad Meter win nonetheless.

The supply and procurement organizations had a strong year, too. The supply organization focused on using less materials to produce the same amount of beer. For example, they used 8.2 percent less water to produce one hectoliter of beer in 2011 compared to 2010. They also used 5.2 percent less energy and recycled 99 percent of brewing by-products like spent grains and yeast, which could be sold as animal feed. Many of these initiatives were celebrated externally as "environmentally friendly" initiatives, which they were, but they were really just good business practices. Doing more with less translates directly to the bottom line.

The procurement organization accelerated its efforts to find the best-quality ingredients and packaging, at the lowest costs, with the best payment terms. As the first Global Commodity Director, I played a key role in this effort. During 2010 and 2011, the prices of commodities like aluminum, corn, oil, cardboard, and wheat rose dramatically coming out of the Great Recession. AB InBev was caught off guard. Historically, they did not hedge commodities prices. They locked in a flat price on items like cans and bottles for three to six months with suppliers. Then they would renegotiate prices based on market conditions. When prices were stable to down, this was not a problem. When prices increased dramatically, this was a big issue. The sales team could not raise prices fast enough to offset the added costs, nor could cost cuts in areas like marketing be made.

I inherited a $500 million problem in 2011. AB InBev was supposed to spend $5 billion on commodities in 2011, but they were on track to spend $5.5 billion because of soaring commodities costs. I quickly learned about Principle 4 & 6: get results and take ownership. I was told that I had to fix the problem if I wanted to get a bonus that year. I lost twenty pounds over the next few months working long hours to fix the problem.

Which we did. We developed a program with many of our top suppliers to separate the price of the commodity from the conversion costs. In other words, we stopped buying things like cans. Instead, we bought aluminum and then separately paid our supplier to turn that aluminum into a can. Separating these costs allowed us to do two things:

1. Hedge the price of the commodity for longer periods of time to help with budgeting, and
2. Negotiate with suppliers on the cost and payment terms to convert the commodity to the end good

⁞⁞⁞⁞⁞⁞⁞⁞⁞⁞⁞

I immediately got to work with our largest aluminum, malt, corn, packaging, rice, and bottle suppliers. Many quickly got on board, as they liked not worrying about what their commodity costs would be, and they could compete on just the cost to convert the commodity to cans, barley, beer boxes, etc.

Some took a little bit of time. For example, I had to fly to Wuhan, China (yes, the same Wuhan of coronavirus fame), to meet with one of our largest rice suppliers. My goal was to get him to tie his price to a Chinese rice exchange so we could hedge that price moving forward.

The owner worked in a dingy office. A dingy dog sat at his feet. He smoked cigarettes at his desk as we spoke through a translator from AB InBev's Chinese operation. I had seen movies where businessmen smoked at their desk, but I'd never seen it in real life. The rice mill operator politely declined my pitch, but he did invite me to lunch.

We ate in a private room, surrounded by colleagues. There were probably ten courses of food over lunch. Rice wine was served with each course. Per the tradition of Ganbei, the rice wine needed to be "cheered" and chugged before you could eat the course. I'm not a huge rice wine fan—as you might guess, I'm more of a Budweiser kind of guy—but I couldn't refuse. The main course was a giant fish. I learned that I was the guest of honor, so I was served the head. I was suddenly grateful for all the rice wine that I'd been served.

After the tenth rice wine, everyone was in a good mood. The owner of the rice company was apparently impressed with my ability to drink and also eat the fish head. He sat next to me and summoned our translator. He agreed to tie his prices to the exchange. This was turning out to be a great day. It was barely 1 p.m. and I had a new rice contract and a new understanding of how business gets done in China. We ordered one last round of rice wine to celebrate.

Cultural differences are a real thing. This was not the only time I felt like the proverbial "fish(head) out of water." I speak pretty fast. I have an optimistic American spirit that anything can be accomplished, on tight deadlines, with hard work and persistence. I use American slang. I sometimes have to remind myself that not everyone does. On a follow-up call with our Chinese team, I mentioned that I thought one of our suppliers was "ripping us off" and we needed to find more "bucks" in the contract "ASAP." I thought I was pretty clear. After a few days, I didn't hear anything back. I called my local Chinese contact to figure out why there was a delay. He informed me that "no one understood a thing I asked them on the prior call." Phrases like "ripping us off" and words like *bucks* and *ASAP* were not part of the English-language curriculum for most Chinese. To make matters worse, in China, I was told people tend to not question individuals in an authoritative position or ask for clarification. It is better to nod politely and hope for further information afterward than to question someone. Therefore, I was advised to email clear follow-ups, in plain English, with explicit deadlines. I did, and results improved dramatically.

Cultural differences weren't unique to China. I was once on the phone with a Belgian colleague and asked him to "swing by my desk" so we could talk in person. After fifteen minutes of waiting, I went to his floor. When asked why he didn't stop by, he responded, "I don't have a swing." He legitimately thought I was asking him to swing, like a child on a playground. From then on, I asked my Belgian colleagues to meet me at the corporate café.

One of the Belgian colleagues I was fascinated by was a guy in the IT department named Ronald. Ronald was the guy who fixed my computer when I had issues. Every time that I saw him, he had a black eye, or a broken hand, or a limp foot. This was because he was a proud European soccer hooligan for his Belgian pro team, Anderlect. I was generally aware of Europe's passion for soccer. And, of course, as a good American expat, I had done my homework: I'd watched some YouTube videos of European fans getting out of control before, during, or after matches. Many fans brought fireworks and smoke bombs to matches. They taunted and threw things at rival fans in the stands. For this reason, most European stadiums have separate entrances for fans of each team and barriers in the stadium preventing opposing fans from physically reaching each other. Ronald was part of a group that took hooliganism to the next level. To evade the barricades and police at the stadium, he would fight with opposing fans at predetermined places outside of the stadium. This was sport to him. He wore his bruises like badges of honor and was honest about where he got them. This is something I will never understand, but Europeans seem to tolerate it as part of soccer culture.

Business helped bridge the cultural divide. Numbers and math were the same across countries, and the company still had a $500 million financial gap to solve. A joint task force was established and we put a monthly Global Commodity Meeting on the calendar. The CEO, Carlos Brito; the CFO, Felipe Dutra; the VP of Treasury; the Chief Procurement Officer, Tony Milikin; the VP of Operations, Fued Sadala, and I were the meeting participants. Each month, I prepared the total commodity exposure the company had for the next twelve months, and I recommended how we should hedge each commodity.

The standard hedging practice was to lock each commodity twelve months out so we could have better predictability on pricing. The Brazilians referred to this standard practice as what "a monkey would do." In other words, this was a simple system that even a monkey could execute because a monkey just had to buy the commodity twelve months ahead each month.

I was tasked with being "better than a monkey." Based on my market views, and with the committee's approval, I could shorten these hedges to as few as six months or as long as eighteen months. I would then benchmark my performance on these calls to go longer or shorter vs. what would have happened if we hedged out twelve months, i.e., the default monkey time. The goal was to deliver at least $100 million in savings vs. the monkey. With a few key calls on aluminum and wheat pricing, I overdelivered the $100 million goal over the next twelve months. Quickly, I was earning my place among the InBev homo sapiens.

While I was focused on reducing our commodity cost, the rest of the procurement team was fanatical about lowering the conversion cost—i.e., the cost of converting raw materials into beer. At the time, Tony Milikin implemented one of the most sophisticated auction programs to secure favorable terms with suppliers. Every item that AB InBev purchased went through an "electronic-auction" or "e-auction." This system was like an inverted version of eBay. On eBay, bidders place their bids for items and the highest bidder wins. In Anheuser-Busch's e-auction system, suppliers bid to be the lowest-cost provider in real time. Each supplier could see what the going price was for a product or service and decide if they could bid lower. No supplier was spared from this process. Can suppliers. Bottle suppliers. Janitorial services. Legal services. Software purchases. Pens. Paper. Every purchase AB InBev made went through an auction.

After a low price was secured, then AB InBev would auction other terms related to the item. For example, they would then have the suppliers do an auction for payment terms, or how long AB InBev could wait to pay a supplier after receiving a service. Most companies pay a supplier in 20 to 30 days. AB InBev was getting terms to pay in 75 to 90 days. At one point, there was a contest to see who could first get a supplier to agree to a 365-day payment contract. A company in South America was the first to agree.

After payment terms, AB InBev would then auction a "signing bonus." Signing bonuses are more common with professional athletes, but AB InBev realized that they could be utilized in the beer industry, too. The signing bonus was a one-time payment from the supplier to

Anheuser-Busch at the start of a contract. Sometimes it guaranteed that AB InBev would stay with a supplier for a certain amount of time. Many times, it was just another way to enhance AB InBev's margins with more cash. It was good business when AB could get it.

Once they received all of the pricing, payment terms, and signing bonus information from suppliers, AB InBev then negotiated with the leading suppliers in each area. The supplier with the lowest price might not have the best payment terms or signing bonus. If the supplier with the lowest cost could also match the best terms, they could win the deal. Vice versa, if the companies with the best payment terms and signing bonuses could come down on price, they could win the deal. All companies could ask suppliers for better pricing, payment terms, and signing bonuses. Nothing in a capitalist system precludes companies from doing so. AB InBev just implemented these policies as part of their operational DNA better than anyone else.

These procurement enhancements led to record profit margins and cash flow in 2011 and into 2012. The $500 million problem I inherited was solved via better hedging programs, better auction programs, and better cost management across the organization. The 38 percent EBITDA margin target was overdelivered. AB InBev achieved 39.1 percent. This led to record-high cash flow. AB delivered $12.4 billion of it in 2011, far exceeding the $10 billion target. An incremental $1.4 billion of cash flow could be attributed to the increase in payment terms.[3] This allowed the finance team to pay down its debt load and reach a debt to EBITDA level of 2.26, well below the 2.5x target. It also set up the company to make its next blockbuster acquisition, as AB InBev usually got its debt below a 2.0x debt/EBITDA ratio before making another large move.

Before I get to the next blockbuster acquisition, though, I want to touch on the second part of Anheuser-Busch's dream of being the "Best Beer Company in a Better World." Did the concept of "better world" mean that in addition to making profits and running a business, AB InBev also hugged trees, saved whales, and promoted other progressive causes? Or that the inclusion of "better world" was meant to cover up a plot to create a world awash in alcohol and the problems associated with overconsumption? Of course not. By focusing on being the best beer company, Anheuser-Busch would by default create a better world.

AB InBev's 2011 letter to shareholders explains as much.[4]

Anheuser-Busch employs 116,000 people. It paid more than $3.2 billion in salaries and wages to these employees. It also invested $3.3 billion in capital expenditures in their facilities, distribution networks, and system upgrades. These investments "generated jobs and local economic growth." And they paid $12 billion in excise and income taxes, which support government programs around the world.

AB InBev also works to promote responsible drinking. These include "We ID" programs that prevent underage drinking. Designated driver programs encourage people to not drink and drive. Be(er) Responsible Days encourage employees and wholesalers to speak with consumers about drinking responsibly.

Most of this is self-interested, of course. It was only one hundred years ago that alcohol was banned in the U.S.; "[t]he scourge of drunkenness" was the primary reason. Today, alcohol is still banned in many countries. And when Covid hit, alcohol bans spread to more countries still. AB InBev can't, and doesn't, take its ability to sell beer for granted.

Being the best beer company also meant managing environmental risks: "Beer is a product of natural ingredients, and therefore stewardship of land, water and other resources is fundamental to helping ensure the quality of our brands for the long term. We strive to be as efficient as possible in our use of natural resources; we invest in projects and technologies to conserve water and energy and reduce waste."

In simpler terms, if there is no barley, there is no beer. If there is no water, there is no beer. These are real environmental risks. The company therefore works with farmers and governments to secure a steady supply of these ingredients and then uses them as efficiently as possible. It's better for the world *and* makes more money.

So is community involvement. Many companies give back to the communities that purchase their products. Budweiser does, too. Budweiser has been supporting the U.S. military for more than one hundred years. In 2011, Budweiser donated another $2 million to the Folds of Honor Foundation, which gives scholarships to military families.

Anheuser-Busch also used its facilities to help local communities when natural disasters like hurricanes or forest fires hit. They can quickly convert their brewing lines to can water. In 2011, they delivered more than 2 million cans to people in need across forty-two communities. These activities further strengthen connections between consumers and Anheuser-Busch, generating lifelong customers and long-term value.

2011 had been a good year for AB InBev, but 2012 proved even better.

Chapter 7

Modelo-poly

Momentum from 2011 carried into 2012. AB InBev's beer volume returned to growth. Revenue, EBITDA, and cash flow continued increasing. Debt decreased. The Debt/EBITDA ratio fell below 2.0x. The stock price ripped. While the S&P 500 was up 13 percent in 2012, AB InBev's stock price increased by ~50 percent from $60 to $89.

More excitingly, another merger was on the horizon. In the summer of 2012, AB InBev announced that it planned to acquire the world's fifth-largest brewer, Grupo Modelo. Grupo Modelo was Mexico's largest brewer; it owned brands like Corona, Modelo, and Pacifico. AB InBev already owned 50 percent of Grupo Modelo from a 1997 transaction by Anheuser-Busch. But the 1997 deal did not give AB InBev strategic control over the brands or the ability to integrate operations. Buying the remaining 50 percent of the company would.

In June 2012, AB made its pitch to investors. AB InBev would pay $9.15 per share, or a total of $32.2 billion for Modelo. This price represented a 30 percent premium to the share price prior to the announcement and a Total Enterprise Value (the equity plus the debt which equaled a Total Enterprise Value of $32.2 billion) or EBITDA multiple of 12.9x. AB InBev expected to dispose of some of the assets in the deal and also recognize more than $600 million of synergies in the transaction. With the expected synergies, the purchase price was closer to 10.8x and the earnings per share generated by Modelo would be accretive in the first year. $500 million in increased cash flow was also predicted over two years, primarily from working capital (i.e., increasing payment terms for vendors).

AB InBev was bullish on both the Mexican beer market and the ability to export Mexican beers globally. Mexico is the fourth-most-profitable beer market in the world after the U.S., Brazil, and Japan. Beer has a 70 percent share of all alcoholic beverages consumed in Mexico, and Grupo Modelo owned 60 percent of the Mexican beer market, growing its share in each of the past four years. Favorable demographics would continue this growth, as Mexico has the largest middle class in Latin America and 2 million people reach legal drinking age each year.

Mexico is also the largest beer export market. 17 percent of all exported beer comes from Mexico. Mexican beer exports grew at a rate of 12 percent since 1991, double the 6 percent average growth rate of other countries. By 2011, Corona was the number-1 imported beer in thirty-eight countries. It was also ranked as the fourth most valuable beer brand globally. AB InBev was betting that the growth of Corona would accelerate moving forward. It successfully grew Budweiser by 45 percent outside the U.S. over the previous three years, and it hoped Corona could do the same.

This was another classic AB InBev deal that would create significant shareholder value if executed well. Grupo Modelo operated in markets where AB InBev did not have a significant presence, and vice versa. The company was attractively valued. Significant cost savings and working capital savings could be achieved to quickly pay down the debt from the acquisition. The deal would be accretive to shareholders in the first year. Now the company had to execute its well-oiled integration playbook, and I would have a key role in carrying out the plan.

Once the deal was announced in summer 2012, I was one of the first AB InBev employees to fly to Mexico City. I had my work cut out for me. We needed to figure out how we could overdeliver the $600 million in savings and $500 million in working capital promised to investors. These numbers were not pulled from thin air. The math was pretty simple. AB InBev did 39 percent EBITDA margins. Grupo Modelo did 32 percent. This represented a "gap" of 7 percent that AB InBev wanted to not only close, but have Modelo overdeliver. Grupo Modelo had $6.4 billion in revenue, so improving EBITDA margins by 7 percent would deliver approximately $450 million in savings. AB InBev always put "challenges" on top of simply closing the gap, though, so if it could achieve 9 percent savings, they would reach the $600 million number. The $500 million in working capital was a quick exercise in stretching Modelo's payment terms to match AB InBev's.

Fortunately, there were many reasons to believe that the Mexican market could be more profitable than other markets as well. Mexico had its own direct distribution system for selling beer. 80 percent of its beer went through its own network of distributors, compared to fewer than 10 percent in the United States. Modelo also owned many retail outlets where it sold beer, including Modelorama and Extra stores. Finally, 75 percent of the beer it sold in Mexico was in returnable glass bottles.

Most people in the U.S. have never seen a returnable glass bottle, but they are prevalent in emerging markets like Mexico and Brazil. Europe and Canada also use a decent amount of returnable glass bottles over environmental concerns. Returnable glass bottles are a thicker and sturdier version of a typical bottle. Customers put down a deposit when they purchase beer and then return the glass bottles to a store to get their deposit back. The bottles are then washed, rinsed, and refilled with beer to be used again and again. The same bottle can be used fifteen to twenty times before it has to be recycled. This format typically saves the customer money and is more profitable. But it's not perfect. The bottle quickly becomes "scuffed" and loses its premium look. The process of paying a deposit on the bottles, carrying heavy crates of bottles home, storing the crates and bottles until the beer is consumed, and then returning the empty bottles to the store is a pain for the customer. In the U.S. and most developed markets, consumers prefer to purchase thinner glass bottles or cans that can be thrown into a recycling bin. This might cost a bit more, and be slightly worse for the environment, but it's much more convenient.

Modelo was a finance and procurement team's dream for cost savings. When the Modelo deal was announced, I remember Tony Milikin saying with a big grin, "This is going to be fun." Most of the finance and procurement teams dropped what we were doing and saddled up to spend a few weeks in Mexico City. This was our Super Bowl. These teams dreamed of opportunities like this. Negotiating with suppliers or auctioning existing contracts to improve pricing or payment terms was challenging and incrementally improved the business. Moving Modelo's suppliers to AB InBev's costs and payment terms was transformative.

I quickly got to work with my colleagues on understanding contracts with suppliers. We started breaking apart the costs of materials into true commodity costs and conversion costs. For returnable glass bottles, we recognized significant savings when we broke down the components of the bottle into silica, soda ash, limestone, cullet (recycled glass), and natural gas (to fire the furnaces). We paid for those ingredients separate from the cost to actually manufacture the bottles. Bottle costs were benchmarked to similar countries, and the local suppliers were asked to match international prices. If they didn't, bottles would be imported from elsewhere at significantly lower costs. The same went for items like cardboard boxes to transport beer. One of the Modelo family members owned the cardboard box company from which Modelo purchased beer boxes. When the contract was put out to bid, significant savings were realized. The same process followed for aluminum cans, malt, transportation, and every other cost that goes into beer. Grupo Modelo used many of the same suppliers that AB InBev did for materials, so it was easy for AB InBev to improve contract terms. For example, AB InBev and Modelo bought aluminum cans from the same supplier. AB InBev paid the supplier less for those cans because it had greater scale and did a better job at negotiating price. It also had payment terms of ~sixty days, while Modelo was closer to thirty days. Magically, Modelo's aluminum can price and payment terms quickly reflected AB's or the supplier risked losing the business.

There were cost savings on the people side of the business as well. This is a reality of any corporate merger, be it two local plumbing companies or two multinational companies. When companies combine, redundant positions are inevitable. These tend to be back-office roles that can be done in one location, like accounting, finance, legal, and HR. But a company doesn't need two CEOs either, so many senior positions are also eliminated. Similar to the takeover of Anheuser-Busch, generous severance and employee job assistance packages cushioned the blow. It's not easy to let colleagues go, but it lets current and future employees know that the company cares. This helps build back engagement post-merger and attracts new talent to the organization.

I went back and forth to Mexico City multiple times in 2012 and 2013. In addition to finding savings for the business, we worked with the local Grupo Modelo team to ensure the savings were sustainable. Being acquired by another company is not easy. For the employees who stay, they have to learn the language of a whole new organization. They have to learn new routines. New key performance indicators. New compensation structures. New colleagues.

There are challenges for the acquirer, too. As much as possible, the acquiring company tries to embed one culture across a firm. AB InBev

used its 10 Principles to quickly discover which employees were culturally aligned and which ones weren't. Signs highlighting the "dream,
culture, people" principles went up everywhere. Employees who did
not buy into the new culture didn't last long.

One of the funny idiosyncrasies about Mexican culture was that
everyone went home for lunch for about two hours during the middle
of the day. There was nothing in the 10 Principles that stated people
could *not* go home for two hours every day. As long as people still got
results, they could technically work whenever. It just made it difficult
to do business. Meetings stopped. Phones went unanswered. Contracts
weren't signed. This was an adjustment I had to get used to in Mexico.
I'm not sure if this is still the custom in Mexico, but I found it very
different from the other places I had worked.

I also spent a few weekends in Mexico City since it was too far to
travel back to Belgium for the weekend. Growing up, I vacationed in
Mexico a few times. I wouldn't consider a week in Cabo San Lucas or
Cancún really being exposed to "Mexican culture," though. Being in
Mexico City for weeks at a time was a bit more immersive. I attended
a soccer game at the famous Aztec Stadium. I took a bus tour to the
Aztec pyramids outside the city. I attended Mexico's Independence
Day celebrations in the Plaza de la Constitución. I went to the Na-
tional History Museum. I had many dinners and nights in the upscale
Polanco neighborhood. The people, food, and culture of Mexico were
wonderful and welcoming. The one thing that always surprised me,
though, was the number of armed military personnel wherever I went.
At the soccer stadium, there seemed to be more armed guards in the
stands than fans. Armed guards sat on the bus on the way to pyramids.
On Independence Day, you guessed it, more guards. In fact, there were
enough armed guards in the square to overthrow the government and
declare a new independent state, if they wanted. I never experienced
any issues with crime or violence when I was in Mexico, but the mili-

tary presence was a constant reminder that potential violence was never too far away. When AB InBev moved expats to Mexico City full-time once the transaction closed, all of the executives were provided with armored cars and housing in secure neighborhoods. This was obviously for their protection, but it also made it difficult to really experience authentic Mexican culture. In other words, it made it hard to understand the lives and needs of the vast majority of the people who drink their beer and effectively market to them.

But that wasn't my job. My job was to cut costs, and that was time-consuming but relatively simple. By the end of 2013, AB InBev had already delivered the $600 million in savings. Grupo Modelo's EBITDA margins increased from 32 percent in 2012 to 42 percent in 2013. By the end of 2014, EBITDA margins would further increase to 47 percent. By 2015, more than $1 billion of synergies would be delivered, $400 million more than the $600 million promised.[1] Per usual, this would be done with declining beer volumes. Over 2013 and 2014, Grupo Modelo's Mexico beer volume declined by 1.3 percent. Revenue increased by 8 percent due to price increases, but the vast majority of the value created was due to operational efficiencies. The stock market reacted favorably to the operational improvements. AB InBev's stock increased from $85/share at the beginning of 2013 to $115 by the end of 2014. This 33 percent gain paced ahead of gains by the S&P 500 and the broader consumer sector.

The Grupo Modelo merger was good for AB InBev. It was not good for Anheuser-Busch in the United States, though. In fact, AB InBev's handling of the Grupo Modelo acquisition in the United States was one of the first times I personally saw a large cultural disconnect between the Brazilians and Belgians running the company and the local market where they operated. The consequences would be dramatic for the U.S. business moving forward. Let me explain.

When AB InBev acquired Grupo Modelo, they wanted to maintain the ability to sell Corona and Modelo in the United States. They knew that U.S. regulators wouldn't like it, though. Combining the largest and third-largest brewer in the U.S. would create highly concentrated and potentially anticompetitive markets. AB InBev's U.S. market share was 40 percent; Grupo Modelo's was 7 percent. That's pretty high. But in certain markets it was even higher. In some places, AB's market share could be more than 60 percent and Grupo Modelo's could be more than 20 percent.

To understand how concentrated a market is, and if it is potentially anticompetitive, the Department of Justice uses something called the Herfindahl-Hirschman Index (HHI).[2] Markets in which the HHI is above 2,500 are considered concentrated, and that's a no-no.

Prior to the Grupo Modelo deal, the U.S. beer industry had an HHI of 2,234. Close, but okay. Post-deal, the HHI would go to 2,800, or an increase of 566 points. More troubling for AB, the Department of Justice looks at the HHI concentration in twenty-six major metro areas in addition to the total U.S. In twenty out of twenty-six cities, the HHI score for a combined AB InBev and Grupo Modelo exceeded 2,500. In Oklahoma City, it was 4,886, an increase of 1,000 points. Apparently, people in Oklahoma City drink nothing but Corona and Bud Light. It was unlikely the DOJ would let the merger through.

So AB InBev got creative.

When the deal was announced, AB got ahead of potential DOJ concerns by proposing an innovative structure. AB InBev would continue to produce Corona and Modelo in Mexico. It would then sell it to a separate import company in the U.S. called Crown. Crown was a joint partnership between Modelo and a U.S.-based company called Constellation (which also owned a premium wine and spirits portfolio in the U.S.). Crown could then market and sell the beer at whatever price it wished. Since Crown controlled the end price of Corona and Modelo in the market, the market would remain competitive. After ten years, AB InBev could buy back the rights to import Corona and Modelo into the U.S., giving them 100 percent control of the supply chain. Crown's CEO was concerned that its "number-1 competitor will now be our supplier," but AB InBev thought a deal could be struck.

Although this structure was unusual, it still might have worked if it weren't for a pricing "Conduct Plan"—essentially a playbook for how to get competitors to "voluntarily" price their competing beers—the Brazilians hatched in the U.S.

Here's how it came about. In 2011, the few remaining Senior Sales Executives from the old Anheuser-Busch left the company. After the acquisition, they had three-year contracts to help with the transition (similar to many marketing executives), which allowed them to accelerate retirement packages and pension vesting if they stayed until 2011. People like Dave Peacock, U.S. President, and Evan Athanus, U.S. VP of Sales, were among the highly experienced and admired folks who left in 2011. From 2008 to 2011, they kept the sales and marketing functions operating as smoothly as possible while other operational efficiencies were found. When they left, they were largely replaced with Brazilian executives. One of those executives was David Almeida. David was in his midthirties and a rising star in the organization. When AB recruited new talent, they said that they wanted people who were "Driven" and "Ambitious." It was well known that "Driven" and "Ambitious" and David Almeida both shared the same first initials. In other words, the company wanted to find more David Almeidas.

David grew up in Brazil, went to the University of Pennsylvania for college, and then was an investment banker in New York City. After one year, he returned to Brazil and joined Ambev's finance team. He quickly worked his way up through the finance organization and became VP of Mergers & Acquisitions in 2007. Throughout 2008 he led the acquisition of Anheuser-Busch and then was promoted to Chief Financial Officer of Anheuser-Busch in the U.S. He was thirty years old. The previous CFO of Anheuser-Busch, Randolph Baker, was sixty.

Despite being in finance for his whole career, David was not a typical "finance" guy. He was charismatic. He was funny. He was optimistic. He was loud. He regularly greeted people and audiences with a rowdy "GOOOOOOD MORNING." If he didn't get a loud enough "GOOOOOOOOD MORNING" in response, he repeated himself until the decibels and energy level matched his own. His personality was more suited for a sales role, but his finance and deal-making abilities made him more valuable in mergers and acquisitions.

David was viewed as someone who could potentially replace Brito as CEO. To do this, he would need experience outside of finance. Therefore, when Dave Peacock and Evan Athanus left Anheuser-Busch, David Almeida was promoted to Chief Sales Officer and took on both of their roles. AB InBev had a history of stretching top talent into bigger and more challenging roles. Running sales for the most profitable beer market in the world, without any sales experience, would be a major challenge. Especially when the vast majority of David's life had been spent outside of the United States.

The lack of sales experience would prove challenging. The lack of understanding U.S. rules, regulations, and customs would be devastating. The "Conduct Plan" was a perfect example of trying to import business practices from other countries to the U.S. that violated U.S. norms and the law. In short, the "Conduct Plan" was a way to try and coordinate price increases among the major beer suppliers in the United States. The Department of Justice highly frowns upon price coordination, even if it is not done explicitly.

Prior to the Conduct Plan, here's how price increases worked. In late summer or early fall, Anheuser-Busch would announce a price increase. This increase varied by region and by channel. For example, the Southeast might increase prices in bars and restaurants one year while the

West Coast might increase beer prices in convenience stores and grocery stores. These increases were based on commodity inflation, local market dynamics, and supply and demand. Competitors like MillerCoors and Modelo would then make decisions to either match AB InBev on its price increase or not. If they didn't, AB InBev would usually have to rescind its price increase or risk losing sales to competition.

Oftentimes, MillerCoors would follow AB InBev's price increases. Modelo increasingly didn't. In fact, Modelo implemented a "Momentum Plan" in 2008 that sought to increase its market share in the United States. It planned to do this by selling more beer after "shrinking the price gaps" between brands like Modelo and Corona and domestic beers like Bud Light and Coors Light. For the next several years, Grupo Modelo held its beer prices flat. Bud Light and others increased their prices. This narrowed the price gap between the brands, and Grupo Modelo experienced significant volume and market share gains. AB InBev was frustrated.

The Conduct Plan was implemented by David and his team throughout 2011 and 2012 in response. This plan was similar to the pricing plans the company implemented in Brazil. In Brazil, AB InBev has more than 60 percent market share. The government is not as concerned about industry concentration or consumer pricing. When AB InBev moved pricing in Brazil, competition followed. If they didn't, AB InBev could quickly undercut competition and pressure their margins until they did follow. Competition conducted themselves accordingly.

When the Department of Justice rejected the proposed AB InBev and Modelo U.S. importation agreement in January 2013, they cited the "Conduct Plan" as a major reason. Specifically, they state:

> The specifics of ABI's pricing strategy are governed by its "Conduct Plan," a strategic plan for pricing in the United

States that reads like a how-to manual for successful price coordination. The goals of the Conduct Plan include: "yielding the highest level of followership in the short-term" and "improving competitor conduct over the long-term." ABI's Conduct Plan emphasizes the importance of being "Transparent—so competitors can clearly see the plan"; "Simple—so competitors can understand the plan"; "Consistent—so competitors can predict the plan" and "Targeted—consider competition's structure." By pursuing these goals, ABI seeks to "dictate consistent and transparent competitive response." As one ABI executive wrote, a "Front Line Driven Plan sends Clear Signal to Competition and Sets up well for potential conduct plan response." According to ABI, its Conduct Plan "increases the probability of [ABI] sustaining a price increase." The proposed merger would likely increase the ability of ABI and the remaining beer firms to coordinate by eliminating an independent Modelo—which has increasingly inhibited ABI's price leadership—from the market.

The complaint went on to summarize all of the reasons why the DOJ deemed this merger illegal. Competition would go down. So would quality and innovation. Price would go up. Consumers would suffer. All bad stuff.

||||||||||||

There was no coming back. AB InBev dropped its supply and import proposal with Crown. By April 2013, AB InBev and the U.S. government agreed to terms for the merger to go forward. AB InBev had to sell not only the import rights in the U.S., but the breweries in Mexico that supplied the beer. But to who? Constellation seemed the likely choice.

Wall Street loved this deal for Constellation. Constellation's stock increased by 25 percent between January 2013 and April 2013 as traders bet that Constellation would be the beneficiary of the DOJ's investigation. Ten years later, Modelo dethroned Bud Light to become the number-1 beer in America. Over this same time period, Constellation's stock would increase almost 6x. It was one of the best-performing companies in the CPG industry. AB InBev's stock would decrease by ~33 percent over this same time period and was one of the worst.

The effects of the botched Grupo Modelo transaction in the U.S., caused by the Brazilians' misunderstanding of cultural and regulatory norms, weren't immediately felt, though. AB InBev still retained the rights to sell Corona and Modelo everywhere outside of the U.S. Large synergies could still be realized in Mexico. There were still large acquisition targets like South African Breweries that could be purchased. So AB InBev moved on in 2013.

I moved on midway through 2013 as well. After two years on Tony Milikin's team and helping with the global integration of Grupo Modelo, I had the opportunity to join David Almeida's team in St. Louis. Even though the "Conduct Plan" prevented AB InBev from owning some of the most popular beers in America, David was still viewed as "Driven and Ambitious" and a successor to Brito. His Modelo mistake was a learning experience from which he could recover.

Other Driven and Ambitious people in the organization were still advised to work with David. I was labeled a "People Bet," which meant that AB InBev execs thought I had the potential to reach the Executive ranks of the organization. To get there, it helped having sales experience and exposure to people like David.

And the U.S. needed more Americans and "People Bet" talent in sales. Constellation was 100 percent focused on growing their share in the U.S. market. As the largest U.S. brewer, AB InBev was most at risk of losing, and lost beer sales are hard to recover.

Chapter 8

There Isn't Even Uber There

"**F**TF!!!!" David Almeida screamed at the May 2013 morning sales call in St. Louis. The room of twenty people, joined by another eighty people on the phone, screamed "FTF!!!!" back. Then he did it again. The first response scream of "FTF!!!!" was not loud enough. It had to be repeated until David felt everyone matched his level of enthusiasm. David implemented "FTF" as a rallying cry for the sales organization. Technically, it meant "Fuel the Future." This meant that AB InBev was launching new brands, and working harder than ever, to revert volume and market share losses in the U.S. In reality, "FTF" stood for "Fuck Those Fuckers." AB InBev was going hard at MillerCoors and Grupo Modelo to maintain its leadership position, and FTF was a call to not let anyone stand in the way.

This was one of the first sales meetings I attended in my new role as Sales Strategy Director for the U.S. In this role, I was responsible for setting the one- and three-year sales plans for Anheuser-Busch in the U.S. I was also responsible for executing special projects for David Almeida and his right-hand man, Ricardo Melo.

2013 was not starting out how David had planned. 2012 was David's first full year as Chief Sales Officer of Anheuser-Busch. And it had been Anheuser-Busch's best year in the U.S. since the merger. Beer volumes increased and profits reached all-time highs. Was this

David's doing? Not really. David inherited a strong innovation pipeline from the legacy Anheuser-Busch execs who were wrapping up their three-year transition agreements.

Bud Light Platinum and Bud Light Lime-A-Rita were both launched in early 2012. They had been in the works well before David took over sales at the end of 2011. Both were unquestionably a success. These products were the number-1 and -2 new innovations in the entire beer category in 2012. Bud Light Platinum achieved more than a 1 percent share of the entire beer category in 2012, which made it about half the size of Michelob Ultra at the time. This was a massive innovation launch that has not been matched by Anheuser-Busch or any other brewer since. It usually takes decades to build a brand with more than 1 percent share of the beer category, not one year. Bud Light Platinum was a more premium version of Bud Light. It was higher priced, had higher alcohol content, a bright blue bottle, and was slightly sweeter than Bud Light. It was made for nighttime "party" occasions that were currently being won by spirits brands. The Super Bowl ad that launched the brand even noted that it had "top shelf taste." Today, consumers can still find Platinum and its "top shelf taste" in stores across the U.S.

Bud Light Lime-A-Rita was introduced the same year. Bud Light Lime-A-Rita was a flavored malt beverage, or FMB. FMBs were an emerging category in beer. They were known for being sweeter than beer and for having more alcohol content. Many times they tasted like mixed spirits drinks. Brands like Mike's Hard Lemonade, Smirnoff Ice (you might recall "getting iced" as a fad in 2010 and 2011), Four Loko, and Twisted Tea had popped up over the past decade. Anheuser-Busch finally had a response. Bud Light Lime-A-Rita was made to taste like a margarita in a can. They quickly grabbed 25 percent of the FMB category and were the number-1 FMB brand by the end of 2012.[1] People loved the taste of a margarita in the convenience of a can. They still do, and the "Ritas" remain in many stores.

Unfortunately, AB's 2013 innovation pipeline was not as robust. Anheuser-Busch launched Budweiser Black Crown to try to repeat the success of Bud Light Platinum. Black Crown was also higher in alcohol and more flavorful than regular Budweiser. It was supposed to be paired with food, but there was a botched Super Bowl rollout of the brand. The marketing team made it look like a nightlife brand, similar to Bud Light Platinum. The ad dubbed "Coronation" was the second-lowest-ranked ad of the Super Bowl.[2] Consumers were confused and didn't really know where to drink it. It never reached more than a third of Platinum's size. It was out of the market within a few years.

Beck's Sapphire was the other innovation launched at the 2013 Super Bowl. Never heard of it? Neither did anyone else. The Super Bowl ad featured a fish singing the song "No Diggity" to a Beck's Sapphire bottle. It was also ranked as one of the worst ads of that year's Super Bowl. Beck's Sapphire didn't perform well in the market and was also discontinued after a few years.

By May of 2013, it was clear that the U.S.'s sales and marketing goals for the year were in trouble. This was the year when the U.S. was supposed to get back to sustainable volume growth and start gaining share of the beer category once again. Almost halfway through the year, though, AB's beer volumes were down 3 percent and they ceded more than 0.5 percent of market share to competition. FTF was a good rallying cry, but AB was the one really getting F'd.

I quickly learned a major difference between AB's Finance/ Procurement team and the Sales team. The Finance and Procurement teams saw the world in black and white. They needed to deliver clear, measurable financial results that showed in the financial statements. If they got a lower price on an aluminum can contract, it immediately showed up as improved margins on the income statement. If they got better payment terms from a barley supplier, their working capital improved on the cash flow statement. If the goals were not hit, employees took the results personally and looked for opportunities elsewhere to improve the business. There was nowhere to hide results.

In sales and marketing, there were clear goals to achieve in the amount of beer sold and the market share to gain versus competitors. The sales and marketing teams tended to spend more time explaining why they missed their goals, rather than how they were going to hit them. There were always exogenous factors to blame when sales and marketing did not perform. I quickly learned that most sales presentations opened with a macroanalysis of the economy and why it was impacting beer sales. In 2013, weather was colder than usual to start the year, and people don't drink as much beer when it is cold outside. Gas prices were elevated in 2013, impacting disposable income for things like beer. Labor participation rates were still low. Competition wasn't following the "Conduct Plan." You get the gist.

Marketing tended to be even fluffier. They used consumer surveys to see how many people were "aware of a brand." Brands like Bud Light had almost 99 percent awareness among people who drank alcohol. Specialty brands like Stella Artois might have only 33 percent awareness. After awareness, they used survey data to show how many people "consider" drinking a brand. 99 percent of people might be aware of Bud Light, but only 50 percent might consider drinking it. After consideration, they measure "past four-week consumption" or the number of people who actually drank the brand in the prior four weeks. Consumers are also asked to highlight their "favorite brand," "brands worth paying more for," and many other things that marketing would use to justify the effectiveness of their ad spend. The worse brands perform, the more creative brand teams become in finding metrics to show the marketing plan is working. Sales down 10 percent nationwide? Don't worry, the percentage of Hispanic women aged 18–39 in North Dakota who are aware that Hoegaarden exists is up 13.4 percent since last year. Our marketing is a success!

By mid-2013, there was a lot of creativity on both the sales and marketing side justifying why AB InBev's volume and revenues weren't hitting targets. The one thing sales and marketing execs agreed on was that it wasn't their fault. It wasn't their bad innovation pipeline (it was). It wasn't the sales plans for the year (these were also bad). It wasn't marketing that missed the mark (this definitely missed the mark). The mostly foreign execs thought there must be an external problem. And while sales and marketing could pitter-patter for hours on all the factors hurting sales, they finally settled on one critical part of the AB InBev ecosystem on which they could place the blame: wholesalers.

Whipping the Hitch That Pulls the Beer Wagon

The relationship between Anheuser-Busch and its wholesalers is complex and born from strange historical circumstances. But for the past century, it's worked, both for Anheuser-Busch and the independent, mainly family-owned group of more than five hundred wholesalers currently delivering its products to bars, convenience stores, and grocery stores across the U.S. InBev's post-merger war with Anheuser-Busch's legacy wholesalers was an early indication that InBev didn't understand the American beer business, and though InBev may try to shift blame to others, it was Anheuser-Busch's brands that would ultimately pay the price.

The history of the Anheuser-Busch and wholesaler relationship goes back to Prohibition. Before Prohibition, brewers and distillers were generally allowed to manufacture, distribute, and sell alcohol with little regulation. They could do one step, or they could do it all. That meant Anheuser-Busch could make the beer, ship the beer, and own the bars and restaurants where the beer was sold. And, for a time, it did.

But in the early 1900s, there was a rise in social problems caused by alcohol. Unlike today, the vast majority of alcohol (over 80 percent) was consumed in dodgy, mostly unregulated bars and restaurants. Vertical integration made alcohol taxes easy to cheat. Workers spent their wages at the bars instead of on groceries for the week. Alcohol abuse led to domestic violence and other crimes. The bars became easy targets. The Woman's Christian Temperance Union and other religious-inspired movements advocated for the elimination of alcohol to rectify these social ills. These movements got their wish when Congress passed the Eighteenth Amendment in 1920, outlawing the production, transport, and sale of alcohol in the U.S. (but interestingly, not the consumption).

But Prohibition did not solve society's drinking ills. For starters, people did not stop drinking. Instead, alcohol production and consumption went underground. Gangsters like Al Capone controlled vast empires of alcohol imported from Canada or the Caribbean and then distributed across the U.S. Moonshiners in places like Kentucky and Tennessee also continued producing and selling alcohol domestically.

Many people were already advocating for Prohibition to be repealed by the late 1920s. The Great Depression accelerated Prohibition's demise. When the Great Depression arrived in the early 1930s, the U.S. government was looking for ways to create new jobs. Legalizing alcohol manufacturing and sales was one of the opportunities. The Twenty-first Amendment was passed in 1933, and the regulation of alcohol sales was granted to the states. To resolve the historical issues regarding manufacturers owning bars and restaurants, many states implemented a "Three Tier System," which was meant to prevent producers from encouraging public drunkenness.

The three-tier system legally separated the manufacturing, distributing (or wholesaling), and retailing of alcohol into individual tiers. Each tier would be independent of each other. Manufacturers could not own distributors or retailers. Distributors and retailers could not own each other either.

Post-Prohibition, the distributing tier emerged as a powerful and efficient way for manufacturers to sell their products across the country. Before Prohibition, there were more than three thousand breweries in the United States. The vast majority were local. Beer brands rarely traveled over county lines, let alone state lines. Opening new brewery-owned bars was expensive. After the Twenty-first Amendment, only fifty breweries remained in the United States. Increasing distribution in grocery stores, convenient stores, and restaurants was the most efficient way to expand.

This relationship proved incredibly profitable for both Anheuser-Busch and its wholesaler network, which distributed its products. Anheuser-Busch quickly found local wholesalers across the country. Some wholesalers were already selling food or other items to grocery stores and restaurants. Selling beer was a natural addition. Other wholesalers were entrepreneurs looking to capitalize on this new government-regulated distribution tier. Some of these entrepreneurs previously bootlegged alcohol during Prohibition. They already knew the local restaurants operating speakeasies. Legally distributing beer was a better business model. They quickly negotiated contracts with many of the largest breweries at the time, including Anheuser-Busch.

Initially, the contracts were not exclusive. Anheuser-Busch retained the rights to sell beer to multiple wholesalers in a territory. The wholesalers would then compete with one another to sell into grocery stores, convenience stores, package liquor stores, bars, and restaurants. Anheuser-Busch initially signed distribution agreements with more than seven hundred wholesalers, who sold its beers from Nome, Alaska, to Key West, Florida, and every legal county in between. Wholesalers also had the ability to distribute any other beer brand they wanted.

Celebrities and athletes even started owning wholesalers, sometimes in exchange for providing services to Anheuser-Busch. Frank Sinatra was famously given the opportunity to buy the wholesaler in

Long Beach, California, after singing at an Anheuser-Busch corporate event. Roger Maris was allowed to purchase the Anheuser-Busch wholesaler in Gainesville, Florida, after helping the Cardinals win a World Series in 1967. Gussie Busch, CEO of Anheuser-Busch at the time, famously stated in 1967, "Anybody who hits thirty-three homers and drives in one hundred runs deserves a beer distributorship."

As Anheuser-Busch grew, so did its wholesalers. By the 1960s, Anheuser-Busch was the largest brewery in the country. By default, its wholesalers were the largest beer wholesalers. Then Anheuser-Busch sweetened the pot.

In the 1970s, wholesalers got an even bigger benefit: exclusive rights to distribute within their territory. This wasn't an act of simple generosity. Anheuser-Busch's largest competitor, Schlitz, made a major mistake. To cut costs, Schlitz changed the brewing process for its flagship beer. The reformulated beer was a disaster. It tasted bad and spoiled more quickly.

Anheuser-Busch quickly capitalized on its competitor's mistake. It established a "somebody still cares about quality" marketing campaign.[3] It also worked to ensure quality products throughout its supply chain. For wholesalers, that meant asking them to invest in climate-controlled warehouses so Anheuser-Busch beer would retain its flavor and not spoil as quickly. But climate-controlled warehouses aren't cheap. And wholesalers were wary to make this huge investment, only to have Anheuser-Busch cancel their contract on a whim. To solve this problem, Anheuser-Busch and its wholesalers negotiated a Wholesaler Equity Agreement, or WEA. Moving forward, Anheuser-Busch wholesalers would need to uphold certain standards, like building refrigerated warehouses, using "Maximum Efforts" behind Anheuser-Busch products over other products they carried, investing a certain amount of marketing dollars into their local market each year and servicing accounts a defined number of times each week. In exchange, wholesalers were given the right to exclusively distribute Anheuser-Busch products in their territory. The agreement was groundbreaking. Now that wholesalers had "franchise protection," or the right to distribute the brands in perpetuity in their defined territories, their businesses were much more valuable. Wholesalers could now sell their business for two to three times more with franchise protection than without it.

The incentives were now aligned between Anheuser-Busch and their distribution network. The next few decades would see unprecedented growth and prosperity for both. Anheuser-Busch's "Somebody still cares about quality" marketing campaign sealed the demise of Schlitz. Anheuser-Busch became the uncontested largest brewer in the U.S., doubling the market share of the next-closest brewer by the end of the century. The Anheuser-Busch distribution network fueled this growth across the nation.

The "maximum efforts" clause and the requirement to spend local marketing dollars set the Anheuser-Busch wholesaler system apart. Maximum efforts was a simple concept that said wholesalers must put "maximum efforts" behind Anheuser-Busch brands before selling other brands. For example, if there was an opportunity to build a beer display in a grocery store, that beer display must be for Anheuser-Busch brands before other brands. If there was an open tap handle at a bar, Anheuser-Busch brands must first be offered to the bar before other brands. If a convenience store owner wanted a neon beer sign in their window, an Anheuser-Busch neon would have to first be offered. If Anheuser-Busch employees visited a wholesaler's market and saw other brands on display, or other neon beer signs, the wholesaler could be taken "out of compliance" and risk losing their contract with Anheuser-Busch if the issues were not immediately remedied.

Wholesalers' local marketing spend requirement ensured Anheuser-Busch brands felt relevant and local to each market. The WEA mandated that wholesalers spend a certain amount of "cents per case" sold in their local market. In other words, for every case of beer sold, whole-salers would have to spend a certain amount of that case on local marketing activities. These could be beer samplings at local retailers. It could be signage for bar owners promoting a "trivia night" sponsored by Budweiser. They could sponsor local bowling leagues. Wholesalers began sponsoring the events that mattered to people in their market. In South Dakota, it might be the Sturgis Motorcycle Rally. In Tampa Florida, it was the Gasparilla Pirate Fest. In Texas, it was every rodeo. Anheuser-Busch beers would become synonymous with many of these events. Local wholesalers would activate these events by bringing "Bud Girls" to hand out free beer. They would purchase custom neon signs for the events and print custom banners. They would bring in local and national celebrities associated with Anheuser-Busch, like NASCAR drivers or Powerboat racers. They could even request the famous Budweiser Clydesdales to attend—a four-hooved spectacle that was known to draw more than ten thousand people on its own. Leading up to an event, Anheuser-Busch's sponsorship would be promoted via grocery store displays and bar promotions.

Due to wholesalers placing "maximum efforts" behind AB's brands, and making these brands very relevant in each local market, AB brands represented the vast majority of a wholesaler's revenue. By 2000, many wholesalers dropped all other beer brands and were exclusive to Anheuser-Busch. Across the AB wholesaler network, 95 percent of their revenue was attributable to AB brands. For many, this number had been less than 50 percent in the 1960s, prior to the WEA.

Anheuser-Busch relied on wholesalers to make their beers part of the fabric of local communities across the country. Many local wholesalers are prominent families in small towns across the country. Their sponsorships and donations allow many local events to happen. They also tend to be one of the largest local employers in each town. Historically, there was strong trust between Anheuser-Busch and its distributors, and they worked together to embody the "making friends is our business" spirit.

In 2013, this partnership was fraying. David Almeida didn't believe that the decentralized wholesaler approach, which had worked for more than forty years, was working anymore. He wanted to "steer from the center." He wanted to control the events that wholesalers sponsored, the brands that they placed in every account, the displays that were placed in every grocery store, and the local marketing spend that each wholesaler was required to spend on things like neon signs.

He did this by mandating programs that could be enforced through the Wholesaler Equity Agreement and an incentive program called Ambassadors of Excellence (or AOE). If wholesalers didn't comply or had low scores, they could be marked out of compliance, lose incentive payments, and risk losing their license to distribute AB brands.

One program was called King of Distribution (KOD), which was developed in St. Louis and cascaded beer brand and package distribution targets to every bar, convenience store, and grocery store in the country. Unfortunately, the KOD algorithm was not very good. It was constantly criticized for asking wholesalers to place brands like Budweiser Chelada, which is a mixture of Budweiser and clamato juice typically enjoyed by Hispanic consumers, into fine Italian restaurants. Bud Light Lime-A-Rita was targeted for Chinese restaurants. In what was a shock to almost no one, most of this beer did not sell and sat in stores past its expiration date. Wholesalers had to swallow the cost. When wholesalers lose money, they are not happy, so KOD was not a very popular program. Wholesalers wanted to sell what sold in their individual market.

POC Level Planning was another unpopular program. POC stands for Point of Connection, or the place where a consumer purchases or drinks beer. This could be a bar, convenience store, or grocery store. Historically, wholesaler sales reps planned the displays and promotions that made sense for their accounts. Sports bars got Super Bowl signage and promotions in January. Grocery stores got Fourth of July displays in the weeks leading up to the holiday. Similar to KOD, POC Level Planning was a program developed and controlled by St. Louis. People in St. Louis would cascade POC level display targets across the country and then ask wholesalers to execute them. Many POC level display targets did not make sense, or changed too frequently for the consumer to even notice. For example, if a local sports team made the playoffs, the wholesaler would want advertising promoting the playoff run in accounts. POC Level Planning didn't account for playoff runs, though, and would demand different advertising that was less relevant at the time.

At the end of 2013, Anheuser-Busch received its annual wholesaler engagement survey back from wholesalers. This survey asked questions related to wholesalers' happiness with marketing programs, sales programs, innovation launches, and many other programs. 2013 had some of the lowest scores in the history of the survey.

When most organizations receive low scores, they look to improve the programs contributing to the low scores. David Almeida and other senior Anheuser-Busch leaders had different ideas. They figured that the wholesalers weren't "aligned" enough behind the programs. The programs weren't the issue. The wholesalers' resistance was.

Therefore, Almeida ramped up a program to try to purchase as many Anheuser-Busch wholesalers as possible. Even though the three-tier system generally prohibited breweries from owning distributors, there were many state-level exceptions and carve-outs. Certain states allowed breweries to own a distributor if they did not have a brewery in the state. Other states said breweries could own their distribution as long as they did not also distribute spirits. In 2013, AB owned less than 10 percent of its distribution by volume. It historically operated a small number of wholesalers to train and develop employees and also establish best practices that could be shared with other wholesalers. But legally, AB could own up to 50 percent of its volume. Almeida and Anheuser-Busch wanted to own this 50 percent. Then they could solve their unpopularity problem.

Wholesalers were not happy about AB's plan to buy their distribution network. Most wholesalers are family-owned businesses that pass down from generation to generation. Additionally, when a wholesaler sells their business, the wholesalers in adjacent territories are the most logical buyers. This is because there are synergies to wholesalers owning more territory. They can operate out of a single warehouse. They can better service retailers that have locations across a wide territory. They can invest more marketing dollars across the market.

When Anheuser-Busch buys a wholesaler, none of these benefits are realized. There are still the same number of wholesalers, but now the independent wholesalers do not have an ability to expand. Instead of being acquirers, they now only have the option to be acquired by Anheuser-Busch. And wholesalers did not trust Anheuser-Busch to be a fair player operating next to them. Since Anheuser-Busch wanted to buy more wholesalers, they could theoretically do things in adjacent territory they owned to decrease the value of neighboring independent wholesalers, essentially forcing neighboring wholesalers to sell at depressed valuations. Some of those actions could be lowering the price of beer in the Anheuser-Busch–owned territory so customers would drive to that territory to buy beer. Anheuser-Busch could also increase its marketing spend in its owned territories while decreasing marketing spend in non-owned territories.

As AB started inserting itself into states and territories where it historically did not have a presence, it experienced a similar effect to when a body receives an organ transplant—rejection. The Anheuser-Busch wholesaler network aggressively fought David Almeida's plan to acquire 50 percent of them. Since the wholesalers are local and some of the largest private employers in a state, they wield outsized political influence to fight.

In Kentucky, Anheuser-Busch tried to buy a very small rural wholesaler in Owensboro, population sixty thousand. The wholesalers in Kentucky quickly organized state legislation to not only reject this acquisition, but force Anheuser-Busch to sell the wholesaler that they'd owned in Louisville since the 1970s. Similarly, Anheuser-Busch bought a wholesaler in Lima, Ohio, which is in the rural western part of the state. Wholesalers in Ohio quickly worked with legislators to prohibit Anheuser-Busch from owning any additional wholesalers in the state. More states proactively passed legislation in 2014 and 2015 preventing Anheuser-Busch from owning wholesalers. By the end of 2015, Anheuser-Busch was able to own only ~20 percent of its distribution, down from ~50 percent at the end of 2013.

The opportunity to own and operate wholesalers was quickly disappearing. David Almeida's frustration with wholesalers was not. Instead of fighting the system, or trying to buy the system, I wondered why AB couldn't just work better with its wholesaler system. At AB's 2014 annual company meeting, I asked this exact question. Specifically, during a Q&A session in front of approximately four hundred people from AB's sales and marketing teams, I asked David if wholesalers were the problem, or if AB's King of Distribution and POC Planning Central programs were the problem. Maybe if we had better tools and programs that were clearly explained and gave wholesalers local market flexibility to execute, that could lead to a better partnership and more sales. David gave a standard company response onstage, saying that AB had the best technology and information and that wholesalers would eventually come around.

Offstage, David pulled me aside and let me know he almost fired me for asking the question. He didn't like being challenged in front of so many colleagues. Lucky for me, David said he thought more about my question, though, and saw there was some merit to it. Now that AB could not own its wholesalers, we were essentially in a marriage with them. AB could make the choice for a good marriage or a bad marriage, but there'd be no divorce. Moving into 2015, there would be more flexibility for wholesalers to execute local programs. David was at least willing to listen to me and work with wholesalers. I don't think he ever really understood them, though. This improved relationships short term, but there were still issues on the horizon.

The Move

In addition to wholesalers, David and the Brazilian executives had another scapegoat for not being able to grow beer volumes and revenue—St. Louis. St. Louis had been the home of Anheuser-Busch since 1852. Tens of thousands of people from across the U.S. and the globe worked for Anheuser-Busch in St. Louis over the decades. They grew Anheuser-Busch to be the largest brewery in the world. St. Louis was almost a microcosm of the U.S. It was an immigrant town on the Mississippi River. There were urban areas, suburban areas, and rural areas all within a thirty-minute commute of downtown. Being in the geographical center of the country, and the Gateway to the West, was also a big benefit. AB employees could easily access the majority of the country via quick flights. Despite this, in 2014, David Almeida and other Brazilian and European AB execs decided that St. Louis was a liability.

They especially saw it as a liability from a marketing perspective. The marketing team was one of the last teams in the U.S. that was predominantly led by Americans, albeit ones who recently joined the company. That came to an end in 2014. Paul Chibe was the Chief Marketing Officer for Anheuser-Busch entering 2014. Chibe joined Anheuser-Busch in 2011. He came from Wrigley, the chewing gum company, where he successfully gained market share over numerous years. But he clashed with the Brazilian management team in the

U.S. and left in early 2014. He was replaced by a Belgian named Jorn Socquet. Socquet had worked at AB InBev for numerous years and was previously the head of marketing in Canada. Socquet quickly fired many of the remaining marketing people based in St. Louis. Many were the last remaining connections to the old Anheuser-Busch. These were people who were not executives at the time of the takeover, but a level or two below who did a lot of the work. They developed the consumer insights that led to the brand campaigns. They worked with the marketing agencies to tweak commercials to hit the right humor and tone. Many were St. Louis natives or people who had lived in St. Louis for most of their adult life.

Jorn had a difficult time recruiting new marketing folks to St. Louis. Many of Jorn's contacts were based in Europe, Canada, and New York City. Most of them worked for InBev. And that's who he wanted, not people from St. Louis. Very few of them wanted to come. Especially not in 2014. That August, Michael Brown, an eighteen-year-old black male, was killed by white police officers in Ferguson, Missouri, a suburb of St. Louis. Race riots ensued for weeks. Buildings burned. One of those buildings was a convenience store that sold beer, images of which became synonymous with the riots. I know it sold beer because there was a clear Budweiser banner on the building that burned with the store. As national media homed in on St. Louis, I remember seeing this image more than any other.

The riots and protests weren't confined to Ferguson. I lived in the Central West End of St. Louis, ten miles from Ferguson and close to downtown St. Louis. Protestors marched through my neighborhood en route to I-64, which is the major highway through St. Louis. They shut down the highway as I watched the outside scene unfold on my TV.

Many of the foreign-born Anheuser-Busch executives were exposed to these protests as well. As were their kids and spouses, who didn't necessarily love St. Louis. Many of them had lived in large cosmopolitan cities like São Paolo, Rio de Janeiro, London, Brussels, New York City, and Toronto. St. Louis was not those cities. Many of the husbands and wives didn't want to be in St. Louis and were eager to move at the next career opportunity. The riots in St. Louis gave them even more reason to get out.

Since other foreign executives' networks were in many of the cities mentioned above, they shared Jorn's concerns about the ability to recruit talent to St. Louis. To address the so-called "talent issue" that was holding the company back from achieving its sales and marketing targets, David Almeida and other foreign executives convinced AB's CEO, Carlos Brito, to move the North American Sales & Marketing office from St. Louis to New York City. They argued that the move to New York City would allow the company to recruit better talent. It could more easily share resources with AB's global office based in New York. It would be closer to new brand agencies that AB's teams wanted to leverage. It would also be closer to many of the sports and music groups that AB wanted to partner with moving forward. Finally, AB thought that it would be better for the Sales & Marketing teams to be in a major metropolitan center, so it could spot "new trends" developing.

The move to New York was announced by David Almeida at the end of 2014. All the Sales & Marketing teams were called to the corporate conference room in St. Louis. Everyone was shocked. People who grew up in St. Louis and lived there with their families were crying. Younger people with no ties to St. Louis and no families were more excited. I was in the middle. I didn't have any ties to St. Louis. I didn't have many friends in St. Louis beyond my work colleagues who would also move to New York. But I also had a young family. My first son, Graham, was a few months old. My wife and I planned to have more kids. New York is not an easy place to raise kids. It is fine when kids are young. But not when kids grow older and need space to run and play. I grew up in the suburbs of the Midwest. Kids played in the woods and rode their bikes through the neighborhood until the streetlights came on. St. Louis offered this upbringing. New York did not.

Beyond the family concerns, I also had concerns about the business moving to New York. Prior to announcing that all sales and marketing was moving to New York City, it was announced that the craft brewery and high-end brands team would move from St. Louis to Chicago. This made sense to me. Goose Island Brewery, which is headquartered in Chicago, was recently acquired, and an entire high-end team was assembled to acquire more craft breweries and also focus on developing brands like Stella Artois, Shock Top, and Hoegaarden. Anheuser-Busch would never acquire a craft brewery in St. Louis, so moving the craft and high-end team to a city where a craft brewery was owned made sense. They could work with the local brewery, understand the craft consumer, and share best practices with future acquisitions, mostly in major urban areas. But the craft and high-end team's move to Chicago was scrapped when the broader organization decided to move to New York. Everyone was now moving to New York, from people working on Goose Island to people working on Busch Light.

New York was appealing to the foreign executives, but was hardly representative of the median AB consumer.

In fact, New York might as well be on a different planet compared to most beer markets in the U.S. Whereas Anheuser-Busch had almost 50 percent of the beer market across the U.S., it had less than 25 percent of the beer market in New York City. Anheuser-Busch's number-1 customer across the U.S. was Walmart, but there is not a single Walmart in all of New York City. There also aren't large supermarkets like Kroger, Publix, H-E-B, Vons, or Albertsons. And there aren't many traditional convenience stores like Circle K, Sheetz, or Casey's. Instead, there are small grocery stores and smaller deli/bodegas that sell a limited selection of beer. A lot of these beers are imports like Corona, Modelo, and Heineken. Those brands overindex market share in New York relative to their total share across the U.S., which reflects New York's more cosmopolitan and foreign customer base. Those brands didn't have any magical marketing in large metro areas like New York, they just better fit the premium, high-end, and import consumer. AB brands like Stella Artois and Hoegaarden could eventually win some of those consumers with better marketing and a more focused sales push in New York. Other brands would have a more difficult time.

The New York market is therefore very disconnected from the realities of most beer markets in the U.S. I didn't see any "trends" of New York–style grocery stores or bodegas spreading to cities across the U.S. New York City might as well be a retail city-state. I can't think of another market that is remotely like it. Even cities like Miami and Los Angeles have Walmarts, large grocery stores, and convenience stores. A newly hired New York team, who knows only the New York market, would have a difficult time connecting with wholesalers, retailers, and everyday consumers across the U.S. who shopped and bought beer in completely different stores.

In many ways, this wasn't a coincidence. The cosmopolitan European and Brazilian leadership never connected with AB's core consumer, and desperately wanted a way out. So they convinced themselves that it was St. Louis itself that was the problem to justify the move. When David Almeida announced the move, he mentioned multiple "trends" that AB's teams in St. Louis might be missing. He noted that Uber still wasn't in St. Louis in 2014. I still don't know what Uber not being in St. Louis had to do with beer sales, but it helped get approval for a new twelve-story office building in New York. Everyone got ready for the move. The marketing teams seemed to quickly embrace the "new trends" that were apparently developing in New York.

One of Jorn's first hires during the transition to New York was a

new Vice President of Bud Light, Alex Lambrecht. Alex was originally
from Belgium. He worked at Anheuser-Busch InBev for seven years.
All his experience was from outside of the U.S. He worked in marketing in Belgium and China before coming to lead the largest brand in
the U.S.

Many of the existing Bud Light sponsorships and brand programs
were immediately terminated. Especially ones that did not make
sense for the New York City market. Ultimate Fighting Championship (UFC), which Bud Light had sponsored since 2008, was deprior-
itized and eventually dropped. Many country music festivals were not
renewed. I was in charge of events for Anheuser-Busch at the time,
so I was involved in many of these discussions with the brand team. I
remember asking Jorn and Alex why we were not renewing some of the
most popular sporting and concert events. They said that Bud Light's
priorities were changing and going in a "different direction." Some of
the new sponsorships would be electronic gaming, or egaming, and
techno music festivals. When I asked if people at these events drank
more beer than people at UFC and country concerts, I was met with
blank stares. I then got muffled answers about how Bud Light was
growing its user base beyond traditional areas.

Fine. Brand teams do this all the time. They come up with new
things to sponsor and new ways to authentically reach new audiences.
Brands have only so much money to spend on advertising, and they
have to make sure they get bang (or beer) for the buck. They usually
don't do this at the expense of existing partnerships and consumers
who buy more beer. If a similarly sized country music festival sells ten
thousand beers and a techno festival sells one thousand, logic says a
company should keep sponsoring the country festival. Why give up
ten thousand loyal customers to potentially gain a thousand new ones?

To me, Jorn and Alex didn't understand the U.S. consumer. They
were using their own Belgian cultural biases to drive Bud Light in

a new direction. For example, Belgium had a famous techno festival called Tomorrowland. This was a big event in Europe and sponsored by InBev's brand Jupiler. Jupiler is the equivalent of Bud Light in Belgium. Jupiler was gaining traction with techno festivals, so Jorn and Alex thought Bud Light might be able to do the same. This was a simple cultural misunderstanding, as a U.S. techno concertgoer might drink a Bud Light, but a U.S. country music or rock concertgoer is probably going to drink a lot more Bud Light. Also, InBev used to copy what Anheuser-Busch was doing in the U.S., and export best practices globally. It seemed strange to me that Anheuser-Busch was now copying what a small brand in a small European country was doing and bringing that to the U.S. as a "best practice."

Although Jorn and Alex didn't know a lot about the U.S. and the U.S. consumer, they were at least willing to admit when they made mistakes. In 2015, they made a large mistake with Bud Light's "Up for Whatever" campaign. Bud Light changed its tagline to "Up for Whatever" when Jorn and Alex took over the brand in 2014. It tried to make Bud Light the official beer of when consumers were up for whatever. This could be "Up for" a techno concert, an egaming event, or basically anything. They even created Whatever, USA, a fictional town in a real location. In 2014 it was in the mountain town of Crested Butte, Colorado. In 2015, it was on Catalina Island off the coast of California. Consumers won trips to Whatever, USA, after submitting videos highlighting how they were "Up for Whatever." Once in the fictional town, consumers could eat ice cream with Vanilla Ice or eat hot dogs with Snoop Dogg. They washed this food down with Bud Light, because that's what consumers drink when they are "Up for Whatever."

The campaign hit a lot of bad publicity in April 2015. That year, Bud Light printed 140 slogans on their bottles highlighting moments when consumers were "Up for Whatever." These moments included more New York–friendly sayings like "The perfect beer for drinking in your backyard, even if your backyard is a fire escape," but also sayings like "The perfect beer for busting out all two of your dance moves" and "The perfect beer for singing loud, even if you don't know the words." The sayings weren't very good. Some were quite bad.

Most of the labels were corny, but one was disastrous. It stated that Bud Light was "the perfect beer for removing 'No' from your vocabulary for the night." This caused a social media firestorm. The label was first posted to Reddit and soon spread across the internet. The brand was accused of promoting "rape culture" by advocating for the removal of "No." Major media outlets from *The Wall Street Journal* to CNN to *The New York Times* all covered the backlash. This occurred well before the #MeToo movement that started two years later.

Anheuser-Busch's response was swift and clear. They released the following statement one day after the Reddit post:

> The Bud Light Up For Whatever campaign, now in its second year, has inspired millions of consumers to engage with our brand in a positive and light-hearted way. In this spirit, we created more than 140 different scroll messages intended to encourage brand engagement.
>
> It's clear that this particular message missed the mark, and we apologize.
>
> We would never condone disrespectful or irresponsible behavior. No means no.
>
> As a result, we have immediately ceased production of this message on all bottles.

Anheuser-Busch and the Bud Light team made a mistake. But they took clear responsibility. They admitted they erred, and the firestorm immediately died down. A handful of bloggers and Twitter users continued to badger the brand, but most of the criticism seemed to be from far-left fringe advocacy groups seeking to use the misstep as a platform for themselves; following the apology, even *The New York Times* closed its piece by joking that the bottles may someday become collectors' items.[4] Consumers didn't boycott the brand, and Bud Light remained the top-selling beer in the United States.

They say that learning in public is painful, but the lessons stick. But for Bud Light, the learning might not have been painful enough. Eight years later, it seemed to forget its playbook for responding to controversy: acknowledge, apologize, and move on.

One month later, in May 2015, AB opened its temporary office in NYC and started officially moving people from St. Louis to New York City. The Bud Light team avoided disaster right before the move to NYC, but more problems were brewing for the company both inside and outside the organization.

Chapter 9

On Top of the World

The move to NYC was swift. People with families wanted to get to NYC before the school year began. Younger people without families wanted to experience summer in NYC. The move from St. Louis to NYC was effectively completed by July 4. This also allowed managers to interview new employees more easily, as a number of people did not make the move to NYC. The employees who didn't make the move either left the organization or found roles in the functions that remained in St. Louis.

The move to NYC changed the company culture immediately. People dressed differently. Polo shirts and loafers were out. Trendy T-shirts and designer sneakers were in. Weekend activities like fishing and camping were replaced with trips to the Hamptons and late nights at clubs in Brooklyn. New employees joined from Google, Facebook, and other tech startups.

Working in New York City changes people. It is not an easy place to work. The commutes are not easy. Many people drive to a train station, rush to catch the train, fight for a place to sit or stand, run from a commuter train to a subway at Grand Central or Penn Station, emerge from the subway to wind, rain, snow, or heat, avoid bikes and cars while crossing streets, wait for elevators, before finally arriving at work. This process repeats itself in reverse on the way home. Every day.

This commute also makes it difficult to connect with coworkers outside of the office. Whereas people in St. Louis regularly got together after work and built strong internal networks, it didn't happen nearly as often in NYC. AB has a great beer garden right on campus in St. Louis. This was regularly used by teams at the end of the day or week. In St. Louis, AB is surrounded by a neighborhood called Soulard where people regularly supported local bars. People didn't have to rush to make trains or have weekend plans in the Hamptons. There was time to connect and it was easy to do so. People felt connected to the company and loyalty to the teams. St. Louis felt like a place where one could build a career. In New York, it felt like people just had a job. That job filled the time between commutes and plans people had outside the company.

In St. Louis, AB was THE company. There was no better place to work in St. Louis than Anheuser-Busch. Everyone in St. Louis wanted to be the Bud man. Many people from across the country moved to St. Louis to be the Bud man as well. In New York, AB was just another faceless corporation working in a faceless building. People could try it on like they try on a set of clothing. If it worked, people might stick around for a bit. If not, then people could easily find a new job. Google, Facebook, McKinsey, and Goldman Sachs were right around the corner. Finding talent was never the problem. Keeping good talent was very challenging.

Change was a constant theme in 2015. Shortly after the summer move from St. Louis to New York, AB InBev announced in October that it was acquiring South African Breweries–Miller (SABMiller). This acquisition would be the crowning achievement of Carlos Brito's tenure as CEO. "Megabrew" is what the press dubbed the new organization. And "Megabrew" it was. AB would pay $120 billion for SABMiller. This price represented a 50 percent share premium and a 17.8x EBITDA multiple (this was quite rich compared to the 30 percent share premium and 12.8x EBITDA multiple AB paid for Grupo Modelo a few years earlier). The combined company would generate $64 billion in revenue and $24 billion in EBITDA. This would make it the number-5-largest CPG company in the world by revenue, and number-1 by EBITDA.

Megabrew created the first truly global beer company. Anheuser-Busch's footprint was in North America, Brazil, Argentina, Western Europe, and China. SABMiller was concentrated in Africa, Eastern Europe, India, Colombia, and Australia. SABMiller owned brands like Castle in South Africa, Aguila in Colombia, Pilsner Urquell in the Czech Republic, and Carlton in Australia. It would now sell one of every four beers globally. They owned seven of the top-10 largest beer brands in the world. They operated in more than 150 countries and had the number-1 or -2 beer brand in the vast majority of those countries.

To get the deal done, AB would have to sell certain assets to appease regulators. For example, SABMiller owned 58 percent of MillerCoors in the United States. MillerCoors owned brands like Miller Lite, Coors Light, and Blue Moon. MillerCoors was the second-largest brewer in the United States after AB. The U.S. government had already blocked Anheuser-Busch's ownership of the third-largest brewer in the U.S., Grupo Modelo, so there was no way it would allow AB to own the number-2 player. AB therefore sold the 58 percent stake of MillerCoors to Molson Coors, which is a Canadian-American brewer.

As part of the deal, U.S. regulators also limited Anheuser-Busch's ability to own more distributors in the U.S. To ensure fair competition and access to market for non–Anheuser-Busch brands, AB could not own more than 10 percent of its distribution in the U.S. This was a far cry from the 50 percent that David Almeida once dreamed about owning in the U.S.

AB would also have to raise more than $100 billion in debt to acquire SABMiller. This debt is more than 3x what AB paid for Grupo Modelo and more than 2x what they paid for Anheuser-Busch. SAB-Miller was a much more efficient company than Grupo Modelo and Anheuser-Busch, and therefore there were not as many synergies available to help pay down this debt. For example, AB found more than $1 billion in synergies for its ~$30 billion purchase of Grupo Modelo. It was targeting only $2.4 billion in synergies for its $120 billion SAB-Miller Purchase.

They were therefore relying much more on organic growth to help pay down this debt. Organic growth would come from places like Africa. Africa accounted for 6.5 percent of the world's beer volume in 2014. By 2025, it was estimated to account for 8.1 percent. Analysts forecast that the African beer market would grow 44 percent over this time period, compared to 16 percent for the rest of the world. AB could accelerate this growth, as it could now bring its global premium brands like Budweiser, Corona, and Stella Artois to the African continent.

Accelerating growth, especially in emerging markets, comes at a cost. Emerging markets for beer tend to be less profitable than mature markets. At AB InBev, the mature U.S. market did the plurality of the revenue and profits of the company. It had 40 percent EBITDA margins. Its China market did closer to 20 percent EBITDA margins. SABMiller's Africa market had EBITDA margins in the low 20 percent range also. The cash generated from markets like the U.S. would not only be used to pay down debt, but a lot of it would be reinvested in places like Africa and China moving forward. The U.S. would be the cash cow for the rest of the company. Its success was critical for broader company growth, but it might not get all of the resources it deserved to increase, or even maintain, its own business.

Investors did not seem concerned about a lack of focus in the U.S., though. Shortly after the deal was announced, AB InBev's stock hit a new high of $130/share in November 2015. Investors and analysts cheered AB's new toy. The price they paid was high, but AB InBev had a history of overdelivering synergies, paying down debt sooner than anticipated, and increasing dividends to shareholders. The same was expected with SABMiller.

Internally, the company was more concerned. After fifteen years of acquisitions, there were no more transformative beer companies left to buy. Yes, the company could potentially buy other companies in the beverage space like Coca-Cola, Pepsi, or Diageo. But before doing that, they had to prove that they could organically grow the beer business. They had no choice. There was a +$100 billion bar tab to pay.

Chapter 10

Fuel the Future

There was one last big change in 2015, and that was in the sales department.

With SABMiller acquired, AB InBev now had to prove that it could build brands. The Chief Sales Officer would play a pivotal role. The pressure was on to deliver. The higher-ups sensed it was time for a change. David Almeida, a finance guy, would return to his roots in a new finance role. But his replacement was not the fresh blood many had hoped for; it was Alex Medicis, another Brazilian who didn't seem to understand either the U.S. market or any of the AB brands. As a result, Anheuser-Busch's domestic performance would be undermined by two trends: another foreign executive who didn't understand the technical operation of the domestic market and a New York–based marketing team that didn't understand the median Bud Light consumer.

I saw it all unfold in real time. After four years leading sales in the U.S., David Almeida was promoted to Global Chief Integration Officer. He would leave the U.S. business and lead the combination of Anheuser-Busch and SABMiller around the world. This meant integrating AB's culture into SABMiller, having similar reporting tools, ensuring procurement realized the targeted savings, etc. This returned David to his finance roots and a place he could drive value in the organization. It was time for a change.

FTF, or "Fuel the Future," was David's rallying cry. He wanted to grow beer volumes and take share from competition. Wholesalers, AB's marketing team, and the City of St. Louis were not going to stand in his way as he altered relationships with all of them. The future was not looking bright for the U.S., though. AB's volume declined by 1.7 percent, and it lost 0.65 percent market share in 2015. The market share loss was the worst loss in recent company history. It was an acceleration from the −0.2 percent in 2012 and −0.5 percent losses in 2013 and 2014. Almost two share points had been lost in four years. This is a huge amount in an industry that spends hundreds of millions of marketing dollars each year to maintain its share in the industry. The sales and marketing programs devised by the Brazilian and Belgium leadership teams weren't working, though. They were costing the company a lot of money. Profits in the U.S. declined by 4.3 percent in 2015. This would not be sustainable with the new $100 billion debt placed on the company by the SABMiller transaction.

There was a lot of speculation about who the next Chief Sales Officer would be. Many hoped it would be someone with experience in the U.S. market. Someone who understood wholesalers. Someone who understood retailers. Someone who understood the customers who purchased Budweiser and Bud Light and Michelob Ultra and Natural Light and Busch Light. Someone who understood marketing that connected to those customers. Someone who could guide Belgian-born Chief Marketing Officer Jorn Socquet and VP of Marketing for Bud Light Alex Lambrecht. It was not.

Alex Medicis was named the new Chief Sales Officer in the United States. Very few people had ever heard of Alex before. He spent his entire life in Brazil. Was born there. Went to school there. Worked there. He led sales for AB InBev in Brazil before being promoted to Chief Sales Officer in the United States. Being Brazilian was about the only thing he had in common with David Almeida. Whereas David was very high energy and was constantly chanting things like "FTF!," Alex gave more of a "WTF?" impression to people.

I first met Alex in St. Louis at the end of 2015. There was a hand-over meeting between David Almeida and Alex. All of the top sales and marketing people from across the country attended. The goal was to provide Alex with a full overview of the sales and marketing or-ganizations in the U.S. The night before, one of my colleagues met Alex in the lobby of the hotel where everyone was staying. I asked my colleague what his first impression was. "Sleepy" was the response. He thought that Alex might just be tired from the flight from Brazil to St. Louis.

He wasn't. Alex was low energy. Low energy isn't necessarily bad, depending on the role. It is not common in a Chief Sales Officer role, though. Chief Sales Officers need to create a vision for how the com-pany can grow. "Fire up the troops" to carry out that vision. Get sales-people motivated to sell. Run through walls to get the customer what they need. Negotiate with wholesalers on plans to put the right beer in the right account at the right price. Work charismatically with retailers to sell new innovations and brand programming. David Almeida had a lot of the intangibles typically seen in Chief Sales Officers. He just didn't have the experience or knowledge of the U.S. to win in the mar-ket. Alex had neither.

The Brazilian beer market is completely different than the U.S. market. In the U.S., more than 80 percent of the beer purchased is from grocery stores, convenience stores, and package liquor stores. Only 20 percent of the beer is purchased in bars and restaurants. In Brazil, it was the opposite. The vast majority of sales were through bars and restaurants. In the U.S., Anheuser-Busch had to work through the three-tier system, selling to independent wholesalers who then sold to retailers. In Brazil, AB InBev owned its distribution network and could sell directly to retailers. In the U.S., Anheuser-Busch could not contract directly with retailers for shelf space or pricing programs. In Brazil, AB InBev commonly had "exclusive" contracts with retailers that prevented competition from being sold in the account. In the U.S., AB InBev was the market share leader, but had only 40 percent of the market and faced stiff competition. In Brazil, AB InBev had almost 70 percent share of the market and competition was relatively weak. In the U.S., there were thousands of brewers, tens of thousands of brands, and many different styles of beer like craft, ciders, flavored malt beverages, and hard seltzers. In Brazil, there were fewer than five hundred breweries and the beer market consisted mostly of lagers.

During the handover meeting, Alex's lack of understanding was evident. During a presentation on AB's strategy to grow sales at top retailers like Walmart, Kroger, and 7-Eleven, Alex asked why we couldn't just go to these retailers and ask them to put incentives in place for their employees to grow Anheuser-Busch's share of their beer category. David promptly explained that he thought the same way four years ago when he was promoted to Chief Sales Officer. He said that he learned that retailers don't care about an individual beer company's market share. They care about the overall growth of their beer category and want to work with the companies that can best grow the overall category. Also, paying retailers incentive dollars to grow share is illegal in the U.S. Alex dismissed this answer, seemingly believing that people in the U.S. just weren't trying hard enough to win. Alex had obviously been successful in Brazil. What works in Brazil would not work in the U.S., though, especially with an unwillingness to listen.

A month later, in January 2016, Alex unveiled his strategy to turn around results in the U.S. He did this at the annual Sales and Marketing COMmunication (SAMCOM for short) meeting. This meeting was the highlight of the year for Anheuser-Busch and its wholesalers. It is everything a beer communication meeting should be. Thousands of people. A fun city (think Nashville, New Orleans, Las Vegas). Hosted in a massive convention hall filled with booths and displays dedicated to showcasing each Anheuser-Busch brand's plans for the upcoming year. The display area spanned multiple football fields. Each brand had a quarter of a football field to build a killer themed area. Busch Light's display usually had fishing, hunting, and NASCAR themes. People could meet celebrities like fisherman Kevin VanDam or NASCAR driver Kevin Harvick. Budweiser World featured the Anheuser-Busch Clydesdales and former Major League Baseball players. Michelob Ultra had workout-theme displays and celebrity fitness trainers. There was also a lot of beer. Unlimited beer in fact. And free. This made the event a feel-good place to start the year.

In between visits to the convention floor and the free beer, there were presentations. The presentations were in a massive auditorium built for the event. Speakers spoke on a big stage surrounded by massive TVs showing videos and slide presentations. If you have ever seen a video of Steve Jobs unveil an Apple product, that is how SAMCOM looked and felt. Big. Important. Energetic. Seamlessly choreographed. Suspenseful. Magical.

Presentations started with an overview of Anheuser-Busch InBev's global goals for the year. Carlos Brito, Anheuser-Busch's Global CEO, gave these highlights. Then he handed the presentation over to the CEO of North America for a quick review of the North American goals. The main presenters were really the U.S.'s Chief Sales Officer and Chief Marketing Officer and their direct reports. The marketing team was responsible for all of the TV commercials, social content, events, and innovations that get consumers to purchase Budweiser, Bud Light, Busch Light, Michelob Ultra, and all of the other Anheuser-Busch brands. The sales team was responsible for selling these programs, products, and pricing into the network of five hundred Anheuser-Busch wholesalers and thousands of retailers across the country.

The marketing team presented right after the CEO of North America. The presentations were always highly anticipated, especially the Bud Light presentation. This is because Bud Light usually revealed its Super Bowl commercials at SAMCOM. Anheuser-Busch employees and wholesalers were the first to see what +100 million people would tune in to the Super Bowl to watch. The 2016 Bud Light presentation was especially highly anticipated. This is because Bud Light had just spent more than one year redoing its Visual Brand Identity (VBI) and was launching a new campaign to replace the tarnished "Up for Whatever" campaign. It's a big deal when a brand does a new VBI. This entails changing the logo of the brand, the look of the brand, the packaging of the brand, the slogan of the brand. It is not supposed to change the mission or identity of the brand, but evolve the look and image. Bud Light had undergone about ten VBI changes over its thirty-five-year history. This was the first VBI update in eight years, and the first update since InBev purchased Anheuser-Busch.

Bud Light unveiled its new VBI, and it was received fairly positively. Its old logo had the words *Bud Light* in white enclosed in a blue shape that looked like a guitar chip. The Bud Light letters were angled forward. There were some silver and red boomerang shapes at the front of the chip. The chip and the angle were supposed to give the brand energy. It did for a while, but it looked a bit dated after eight years. The new VBI was much simpler. It did a nice job of honoring the heritage of Bud Light while also moving it forward. It ditched the chip and the boomerang shapes. Instead, it had a simple rectangle box, with rounded corners, and large Bud Light block lettering. This lettering harkened back to the lettering used when the brand launched in 1982. On packaging, it also included an oversized image of the Budweiser design and creed, which states: "This is the famous Budweiser beer. We know of no other brand produced by any other brewer that costs so much to brew and age. Our exclusive Beechwood Aging process produces a taste, a smoothness, and a drinkablity that you will find in no other beer at any price."

This image and creed was similar to one used in the 1980s when the brand was launched as Budweiser Light. The new image and design would roll out immediately. Hundreds of millions of dollars would be spent getting the new logo and branding in front of consumers. We're not just talking new TV commercials. Every bar or restaurant with an old Bud Light logo neon sign needed to have the sign replaced. Every delivery truck with the old logo would be repainted. Every Bud Light tap handle with the old VBI needed to be pulled and replaced with a new one.

Bud Light also launched a new marketing campaign alongside the new VBI—The Bud Light Party. This wasn't your typical Bud Light Party. In 2016, during a hotly contested presidential election, the Bud Light Party would be an alternative to the Democrat and Republican parties. It was a party that was supposed to bring all Americans together. Because that is what Bud Light had been doing for almost thirty-five years. It was the most popular beer in America because it was enjoyed by people of all backgrounds. Studies show Democrats and Republicans drank it equally. The first Bud Light Party commercial would launch during the Super Bowl, and the first people to see it were the people who attended SAMCOM.

The ad featured Amy Schumer and Seth Rogen, two popular comedians at the time. Even this decision was more controversial than the New York ad executives likely realized. Both comedians, of course, are notoriously liberal, outspoken critics of President Trump. And so an ad campaign that may have appeared "unifying" to New York elites in fact felt out of touch and condescending to consumers in Red America.

But the commercial nonetheless strived to be as apolitical as an apolitical ad can be. It opened with Amy and Seth making a political-looking speech in front of a government building. The opening line from Amy is "They say we are nation divided. They say we disagree on everything." Then Seth notes, "That's not true. We agree on a lot." The ad goes on to highlight that Americans agree on beer and "nothing brings America together like Bud Light." Using Bud Light's humorous voice, Amy then declares that they are forming the "Bud Light Party," and Seth claims that the party will have "the biggest CAUCus in the country." This double entendre is then played out over the course of the commercial. It ends with Amy stating, "America has seen the Light" and Seth finishing with "and there's a Bud in front of it."

The commercial was fine. It ranked number 10 on *USA Today*'s Super Bowl Ad Meter. Not bad, but not the number-1 ranking that Bud Light was accustomed to. The audience at SAMCOM was lukewarm about the Bud Light Party campaign, though. This was supposed to be a one-year campaign during a hotly contested presidential election. Bud Light would produce numerous hopefully funny commercials hitting on social issues. After the election, Bud Light would move to an entirely new campaign. Wholesalers worried that the one-year campaign could potentially alienate customers, especially if the commercials did not hit the right amount of humor and veered too political.

Wholesalers were right to be worried. A new marketing agency, Wieden+Kennedy, was producing the ads. Wieden+Kennedy was based in New York City. Prior Bud Light marketing agencies tended to be based in the Midwest. Now that the Bud Light team was in New York, they wanted to work with New York agencies. Wieden+Kennedy was one of the highest-regarded agencies in New York. It produced TV commercials and digital campaigns with clients like Nike, Coca-Cola, Proctor & Gamble, and Facebook. It was one of the more progressive agencies in New York as well. It was the first global agency to get B Corp certified, a designation that measures a company's entire social and environmental impact.[1] It highlighted that it got this certification "alongside the likes of Ben & Jerry's," which touts on its website how it sells ice cream to promote its own "progressive, nonpartisan social mission."

The Bud Light Party campaign was supposed to last through the 2016 election. The Bud Light Party released commercials highlighting issues like gender pay equality and same sex marriage. To address gender pay equality, Bud Light and Amy touted that "Bud Light costs the same no matter if you are a dude or a lady." The Supreme Court legalized same sex marriage in 2015, so Bud Light's ad highlighted the similarities of gay and straight weddings. Interestingly, the gender pay equality ad ran nationwide. The same sex marriage ad only ran in New York and Los Angeles.

Regardless of where the commercials ran, consumers were not impressed. Bud Light sales fell almost 5 percent in the first half of the year.[2] They did not get better in the second. Bud Light experienced its worst sales and share performance in the third quarter of 2016, so it switched marketing tracks mid-campaign.[3] The Bud Light Party dropped out of the 2016 race in August, three months ahead of schedule. Instead, Bud Light started a Dive Bar Campaign featuring famous musicians playing in local dive bars. They also leaned heavier into the NFL and football advertising.

Bud Light didn't explicitly take sides on controversial political issues in 2016. It tried to toe the line by creating a party everyone could rally behind. But even that relatively measured approach hurt the brand. The failure of the campaign showed that Bud Light drinkers don't want Bud Light near any political party. They want Bud Light focused on beer, fun, sports, and music. It's amazing that this lesson was not learned. The next time Bud Light leaned into political issues would have much greater consequences. . . .

Bud Light's problems in 2016 were exacerbated by Alex Medicis's new sales strategy. Back at SAMCOM, Alex laid out his sales strategy for selling more Bud Light and other Anheuser-Busch brands after the marketing teams presented their presentations. His strategy was two-pronged. First, he introduced a new distribution program called SAP-SKU Assortment Program (or SAP for short). This would replace David Almeida's KOD, or King of Distribution, program. Whereas KOD used big data and algorithms to recommend the right package type to sell into each account, the SAP program was much simpler. Every account basically had to have twenty-five-ounce cans, six-packs, twelve-packs, and twenty-four packs of Anheuser-Busch's main brands—Bud Light, Budweiser, Michelob Ultra, Busch, and Natural Light. If the account had all of these package types in each brand, then it was a certified SAP account. If not, then it had a goal to become one. At the beginning of 2016, fewer than 10 percent of the accounts across the U.S. were SAP certified. By the end of 2016, the goal was to have more than 30 percent of the accounts in the U.S. SAP certified. Alex showed data that SAP-certified accounts sold more beer than non-SAP-certified accounts, and therefore having more SAP accounts would sell more beer.

His second strategy was to give beer away for free. Seriously. He wanted to bring the "BOGO," or Buy One, Get One free strategy to the beer category. If a consumer purchased a twelve-pack of Bud Light, they could get a second twelve-pack of Bud Light free. This promotion also applied to Budweiser and Michelob Ultra, and consumers could mix and match. The promotions would run over the major holidays like Memorial Day, Fourth of July, Labor Day, Thanksgiving, and Christmas. Promotions like this had never been done in the beer category previously. There were good reasons. The first is that the program could not legally run in ~50 percent of states. Many states do not allow "free beer" because it violates their interpretation of the "three-tier system." If beer companies give away free beer, it technically bypasses the retailer. They might be able to sell it for a penny, but they could not advertise that it is free. Second, many key retailers do not do "BOGO" strategies. For example, Anheuser-Busch's largest customer is Walmart. Walmart does Every Day Low Pricing (EDLP). They do not pulse in large discounts or do "BOGO" strategies like other mass-market and grocery store chains. Walmart's customers want the price to be low every day so they can expect what to spend and therefore live better. Third, and most importantly, giving beer away for free would ruin the profitability of the business. No great products are built by giving them away for free. It's not a sustainable long-term strategy.

Both the SAP distribution program and the BOGO program were imported from Brazil. Alex used both programs somewhat successfully while leading that market. The Brazilian market was very different than the U.S. market, though. AB InBev owned more than 60 percent of the Brazilian beer market, with fewer brands and much less SKUs than the U.S. market. Implementing a distribution program like SAP was therefore much simpler. Brazil didn't have the same legal restrictions on pricing either, and they could run BOGO programs with individual retailers where it made sense. Listening to Alex speak, I was having déjà vu. Jorn and Alex quickly replaced proven Bud Light marketing partnerships with Belgian-influenced partnerships. Alex seemed to be doing the same with Brazilian-influenced sales programs. I was concerned.

Alex was not. To solve the legal issue, he asked the government affairs team to work with targeted states to change their laws. If certain retailers like Walmart didn't want the program, he would first go to retailers like Publix that did. Eventually, Alex thought Walmart and others would join the program if they lost out on sales. As for profitability, he saw the play as merely a short-term sacrifice to grow market share. In fact, his first three priorities announced at SAMCOM were:

1. Grow Share
2. Grow Share
3. Grow Share

After four years of accelerating share losses, Alex wanted to increase Anheuser-Busch's market share by selling more beer, even if some of that beer had to be given away. Once AB started growing share again, it could wean itself off of the BOGOs.

Similar to the recently announced Bud Light Party campaign, wholesalers were concerned about both SAP and BOGOs. SAP would be scored like KOD. If wholesalers didn't comply, they could be marked out of compliance and risk losing their beer wholesaler. Even though SAP was simpler than KOD, it did not permit much flexibility to add additional products to an account. This went for certain package configurations like eight-pack aluminum bottles or thirty-packs that played better in certain markets than others. It also didn't provide much flexibility for new innovation that was launching or some of the craft and high-end brands that AB had recently acquired. Alex just cared about the core SKUs on the core brands.

As for BOGOs, wholesalers were concerned because they did not know how competition would respond (in addition to the questions around legality, retailer acceptance, and profitability). It was a bit of a real-life game theory situation, akin to the Prisoner's Dilemma. The Prisoner's Dilemma involves a thought experiment where two rational actors cooperate for mutual benefit or defect for individual reward.

This leads to four different possible outcomes for prisoners A and B:

1. If A and B both remain silent, they will each serve one year in prison.
2. If A testifies against B but B remains silent, A will be set free while B serves three years in prison.
3. If A remains silent but B testifies against A, A will serve three years in prison and B will be set free.
4. If A and B testify against each other, they will each serve two years.

Four similar outcomes could be applied to the Anheuser-Busch whole-salers implementing a BOGO price action and contemplating the response from their MillerCoors counterparts. Assuming the beer market has zero-sum outcomes, where Anheuser-Busch and Miller-Coors gain and lose customers to each other, the outcomes could be:

1. If neither AB nor MillerCoors implements a BOGO strategy, they sell the same amount of beer as last year at the same price as last year. Revenue remains the same for both.
2. If AB implements a BOGO, but MillerCoors does not, AB gains volume and revenue and MillerCoors loses volume and revenue.
3. If MillerCoors implements a BOGO, but AB does not, MillerCoors gains volume and revenue and Anheuser-Busch loses volume and revenue.
4. If AB and MillerCoors both implement a BOGO, they sell the same volume of beer as last year, but generate half of the revenue since they gave away half of the beer for free.

Historically, MillerCoors almost always responded to Anheuser-Busch pricing actions. If Anheuser-Busch discounted beer ahead of a big holiday, MillerCoors did, too. They wanted to be price competitive and get featured in retailer ads. Based on this history, scenario four was the likely outcome. Anheuser-Busch and MillerCoors would both be worse off.

I would get to experience the wholesaler concerns on SAP and BOGOs firsthand. As SAMCOM ended, Alex Medicis pulled me aside and asked me to run Anheuser-Busch's Western region. This was a big promotion. This region covered Colorado through Alaska. It was based in Denver. I would have a team of more than six hundred people, including people employed by Anheuser-Busch's owned distributor-ships, reporting to me. I would work with more than fifty independent wholesalers, thousands of retailers, and serve millions of consumers. It was the largest geographic region in the U.S., and I would have full sales and marketing responsibility to Grow Share, Grow Share, and Grow Share.

||||||||||||||||

I was on a plane to Denver the next week and officially moved my family from New York to Colorado the following month. I began working with wholesalers and retailers immediately to implement both SAP and BOGO programs. Similar to the Bud Light Party campaign, both of these programs had largely failed by the end of summer.

For SAP, the rigid nature of the program failed. 2016 was the first summer that hard seltzers like White Claw and Truly started to gain significant sales. Funny enough, Anheuser-Busch bought the original hard seltzer in 2015. It was called Spiked Seltzer. It was founded in 2013 and gained traction in the New England area. Anheuser-Busch got into a bidding war with a company called Mark Anthony to purchase Spiked Seltzer. Mark Anthony owned brands like Mike's Hard Lemonade and Cayman Jack. Anheuser-Busch paid more for Spiked Seltzer, but Mark Anthony thought the idea of spiked seltzers was interesting. They therefore created the brand White Claw and made it their big innovation launch in 2016. Samuel Adams did the same with Truly. I remember watching massive displays of White Claw and Truly go up in states like Montana and Colorado during the summer of 2016. I wrote an email to Alex Medicis saying that we needed to accelerate our distribution of Spiked Seltzer to compete. His response to me was "this is not a priority." Spiked Seltzer was not in SAP, so it was not a focus for distribution. White Claw and Truly would go on to dominate the hard seltzer category. They captured more than 80 percent of the category as the hard seltzer category grew to approximately 10 percent of total beer within five years. By

2021, the hard seltzer category was larger than every beer brand with the exception of Bud Light.[4]

The BOGO program didn't work either. Actually, it worked one time. The first time Anheuser-Busch ran a large BOGO program was over Memorial Day weekend of 2016. MillerCoors was caught off guard by the promotion. They did not understand the program or what was happening. Anheuser-Busch was able to get some large retailers like Publix and Winn-Dixie to run the program in states where they legally could, like Florida. I was able to get the program executed in independently owned package liquor stores in states like Colorado and Wyoming.

Remember Alex's top three priorities: Grow Share, Grow Share, Grow Share. In May 2016, Anheuser-Busch grew share of the beer category for the first time in years. This was measured by a company called the Beer Institute that analyzed beer sales from all of the top brewers. Scenario 2 of the Prisoner's Dilemma had played out:

> If AB implements a BOGO, but MillerCoors does not, AB
> gains volume and revenue and MillerCoors loses volume
> and revenue.

May turned out to be a pyrrhic victory. MillerCoors was a rational actor and would not allow its sales and share to slip. MillerCoors quickly learned that Anheuser-Busch was putting all its focus on winning the key holidays with free beer. MillerCoors decided to let Anheuser-Busch win those battles, but it would win the long-term war by keeping prices low every day. In Colorado, for example, Miller-Coors responded to the May BOGO by lowering the price of their twelve-packs and twenty-four-packs every day for the remainder of the summer. I could not match these prices AND do the BOGO program or I would essentially end up in Scenario 4 of the Prisoner's Dilemma:

If AB and MillerCoors both implement a BOGO, they sell
the same volume of beer as last year, but generate half of the
revenue since they gave away half of the beer for free.

Selling less beer at lower prices would be bad for profitability and long-
term shareholder value. Therefore June, July, August, and September
were all bad months for Anheuser-Busch. The summer was lost. Share
losses continued across the organization, and things didn't improve
at the end of the year either. Revenue for the year was flat, but it was
down 2.1 percent in the fourth quarter. Market share for the year was
down 0.5 percent. This was an improvement from the −0.65 percent a
year earlier, but a long way off from the priority of Grow Share, Grow
Share, Grow Share.

Despite the poor results, the sales priorities did not change much
between 2016 and 2017. In fact, Alex doubled down on the SAP and
BOGO strategy. He wanted more execution of both programs. SAP
would be required in more accounts, and it would add a focus on high-
end and flavored malt beverage brands. BOGOs would expand to
more holidays and more retailers. He didn't think that there was an
issue with the programs. He thought that there was a problem with the
wholesaler and retailer execution of the programs. He was repeating a
lot of the same mistakes David Almeida had made a few years prior.
The problems were always external. Never internal.

2017 turned out to be the worst year for Anheuser-Busch since the
InBev merger. Anheuser-Busch's revenue declined by 2 percent. It lost
0.75 percent market share, the most in the history of the company. Annual engagement surveys for both wholesalers and internal employees
plummeted. Mainstream news organizations started to notice. An October 2017 *Forbes* headline stated, "Latest Earnings Hint That Bud and
Bud Light Might Not Ever Get Their Groove Back."[5] *The New York
Post* piled on by claiming, "Drinkers don't care about Anheuser-Busch

anymore."[6] CNN hammered home the point, declaring, "America is falling out of love with Budweiser."[7]

Grow Share, Grow Share, Grow Share was not a long-term strategy that people understood. They especially didn't understand how it was going to attract new customers and grow the revenue and profitability of Anheuser-Busch and its wholesaler network. Investors were also confused. After peaking at more than $135 per share in mid-2016, the stock fell to $110 by the end of 2017. The results from 2016 and 2017 definitely didn't give much hope.

Changes were therefore made in 2017. Anheuser-Busch's board and the global CEO, Carlos Brito, lost faith in where the U.S. was headed, both on the marketing and sales side. The marketing organization needed better programming and leadership after the failed Bud Light Party campaign. Sales needed a strategy that wholesalers and retailers could believe in to grow long-term profitability. Brito realized some of the issues in the U.S. were self-inflicted. Before buying Anheuser-Busch, Brito mentioned that InBev used to come to the U.S. to benchmark and copy the sales and marketing strategies that Anheuser-Busch employed to grow revenue and profitability. They were the best in the world at this. Once they bought Anheuser-Busch, they could no longer copy Anheuser-Busch. They *were* Anheuser-Busch. They were responsible for developing the marketing and sales strategies that would increase customer affinity and shareholder value. They failed to do this over the past five years in the U.S. All key CEO, CMO, and Chief Sales Officer roles had been filled by Brazilians or Belgians during that time. Key VP roles for brands like Bud Light and Budweiser had also been filled with people from outside of the United States. Instead of focusing on what works for the U.S., many of these execs tried to copy the sales and marketing strategies of other countries. This obviously failed. It also meant that AB missed out on leading key trends in areas like hard seltzers, which originated in the U.S. AB InBev's DNA was not customer-centric. It didn't understand how to innovate. It couldn't capitalize on trends happening right before its eyes. Instead it was a flawed follower. It launched inferior products and sales and marketing campaigns that were further hampered by the zero-based budgeting philosophy that constantly reduced resources.

Brito didn't revert back to the old days and appoint 100 percent Americans to turn around Anheuser-Busch, but the pendulum started to swing back.

Marketing changes happened first. The CMO Jorn and the VP of Bud Light Alex were replaced mid-2017. The Belgian CMO Jorn was replaced with a Brazilian CMO, Marcel Marcondes. Marcel had at least worked at the Global AB InBev office in NYC for the past few years as the Global VP of Corona (which Anheuser-Busch owned outside of the U.S.) and New Brands. Prior to that, he had spent his entire twenty-year career in Brazil.

No one really knew Marcel. People hoped that he would put the right people in place to lead the brands. To his credit, he picked the best person he could to lead Bud Light—Andy Goeler. Andy is an absolute legend in the beer industry. He might be the closest thing to Steve Jobs that the beer industry will ever see. He was one of the last remaining senior executives from the pre–InBev Anheuser-Busch days. He started his career at Anheuser-Busch in 1980 at a New Jersey wholesaler. Over the next thirty-seven years, he held various positions across the sales and marketing organizations. In 1982, he was on the original team that launched Bud Light. He then led Bud Light during its rocket ship growth from 1992 to 2002, turning it into the number-1 beer brand in the country. After that, he took over as Budweiser's VP from 2002 to 2006. Then he led all Anheuser-Busch's craft and high-end brands until 2017. He turned Goose Island Brewery, which Anheuser-Busch acquired in 2011, from a small regional brewery in Chicago into a nationwide success. He repeated this with Anheuser-Busch-acquired craft brands like Elysian and Golden Road. Everything Andy touched typically turned to gold. His SAMCOM presentations were always the most highly anticipated and attended. He almost always went over his allotted time, but no one cared. He could story-tell and build brand identities better than anyone. And he always saved a grand finale act for the end of his presentations. One year, he finished his Goose Island presentation by releasing a few hundred pounds of fresh hops from the rafters onto the stage, covering himself in a cloud of hops that would eventually go into Goose Island India Pale Ale beers.

Andy started working his magic almost immediately. He was responsible for the famous "Dilly Dilly" campaign that launched at the end of 2017. "Dilly Dilly" was a catchphrase used in a series of humorous "medieval" commercials that played off the popularity of the popular HBO series *Game of Thrones*. The first commercial in the series was titled "Banquet." In the commercials, subjects present gifts to the king and queen at a royal banquet. The first subject presents a six-pack of Bud Light. The next subject presents a twelve-pack of Bud Light. As each guest brings more cases of Bud Light, the Bud Light King expresses his approval by saying, "Dilly Dilly." However, when a guest presents "spiced honey mead wine" (which was a veiled slight of snobbish wine culture) instead of Bud Light, the King is offended, and banishes him to the Pit of Misery.

The ad proved very popular with audiences. More than one hundred thousand people searched on Google for the made-up name "Dilly Dilly" in November 2017, and thousands more watched the ad on YouTube. Dilly Dilly and Pit of Misery both became memes and popular sayings. Dilly Dilly was used in wedding toasts. Ben Rothlisberger, the quarterback for the Pittsburgh Steelers, used it to call an audible during a nationwide NFL game. "Pit of Misery" was used by hockey teams to banish opposing players to the penalty box. It was the first time since the famous "Wassup" commercials that Anheuser-Busch created a catchphrase that became part of the cultural zeitgeist.

The reemergence of Bud Light in the national conversation happened too late for Alex Medicis, though. He was also banished to the Pit of Misery in November 2017 and left Anheuser-Busch.

The CEO of North America, João Castro Neves, left as well.

No one was really surprised. Anheuser-Busch InBev was a results-oriented company, and the results were not there.

Chapter 11

Scared Dinosaurs

The pressure was on. By late 2017, most of the obvious fat had been cut from all the companies Anheuser-Busch InBev had acquired over the past decade. ZBB (Zero Based Budgeting) would get the company only so far. AB InBev needed to find a way to grow market share. The current sales and marketing approaches weren't working. Starting a price war would only drive profits down for the industry as a whole, without substantially increasing AB InBev's market share—if at all. Investors were running out of patience. By year end, the stock price was down to $111 per share—about a 15 percent drop from its $131 high in 2016.

It was time for a change.

But would fresh blood bring fresh ideas? Ones that resonated with the American consumer? Or would they get mired in European and Brazilian playbooks that didn't, and couldn't, work in the United States?

The next CEO of North America and the next Chief Sales Officer of the U.S. were both a surprise. Michel Doukeris was named the CEO of North America. He was unknown to most people in the U.S. Doukeris grew up in Brazil but his father was Greek. He joined AB InBev in 1996 after undergrad and worked in various sales and marketing roles in Brazil for the next fourteen years. He spent the next six years as the President of Anheuser-Busch's China and Asia Pacific region. In 2017, he joined the Global office in NYC as Global Chief Sales Officer. Even though Doukeris was not well known in the U.S., he was well known across the organization for his "5 and 10 year plans." He learned this style from his time in China, where the government issues economic guidelines for the entire country every five years.

Doukeris was not a communist. He would be considered more of a globalist. More specifically, he thought that the world is more interconnected than we think and there are patterns and "unstoppable trends" that persist across countries and cultures. His Brazilian/Greek heritage, time in China, and time in the U.S. shaped that worldview. He saw trends in the beer industry, and the consumer industry at large, toward premiumization, health and wellness, and purpose-driven branding happening globally. He was committed to acting on a long-term vision in the U.S. that would grow revenue and profitability based on these trends.

He was announced as the new CEO on November 13, 2017. I met him a few days later on November 16. Actually, he met me. We were both at the Fall Anheuser-Busch Wholesaler Panel meeting. The Wholesaler Panel is a group of about twenty wholesalers that meet quarterly with Anheuser-Busch to review joint priorities.

There was a happy hour the night before the panel meeting. I was chatting with a few wholesalers when I was approached by a man I had never met before. I introduced myself and he said, "I know who you are. I am Michel." I immediately realized it was the new CEO of North America, and I apologized for not recognizing him. He looked different in person than he did in pictures. In pictures, Michel's smile looks forced; in person, he seemed much warmer. He was shorter than most of the other Brazilians I had worked with, and his personality was more understated as well. I would say his personality leaned more heavily on his European heritage than his Brazilian heritage. He was more quiet, thoughtful, and reserved compared to many of his Brazilian colleagues. He admits that he is "a little bit shy."

Doukeris sought me out because he wanted to visit me in Denver. The western region I managed was the only U.S. region, out of six, that had "Grown Share, Grown Share, Grown Share" in 2017. To develop his longer-term plan for the U.S., he wanted to learn about some of the things I did in the West to beat competition. He planned to learn from others as well throughout November and December. Then he would present his longer-term plan to wholesalers at SAMCOM in January 2018. I told him that I welcomed the visit.

Later in the evening, I ran into the person whom Doukeris announced as the new Chief Sales Officer—Brendan Whitworth. Doukeris announced Whitworth the same day that he was appointed CEO. I had known Brendan for a number of years. We first met when I was in business school. It was in 2010 on my twenty-seventh birthday. Brendan graduated from HBS two years before me, so we never overlapped. We both played rugby in business school, though, and Brendan returned to campus for some alumni rugby events. My girlfriend at the time, and now wife, threw a birthday party for me after a rugby game. The whole rugby team, their girlfriends, other rugby fans, and rugby alumni were invited. Brendan came for a few beers. He is a hard guy to forget. He's a former Marine. Looks a bit like GI Joe. Full of self-confidence. We had a few beers together before he left with some other alums.

I didn't run into Brendan again for three years. In 2013, I flew from Belgium to New York City to work on a project with our Global Finance team. In the Global office, I turned the corner and ran into Brendan. He had recently joined Anheuser-Busch's Global Sales team from Pepsi. We briefly chatted about our experiences post–business school and about the fun we had playing HBS rugby. Shortly thereafter, we both joined the sales team in the U.S. Brendan became the Vice President for the Northeast Sales Region in 2014 (this was similar to the role I had leading the Western region). He was promoted to VP of Trade Marketing at the end of 2016. He reported into Alex Medicis and was responsible for all of the sales programs like SAP and BOGOs. He often clashed with Alex on these programs and advocated for changes to them. This happened multiple times when Alex was presenting to the Global Chief Sales Officer—Michel Doukeris. Michel obviously liked some of Brendan's ideas and therefore promoted him to Chief Sales Officer.

People in the organization were generally happy to have an American back in the Chief Sales Officer role; not everyone was excited it was Brendan. In addition to clashing with Alex Medicis, Brendan clashed with other people in the organization. He could be quite stubborn. He had a difficult time admitting when he was wrong. And he wasn't a great listener. A few top people left the organization when Brendan was promoted. They did not want to report into him. I was not one of them. I had a fine business relationship with Brendan. We weren't great friends, but we respected each other and worked together to try to sell more beer.

⁙⁙⁙⁙⁙⁙⁙⁙

Two weeks later, I greeted Michel and Brendan at our Denver office. I presented an overview of why the Western region was very different than the rest of the United States. It was geographically much bigger. It was more competitive than many other regions as well. The Western region overindexed in craft beers. It had strong regional value brand competitors like Rainier, Olympia, and Pabst. It was the home of Coors Light, one of Bud Light's largest competitors. Hard seltzers like White Claw and Truly were growing faster in states like Colorado and Montana than anywhere else. Each state was uniquely regulated. States like Colorado and Utah still had laws requiring that lower-alcohol 3.2 percent beer could be sold only in convenience stores and grocery stores. Higher-strength beer could be sold only in package liquor stores. Prices in Idaho had to stay the same for 180 days.

I explained how I used these idiosyncrasies of the Western market to my advantage. I greatly expanded distribution of Anheuser-Busch's recently acquired craft brands like Elysian (based in Washington), 10 Barrel (based in Oregon), and Breckenridge (based in Colorado) across the region to win in craft. I resurrected Rolling Rock as a value brand to compete against Rainier, Olympia, and Pabst. I sandwiched Coors Light with custom Bud Light skiing and rodeo programming that my local marketing team developed. This played well with consumers out west. I further hit Coors Light by accelerating Michelob Ultra in markets like Oregon, which is home to Nike and Columbia. Michelob Ultra's running and workout themes played better in states like Washington and Oregon than Coors Light's "Cold as the Rockies" theme. I did custom incentives to drive distribution of brands like Spiked Seltzer to arrest the growth of White Claw and Truly. I worked with our brewing team to bring more 3.2 percent alcohol beer offerings to Utah and Colorado. All of these programs added up to share gains in 2017.

I then took Michel on a market visit in Denver. We hit many liquor stores so he could witness all of the different craft brands, value brands, and seltzer brands I referenced in my presentation. I also took him to visit stores selling marijuana. Marijuana had been recently legalized in many Western states, including Washington in 2012, Colorado in 2014, and Oregon in 2015. This posed a longer-term threat to the beer industry as beer sales typically declined in the years following marijuana legalization. The marijuana industry did a nice job premiumizing the shopping experience. Many marijuana stores in Colorado looked like Apple stores. They were very modern in their design. They had cool lighting and music. Knowledgeable "Budtenders" helped consumers decide what products would be best for them before they checked out on Apple iPads. More legalization efforts were underway across the U.S. This could be a threat, especially as most beer was purchased in gas stations and liquor stores that did not look like Apple stores. . . . The marijuana industry in Colorado also had well-coordinated campaigns advertising that marijuana was safer and healthier than beer. If marijuana won this PR battle, it would pose another threat to beer.

Michel and Brendan seemed pleased with the visit. They asked me to be a key member of the team that would execute Michel's long-term vision to restore growth. They then granted me a nice stock option package to make it worth my time. The option package would pay well if the stock price increased over the next five years. It would be worth nothing if it didn't.

The following month, in January 2018, Michel laid out his long-term vision to restore growth in the U.S. at SAMCOM. SAMCOM was in New Orleans that year. There was a lot of energy at that meeting, and it wasn't just at the after-parties on Bourbon Street. Andy Goeler was back in charge of Bud Light. The "Dilly Dilly" campaign was shaping up to be one of the most popular since the "Wassup" commercials. It was a cultural phenomenon. At the Super Bowl the following week, the Philadelphia Eagles executed a trick play against the New England Patriots called "Philly Philly" that was inspired by the phrase. The trick play was one of the gutsiest calls in NFL history. It happened on fourth-and-goal toward the end of the second quarter. NFL films described the play as "a play that the Eagles had never called before, run on 4th down by an undrafted rookie running back pitching the football to a third-string tight end who had never attempted an NFL pass before, throwing to a backup quarterback who had never caught an NFL (or college) pass before, on the biggest stage for football."

Philly of course scored on the play. The decision to go for the touchdown instead of a field goal helped propel the Eagles to their first Super Bowl in fifty-seven years. They beat the New England Patriots 41–33. The Philly Philly play was enshrined in NFL lore. The

Eagles' Super Bowl rings contained 127 diamonds, which is the sum of the numbers of the three players who touched the ball executing Philly Philly—RB Corey Clement (30), TE Trey Burton (88), and QB Nick Foles (9). Later in 2018, a statue commemorating Philly Philly, showing the moment Nick Foles asked head coach Doug Pederson if he wanted to run "Philly Philly," was unveiled at the Eagles' Lincoln Financial Field. The statue was commissioned by Bud Light.

Back at SAMCOM, though, Michel unveiled his plans to turn around the U.S. His five-year strategy to do so was coined "Lead Future Growth," or LFG for short. LFG was a play on the popular sports phrase "Let's Fucking Go." People like Tom Brady regularly posted the phrase LFG before big games. Unlike "Grow Share, Grow Share, Grow Share," which didn't have much substance or direction to it, LFG had a clear underlying plan to get the U.S. back to growth. It was five-pronged with a clear hierarchy of focus. I simplify it as:

1. Double the size of Michelob Ultra
2. Double the size of the thirteen high-end craft breweries Anheuser-Busch had acquired
3. Disrupt Corona & Modelo by increasing Stella Artois and other premium brand volume 10x
4. Maintain Bud Light's share of core beer vs. Miller Lite and Coors Light
5. Capture +$1 billion of revenue in the emerging hard seltzer and canned cocktail market with new brands

Michel showed a bunch of graphs and slides on how to achieve these goals. More importantly, he showed what could happen to the revenue trajectory of the U.S. if these goals were achieved. There were strong reasons to believe that revenue could turn around, especially if Anheuser-Busch could accelerate the growth of higher-priced beers like Michelob Ultra, Goose Island, and Stella Artois. People generally liked the strategy. Michelob Ultra was already a top-5 beer brand in the U.S., growing double digits, and priced ~20 percent more than Bud Light. There was a clear opportunity to overtake Miller Lite and Coors Light if it could build on this growth and double its size. Craft beers were still growing double digits, Anheuser-Busch was now the largest craft brewery in the U.S., and these beers generally sold at a 50–60 percent premium to Bud Light. And Stella Artois played in the import category with Corona and Modelo. This segment was also growing and priced ~40 percent more than core beers.

The one large concern was where Bud Light sat in the list of priorities. Bud Light was still the largest beer brand in the U.S. It was the largest beer brand in every wholesaler's portfolio. At the end of 2017, it still accounted for one of every five beers sold in the United States. It had been the largest beer brand in the country since 2001, and subsequently it had always been the number-1 priority for Anheuser-Busch. Now it was clearly listed as the number-4 priority for the company. There was no aspiration to grow Bud Light either. It was supposed to just "maintain" its share of core beers versus Miller Lite and Coors Light, which comprised another 15 percent of the beer industry. As the number-4 priority, Bud Light budgets would be slashed and the dollars would be reallocated to higher-priority brands, even as the "Dilly Dilly" campaign was becoming a cultural phenomenon.

Michel's reasoning was that the entire world was experiencing "unstoppable trends" toward health and wellness, premiumization, and purpose-driven brands. He saw this during his time in China. The Chinese beer market experienced strong growth from 2010 to 2016. Anheuser-Busch gained significant revenue and market share, led by premium brands like Corona and Stella Artois.

Brands that fit into these "unstoppable trend" categories would continue to experience tailwinds, and their segments would grow.

Michelob Ultra was considered a "health and wellness" beer given its low calories and low carbs. Craft beers were seen as premium. Brands like Stella Artois had clear purposes around them with their "Buy a Lady a Drink" campaign. Every time someone bought a Stella Artois, the brand would donate clean drinking water to women in emerging countries. That's why these brands captured the first three priorities.

Michel viewed core beers like Bud Light in long-term secular decline. They did not fit into his "unstoppable trend" framework, even though the Bud Light family of beers had grown volume by 4.3 percent and share by 0.70 percent as recently as 2012 (before the string of Brazilian and Belgian sales and marketing execs took over). Miller Light had gained share of the U.S. light beer category for the last three years, capitalizing on some of the missteps of the "Up for Whatever" and "Bud Light Party" campaigns. Miller Lite's volume trends had been much better than Bud Light and were even returning to volume growth in early 2018. Putting Bud Light as the number-4 priority and aspiring to "maintain share" meant that it would be even more difficult to arrest the growth of competitors like Miller Light. As the number-4 priority, financial and marketing resources would be pulled from Bud Light and reallocated to Michelob Ultra, Craft, and Stella Artois. It was easier to accelerate the revenue growth of smaller brands with momentum than doing the hard work of putting the number-1 brand Bud Light on a sustainable growth trajectory. Many people questioned if this was the right strategy, especially as Bud Light was catching fire with consumers with the Dilly Dilly campaign.

Despite the concerns, people were willing to give Michel's LFG strategy a chance. This was a real strategy to grow the business, backed up by clear financial goals, and with clear targets for Anheuser-Busch and its wholesalers to achieve.

Not everyone was convinced that LFG would be enough. Jorge Paulo Lemann, the architect of the Anheuser-Busch InBev merger, AB

InBev board member, and the controlling shareholder of AB InBev, was worried about his firm in 2018. He built Anheuser-Busch InBev by using cheap debt to acquire good businesses and run them more efficiently via Zero Based Budgeting.[1] After acquiring SABMiller in 2016, there were no beer companies left to buy. AB InBev would have to rely on growing organically to create shareholder value. At the end of 2017, there weren't reasons to believe the U.S. was capable of doing this. And the Brazilians and Belgians had always looked to the U.S. for inspiration on how to grow brands in other markets. If the U.S. business was losing due to more aggressive craft, seltzer, and import competitors that did a better job innovating and capturing U.S. consumer demand, how long would it be before Anheuser-Busch InBev started losing revenue and market share in its other markets around the world? It seemed like it was already starting in Brazil, Anheuser-Busch's second-largest market by revenue. Brazil lost beer volume and market share in 2017 also.

In April 2018, Jorge Paulo Lemann admitted that he was a "scared dinosaur." He was speaking at the "Strategy and Leadership in an Age of Disruption" panel at the Milken Institute annual conference. He admitted that 3G Capital is "learning from its mistakes in the U.S." and will use that knowledge to protect itself in other markets. He further stated that "we bought brands and we thought they would last forever." Brands obviously don't last forever unless they continue to make connections with consumers. They do this by being authentic to their mission and delivering remarkable marketing, products, and services that ensure consumers can't live without the product. Anheuser-Busch had failed to do this over the past five years with its historical brands like Bud Light, but also with innovations that it missed like hard seltzers. Jorge Paulo Lemann was just now realizing this. So he mentioned that AB InBev would have to "adjust to new demands from clients" and the company was behind companies like Starbucks and Nike.

At that point, the panel moderator asked him: "I could see someone making an argument that you and your colleagues are not the people to manage this innovative change because that's not where your expertise lies. How do you approach that?" Jorge responded, "Oh . . . I've had various careers in my life. . . . I was a tennis player, a finance guy. . . . I've been adjusting. I'm seventy-eight, but I'm ready! And I'm scrambling. I am not going to lie down and go away."

It was probably time for Jorge Paulo Lemann to go away. He won the beer war he started when he bought Ambev in 1989. He went on to build the largest beer company, and the largest consumer packaged goods company in the world by profitability. He did this with a strategy of ruthlessly cutting costs of acquired companies. There was nothing worthwhile left to buy because he bought it all. If he wanted to start growing organically, it was time to bring in someone else who specialized in brand building and innovating.

But he didn't. While Michel Doukeris and Brendan Whitworth adopted a strategy of LFG in the United States, Jorge Paulo Lemann, and the rest of the Anheuser-Busch InBev board, adjusted the global company's growth strategy from ZBB to be based on the controversial European philosophy of ESG—or Environmental, Social, and Governance factors. This would prove a disastrous battle plan for winning the next phase of the beer wars and creating long-term shareholder value.

Chapter 12

Stakeholder Capitalism and ESG Adoption

To understand what ESG is, you have to understand where it came from. The acronym ESG may be relatively new to the scene, but the idea that companies have an obligation to "do well by doing good" is not.

Business ethics, of course, is not a new concept. Even the Bible cautions that "Better is a little with righteousness than great revenues with injustice." And even the most fervent capitalist diehards would be pressed to argue that companies should be grabbing pitchforks and red horns if it meant an extra buck in the company coffers—at a minimum, abject evil isn't typically good for business. But where the balance should be struck, and at what cost, has always been up for debate.

During the twentieth century, two schools of thought emerged. One was led by the European Klaus Schwab, the intellectual leader of the "stakeholder capitalism" movement in the 1970s. Under this theory, businesses exist not just to serve their owners, but society as a whole. In this system, society is run by elites from every sector—not just democratically elected politicians, but by churches and nonprofits and billionaires and business leaders. These experts come together to create policies that benefit the world as a whole and then implement them via the power they hold over the various organizations that they run. The purpose of a business is thus not very different from a nonprofit or government agency: making the world a better place. Central planning, but with a better PR department than the communists had.

What constituted making the world a better place, of course, was always a subjective call, and one that was left up to the elites to decide. Should developing countries be forced to cut their energy use, in the name of fighting climate change? By how much? What if that meant forcing Ghanaians to sweat in sweltering summer heat? What if some died? Or had to choose between air-conditioning and sending their children to school? Should food suppliers raise the cost of meats (or eliminate them altogether), to support animal welfare causes? Should farmers be forced to switch to organic fertilizers, even if it means millions will starve? Should we stop drilling for oil, or fracking for gas, or mining for coal, to save the planet? To avoid disrupting indigenous lands? Or increase such efforts so that low-skilled workers aren't put out of work? Should companies increase wages for their employees (or their suppliers' employees), even if that means raising prices on essential goods? Who decides what that raise should be?

The other school of thought was distinctly American: "shareholder primacy." This philosophy was spearheaded by American economist Milton Friedman around the same time. It holds that the purpose of a for-profit company is to make money for its owners. Nothing more, nothing less. As he wrote in *The New York Times*: "There is one and only one social responsibility of business—to use its resources and engage in activities designed to increase its profits so long as it stays within the rules of the game, which is to say, engages in open and free competition without deception or fraud."[1] The use of owners' money to pursue social goals was tantamount to theft, since the owners did not consent to having their investments in the business spent this way. He also believed that doing so was undemocratic, since it allowed wealthy business executives to use their access to corporate money to force social policies on fellow citizens that they did not vote for, and with which a majority of them, almost by definition, did not agree. There was no such thing as simply doing "good," he argued, since "one man's good is another's evil."

Of course, proponents of shareholder primacy also cared about making the world a better place. It's just that they believed American-style free market capitalism was the best way to do it. Capitalism gets a bad rap, but as an economic system, it can't be beat. It has lifted hundreds of millions of people out of poverty, incentivized the development of groundbreaking technological innovation, and enabled nearly all modern-day Americans to enjoy a lifestyle historically reserved for kings.

But in the 1970s, the benefits of shareholder primacy vs. stakeholder capitalism were still very much up for debate. And so, through the next several decades, the intercontinental contrast continued. Europe largely adopted a stakeholder capitalism track, while American companies adhered to shareholder primacy.

Germany, for example, embraced a system of "co-determination," where company workers could elect up to half a company's board and influence how the company is run.[2] They paid their CEOs less and promised more job security to their employees. Europeans taxed more, at least relative to the United States' consistent corporate tax reductions since the 1970s.

America, by contrast, plowed headfirst into free market capitalism. Entrepreneurs flocked to America. Great companies were born. Industries rose to greatness. As a result, America enjoys the largest and wealthiest middle class in the world, with per capita GDP of more than $76,000. But the rich didn't just get richer, the poor did, too. The percentage of Americans living in poverty dropped from 13 percent in 1980 to 2.9 percent in 2018. Today, even the average "poor" person in America owns a car and has air-conditioning, internet access, and at least one TV. 92 percent of all adults own a smartphone; for those under sixty, it's nearly everyone.[3]

Of course, it wasn't all sunshine and roses in the U.S. The merger mania of the 1980s sent stock prices skyrocketing, sometimes at the expense of laid-off employees and increased corporate debt. Then came the tech-driven dot-com boom of the 1990s, punctuated by its 2000 bust. In the early 2000s, banks invented ever-riskier financial products to juice profits—finding ways to slice up risky investments and repackage them so that the parts looked less risky than the whole—eventually leading to the subprime mortgage crisis. But fraud is not unique to shareholder capitalism, and our government has always stood ready to rein in the excess, regulate the bad, and imprison people who break the law.

But the common denominator in all of these trends—good or bad, risky or safe—is that they were designed to increase profits. And despite the bumps, the overarching trend of capitalism has been toward prosperity. That's by design. By focusing on individual gain, the collective wins. As Adam Smith wrote in *The Wealth of Nations* almost 250 years ago, though a man "intends only his own gain," he is "led by an invisible hand to promote an end which was no part of his intention." The pursuit of one's "own interest . . . frequently promotes that of society more effectually."

The view from inside the corporate boardroom was largely the same. Companies competed with one another to make the best products in the most cost-efficient manner. To best one another in a free market system. Board members fought hard to ensure companies met financial targets, yes, but knew the way to do so was to develop new products and to put the customer first. Executive compensation packages were increasingly tied to stock performance, too, meaning C-suite execs were also incentivized, on a personal level, to see the company succeed. And increasing merger activity meant that it was an eat-or-be-eaten mentality more broadly. A company that found itself fat on costs, or short on performance, may soon find itself being eyed as prey by larger companies hungry for growth.

It was a simpler time. For-profit companies existed to make a profit. It was almost tautological. It would have made no sense for the Cabbage Patch doll company to write an open letter to Congress on the human tragedy inflicted by the Cold War. Or for Blockbuster Video to issue a PR statement decrying the Supreme Court's decision in *Planned Parenthood v. Casey* narrowing abortion rights. No one did. It would be like the Roman Catholic Church weighing in on whether JPMorgan Chase should short grain futures on the commodity exchange. Or the White House offering its opinion on the correct interpretation of the Quran. Unimaginable. It just wasn't the role of that particular type of institution.

But don't take my word for it. As recently as 1995, companies were reluctant to even entertain the possibility of supporting social causes. Even one as uncontroversial today as supporting gay rights. A former aide to President Clinton, for example, recounts being tasked with inviting corporate leaders to the White House, with the hopes that they might endorse the president's goals of expanding protections against discrimination and hate crimes against the LGBT community.[4] Typically, corporate types are thrilled at the chance to rub elbows with the president. But by his own account, he got "few takers." At one event, the only attendee was a Hollywood producer, who was gay himself. No other industry "wanted anything to do with gay rights."

Corporate America's reluctance to take sides on the gay rights debate wasn't controversial. It was common sense. As a young Michael Jordan famously responded when a reporter asked why he wasn't endorsing the Democratic candidate in the 1990 North Carolina senate race, he responded, "Republicans buy sneakers, too."[5]

Even after 9/11 hit, companies focused on getting back to business rather than waxing poetic on patriotism or trying to capitalize on trag-edy.[6] Ensuring that their companies could continue to provide goods and services to Americans *was* serving their highest purpose. For the City That Never Sleeps, the greatest tribute was making sure the show could go on. Verizon worked around the clock to rebuild the network that powered the New York Stock Exchange—a telecommunications network as large as the one that serves all of Cincinnati—in just six days.[7] Starbucks reopened two days after the attacks, serving coffee and snacks to workers at Ground Zero. American Airlines undertook monumental efforts to get their planes back in the air as quickly and safely as possible—two of its unions even waived a number of rights of rank-and-file members to aid in the effort.

Companies did not rush to incorporate an image of the Twin Tow-ers into their logo, or get airtime to promote their performative cor-porate sympathy for New Yorkers on *Live with Regis and Kelly*. They focused on their businesses. They got back to work.

Companies knew better than to do otherwise, even on the rare issue that brought Americans together. It would be tasteless. Inau-thentic. And if it ever even crossed a business executive's mind, for a fraction of a second, to say something about 9/11, it certainly wasn't going to be a comment twisting itself in knots over how to express concern for economically privileged New Yorkers while also recogniz-ing how white privilege may have played a role in oppressing minority groups from Afghanistan that ultimately led to the radicalization leading to the attacks. That would be corporate suicide.

In the end, few companies made any public reference to the event at all, outside of business necessity.

One of the few companies that could authentically memorialize 9/11 was Anheuser-Busch.

During the 2002 Super Bowl, just five months after the attacks, Anheuser-Busch ran a sixty-second ad titled "Respect," honoring the victims of 9/11. The ad ran just once. It featured the Budweiser Clydesdale horses pulling a red wagon over the Brooklyn Bridge, down a cobblestone street in Manhattan, and ultimately onto the grass in Liberty State Park in New Jersey. With the Statue of Liberty in the backdrop, the horses look out onto the New York City skyline and slowly bow their heads. There is no voiceover. There is no beer. The only on-screen text comes at the end: "We will never forget."

The ad was iconic. Unforgettable. Twenty years later, it is still counted among the best Super Bowl ads ever aired. It was able to make an emotional connection with a heartbroken country, still reeling from a terrible loss, without feeling opportunistic or promotional.

The fact that Anheuser-Busch was able to accomplish what no other company dared to try was a testament to its authenticity and connection to the American people. The commercial wasn't easy to make. Anheuser-Busch needed to obtain approval from both Congress and then-mayor of New York City Rudy Giuliani to film in New York in the wake of 9/11. The scene of the Clydesdales crossing the Brooklyn Bridge was filmed by a helicopter flying overhead, and gaining permission to enter the airspace was no simple task. Then there're the horses, which had to be transported from the Midwest to New England for training over the winter. Robin Wiltshire, Anheuser-Busch's go-to horse whisperer for twenty-five years, had to train the Clydesdales to bow in unison. "It would rain and my hat would turn to ice," he recalls.[8]

But more than its unrivaled execution abilities or production budget, Anheuser-Busch fundamentally understood Americans. It had spent decades building up trust with the American people. Budweiser was America in a bottle. It had a ninety-year history supporting the U.S. military, dating back to building diesel engines for submarines during World War I and gun and glider parts during World War II. It sponsored Little League Baseball games, brought neighbors together for a barbeque on a warm summer night, and marked weddings, anniversaries, birthdays, and all the celebrations in between. Budweiser loved America. And America loved it back.

Anheuser-Busch was the exception to the rule because it understood the rules. The dos and the don'ts. Focus on your customers. Focus on your product. Earn trust. Also: Do not alienate people. Do not chase social fads. Do not take sides in political debates. And in all but the rarest circumstances—a once-in-a-generation kind of event that aligns with what your company is at its core—do not comment on high-profile news events.

Many companies forgot this after the next crisis that rocked America: the financial crisis of 2008. Wall Street banks had gotten fat by loading up on cheap debt to fuel risky investments. The mind-boggling amount of leverage on their balance sheets meant that there was no margin for error. Even a tiny drop in the value of their assets would lead to cascading failures, wiping out banks and threatening to take the economy with it. Then the inevitable happened. The housing bubble popped. Investment bank Bear Stearns collapsed. President Obama stepped in to bail out the banks. More than $600 billion in free taxpayer money was offered as handouts to prop up the financial sector. Homeowners, however, were still facing evictions and foreclosures with little relief in sight. And workers were facing the toughest job market since the Great Depression. Between October 2008 and April 2009, an average of 700,000 American workers lost their jobs each month.[9]

People were enraged. By the fall of 2011, this collective outrage had found its voice. The cries came from the Occupy Wall Street movement. "We are the 99 percent," they chanted. For fifty-nine days, left-wing populist protestors camped in Zuccotti Park, located in New York's Financial District.

The rallying cry was against the 1 percent. Economic inequality was the enemy. Redistribution of wealth was the goal. And Wall Street banks were the villains under siege.

But redistributing wealth is *expensive*. Particularly for the 1 percent. So Wall Street adopted a different strategy instead. It would divert attention away from financial excess and economic inequality by promising to focus on fighting climate change and gender and racial inequality instead. Restructuring capitalism is hard; hiring a few extra female board members and throwing some donations at social justice organizations is not.

And Wall Street could dangle another prize. Wall Street firms, are, of course, first and foremost investors. That means they own not just their own day-to-day business operations, but virtually all publicly traded American companies as well. BlackRock, State Street, and Vanguard, for instance, are three of the largest asset managers in the world and collectively the largest shareholders in 88 percent of S&P 500 companies.[10] The amount of money they control is staggering. More than $20 trillion to be exact, or roughly the same size as the GDP of the United States. Their money comes from everyday people who have their 401(k) and pension plans invested into funds controlled by these organizations. The number of *companies* they control is staggering, too. Given their huge financial clout, these firms could impose new social and diversity mandates not just on their own, internal operations, but across the entire private sector.

Some of these mandates stemmed from BlackRock, State Street, and Vanguard's largest customers: progressive pension funds. In a truism as old as time, follow the money to understand the behavior. The largest pension programs in the world tend to come from progressive states and countries. In the U.S., California and New York have the largest state pension systems, with more than $700 billion and $550 billion respectively.[11] In Europe, Norway has a $1.62 *trillion* fund. These entities are influenced or controlled by politicians who demand that asset managers who manage their money pursue favored progressive causes. New York City's comptroller, for example, is an elected official who spends his days writing letters telling Amazon to treat its workers better and Starbucks to allow unionization and all companies to adopt climate and diversity goals more broadly. Many of California's pension-fund heads are similarly elected, and use the power of the pension purse string to pursue similarly progressive goals. If these pension funds could marshal not only pension fund money but Wall Street money to the same causes, they would be unstoppable.

It was an offer the Occupiers could not refuse. Wall Street could atone for its sin of greediness by sacrificing the virtues of merit on the altar of Stakeholder Capitalism. Now, identity politics and programs like ESG and DEI would be offered to appease the activist gods.

Perhaps the most public display of this new bargain was the Fearless Girl statue, which appeared in downtown Manhattan one day to stare down the famous Wall Street Bull. At her feet lay a placard: "Know the power of women in leadership. SHE matters." Crowds flocked to the site. Wall Street was abuzz with speculation. Who was this girl?

A PR testament to Wall Street's newfound commitment to social activism, it turned out. The statue was commissioned by State Street, one of Wall Street's largest banks and investment firms, to promote the launch of a new index fund that would invest in companies with relatively high representation of women on company boards. The new fund would trade on the New York Stock Exchange. Its ticker? SHE.

But State Street did more than put up a new statue and launch a new financial product. It also revised its corporate voting policies with respect to all of the companies it invested in. You see, when someone buys stock in a company, they're not just entitled to the financial benefits of ownership, such as collecting dividends and enjoying the financial upside when a stock price increases. They're also given the ability, as business owners, to control the company and its strategic direction. They do this in a variety of ways, but one of the most important is by electing the company's board of directors and voting on various proposals that management and other shareholders put forth. As part of State Street's gender diversity pledge,[12] it promised to start voting out directors at the public companies it invested in unless those companies had at least 15 percent female directors on their boards. And as an investment firm with nearly $3 trillion in capital under its management, State Street had a lot of votes to cast.[13]

The tides were slowly turning.

Climate change was also coming into focus. 2015 marked the year the Paris Agreement would be signed. 195 countries adopted the treaty. Before it was even signed, there were calls for corporate America to do its part. The Obama White House had launched its American Business Act on Climate Pledge in July. By October, eighty-one of America's largest companies had pledged to meet the agreement's goals.[14]

Diversity initiatives were gaining traction, too. In January 2015, the consulting firm McKinsey released a white paper called "Why Diversity Matters" that purported to show a link between gender and ethnic diversity and a company's financial performance. I say "purported" because the study has been thoroughly debunked by academics (hardly a conservative bunch), but the media and public at large had already eaten it up.[15] Companies were starting to be called on to not only make money, but also fight climate change and focus on diversity at the same time. A few years later, these corporate expectations would intensify, putting many firms like Anheuser-Busch in a bind between shareholder and stakeholder priorities. In 2015, Anheuser-Busch didn't have time for competing priorities, as it still had competitors to buy. It had used American free market shareholder capitalism principles to create the world's largest beer company, and shareholders had been rewarded with a record-high share price in 2015.

By 2018, BlackRock, the world's largest asset manager, had not just jumped on the bandwagon, but taken the reins. Its CEO, Larry Fink, wrote a famed letter to America's CEOs imploring them to pursue social and ideological goals in addition to financial ones.[16] "Society is demanding that companies both public and private, serve a social purpose," he wrote. "Companies must benefit all of their stakeholders, including shareholders, employees, customers, and the communities in which they operate." If they don't, they will "ultimately lose the license to operate from key stakeholders." Stakeholder capitalism was now in vogue.

There was something else notable about the letter: It marked one of the first times BlackRock talked about "environmental, social, and governance" matters. The term dated back to a 2004 United Nations report titled "Who Cares Wins," but hadn't really caught on. In 2018, the phrase was still so obscure that Larry Fink's letter didn't use the now-ubiquitous ESG acronym; he had to spell it out.

The New York Times predicted the letter was "likely to cause a firestorm in the corner offices of companies everywhere."[17] A Yale business school professor called it a "lightning rod." Companies, of course, quickly took note. When your largest shareholder tells you to do something—anything—you do it.

Of course, there had always been skeptics. Fink's letter was light on details. And intentionally vague. Socially responsible investing had always existed, yes, but the point was to invest in ways that helped society. It was about giving up a little bit of money (say, refusing to invest in tobacco companies, even though they deliver great shareholder returns) for the greater good. In Fink's version, though, ESG wasn't just good for society, but good for business. Businesses that catered to the environment and whims of diversity advocates would make more money, he explained. Having more women was more profitable. So was having more wind turbines. And selling fewer guns. And everything else favored by the progressive left. Suddenly, socially responsible investing wasn't just socially optimal, but financially optimal, too.

The new stance raised a lot of questions. Was all of this talk of social responsibility meant simply to drive profits? Was this simply a PR wash on American capitalism in the post-recession era? Or was it something more? Corporate goodness for the sake of goodness itself? How were you supposed to balance the various E's, S's, and G's? What was ESG? Fink's letter wasn't clear. But BlackRock did launch ESG specific index funds, at much higher fees than their non-ESG counterparts, to capitalize on the new fad they were pushing.

And soon enough, study after study was published showing that companies that do good in the world make more money for their investors. ESG funds allegedly outperformed their non-ESG counterparts; never mind the obvious fact that ESG funds tend to hold a ton of Big Tech stock, since tech companies have almost no emissions, and Big Tech had been booming for reasons totally unrelated to their green credentials. Companies with diverse boards had higher financial returns; never mind that the studies looked at correlation, not causation, and that big, rich companies were more willing to add a couple women and minorities to the team. Never mind these new ESG funds had short, unproven track records, when most investors demand at least three years of returns data before investing.

The seeds of stakeholder capitalism had been firmly planted. And Anheuser-Busch proved to have fertile soil.

In some sense, it was a match made in heaven. Stakeholder capitalism had deeply European roots, and AB InBev's corporate history already embraced much of this culture. I saw some of this working in Belgium. The Europeans loved their recyclable glass bottles, and Belgian beer brand Stella had long incorporated some degree of social responsibility into its brand, such as through its partnership with charities ensuring access to clean water in developing nations. The other half of the corporate marriage, the Anheuser-Busch side, did not share this heritage. Its advertising and brand image tended to stay away from softer social and environmental causes. It was a rough-and-tumble American beer brand, not an international aid organization. Anheuser-Busch historically stayed in its lane. Brands advertised why the beer was better, colder, and funnier than others. The parent company promoted responsible drinking programs and designated driver programs. It directed its charitable efforts toward U.S. military and first responder–linked organizations, which helped many of its loyal customers and played into brand programming. But like any newlyweds, there was much for each side to learn from one another.

And there was another reason Anheuser-Busch was so receptive to the promise of stakeholder capitalism. 2017 had been a tumultuous year. Profits were down. Leadership was worried. Larry Fink's 2018 letter promised salvation. A way to turn company finances around.

The SABMiller integration was not going as planned. Anheuser-Busch took on more than $100 billion in debt to finance the deal. This debt was denominated in U.S. and Eurodollars. Most of the revenue streams they acquired with the SABMiller deal were in emerging market currencies like the South African rand, Colombian peso, and Indian rupee. After the deal closed, many of these currencies began to decline versus the U.S. dollar as the Trump administration enacted tariffs. This made the U.S.- and Euro-denominated debt difficult to pay off. More rand, pesos, and rupees would need to be generated to pay off the same amount of debt. The investment bank Jefferies estimated that the swing in emerging market currencies cost the company $2.3 billion dollars between the merger and 2019.[18] This exceeded the $2.2 billion in synergies achieved by the deal. Anheuser-Busch was therefore struggling to pay down its $100 billion debt and achieve its targeted net debt/EBITDA ratio of 4.0.

To do this, they had to make changes. They started by slashing their dividend in half and selling off some of the SABMiller assets Anheuser-Busch had just acquired. These assets included the Australian business, which included brands like Carlton and Great Northern.

Financial pressure rarely makes for good deals. And this was no exception. Anheuser-Busch cheaply sold the Australian brands to the Japanese beer company Asahi. The assets they sold amounted to one-third of the value of SABMiller and 50 percent of its profits. Anheuser-Busch sold these assets at an average EBITDA multiple of 10.2x versus the 17.3x they had paid for SABMiller.[19] As a result, these divestitures were highly dilutive to the value of the business. And at the end of them, AB InBev was still left with a mountain of debt. Megabrew was quickly becoming Megabust.

Investors noticed the mounting problems. By the end of 2019, the stock price had declined to about $82, or about 35 percent from October 2016 when the SABMiller deal was announced.

AB InBev, the unstoppable force that rescued companies from falling profits and financial ruin, was now in need of rescuing itself.

It looked to stakeholder capitalism and ESG as its white knight.

One can reasonably wonder whether the new strategy was pursued with an earnest belief that serving societal goals would increase profits or whether it was pursued more cynically. But the truth is that the distinction was never so clear. Yes, Anheuser-Busch executives were truly looking for a way to increase the company's financial success. And this newfangled trend seemed to be a way to do it. But if it didn't work out that way, leadership surely knew that being a good corporate citizen would at least distract investors from its financial woes, at least for a period of time. And once it squeezed all the juice out of ZBB, it was desperate to find another three-letter acronym that promised a path toward growth. ESG seemed a perfect fit.

The timing couldn't have been better. In 2019, the CEOs of 181 American companies joined the Business Roundtable, an ostensibly business-focused chamber of commerce–type group, in redefining the purpose of a corporation. Rather than focus on profits, companies were now obligated to make "a fundamental commitment to all of our stakeholders," from customers to employees to suppliers to communities. A chief requirement was "foster[ing] diversity and inclusion." Companies from Apple to Pepsi to Walmart to, of course, BlackRock were eager to sign on.

Anheuser-Busch signed on, too, at least ideologically speaking. It wasn't allowed to formally join the club since the InBev takeover meant that AB was no longer technically an American company. But it had already taken heed of Fink's 2018 letter, and the transformation was already underway.

The transformation is visible in the company's annual reports—the public reports companies must give to their shareholders to keep them up to date on the business each year. Up through around 2017, the reports were standard fare. Profits. Costs. Geographic reach. Executive compensation. Charts with numbers. Credit risk disclosures. More charts with more numbers. Legal disclaimers. There might be some platitudes about beer's social purpose in "bringing people together for thousands of years," but nothing on stakeholder capitalism, gender equity, structural racism, or net-zero goals. In 2016, the only mention of "diversity" was the diversity of beer that AB brewed; the only mention of "sustainability" was in reference to how sustainable AB's profitability would be. In 2017, diversity creeped in, but only as it relates to "diversity of thought"—the now much-derided concept that the kind of diversity that matters is in ensuring that many different perspectives are heard, not in ensuring that companies can check many different race and gender boxes.

Fink's 2018 letter changed that. In 2018, Anheuser-Busch launched its first global Diversity and Inclusion Policy. It hired its first Global Director of Diversity and Inclusion. It signed the UN Women's Empowerment Principles & CEO Action for Diversity Pledge. It touted efforts to "hir[e] and develop[] diverse talent," although it spoke in broad, aspirational language that steered clear of quotas or numeric targets. It boasted about celebrating LGBT+ rights and fighting domestic violence. The company even hosted "A Day of Understanding," where CEO Carlos Brito shared his "personal insights on diversity, inclusion, and implicit bias."

By early 2020, Anheuser-Busch was producing two annual reports rather than just one: A traditional financial report and a separate ESG report. And it was making the rounds. Its Global Vice President of Sustainability was speaking on panels at the World Economic Forum at Davos—the mecca where global elites gather each year to solve the world's most vexing social and environmental problems—alongside other stakeholder capitalism evangelicals.[20]

Still, in those early, pre-pandemic days, stakeholder capitalism had mostly the same feel-good vibe as the "Save the Rainforest" and "Stop Acid Rain" campaigns I remember as a child from the 1990s. Well-intentioned. Largely unobjectionable. Not particularly interesting. At least to casual observers. Something I'd be willing to buy a tie-dyed T-shirt for to celebrate at my school's Earth Day assembly, but otherwise not something anyone thought about much.

That was all about to change.

Chapter 13

Trust and Wobbles

While Jorge Paulo Lemann and the board at Anheuser-Busch InBev were busy dipping their toes into ESG in 2018–2019, Michel Doukeris, Brendan Whitworth, and the rest of the U.S. team were focused on LFG. Michel was actually off to a good start. 2018 was the best year for Anheuser-Busch from a market share perspective since 2012. Share losses were almost cut in half versus the prior year and revenue trends improved. The success of the Bud Light Dilly Dilly campaign was partly to thank, but so was the acceleration of brands like Michelob Ultra and the craft portfolio.

My team was off to a good start, too. I'd launched a new program with our sales team called "WULTRA"—a combo of "Wall" and "Ultra." The program was simple—build "walls" of Michelob "Ultra" in every store. I know it sounds silly, but that was kind of the point. It was a straightforward, easy-to-understand way to get our fastest-growing brand—the fastest growing in the U.S., in fact—in front of more customers at more locations. I'd also taken Bud Light's Dilly Dilly campaign to as many sporting events as possible. We worked with an NHL hockey team, the Colorado Avalanche, to tweet "Pit of Misery! Dilly Dilly!" every time an opposing player was placed in the penalty box. And it was all working. By midyear, my Western region was outperforming every other region in the United States.

Heading into July 4th weekend of 2018, I received a phone call from Brendan. He was promoting me. He wanted me to take charge of Anheuser-Busch's largest revenue region—the Southeast. It was head-quartered in Atlanta, Georgia, and spanned from Mississippi to the Carolinas and from Tennessee down to Florida. It was responsible for almost 25 percent of Anheuser-Busch's sales, or about $3 billion in revenue. It was one of Anheuser-Busch's highest-share and most prof-itable beer markets. The Southeast is made for beer drinking. It is the home of college football, the birthplace of NASCAR, and the spring break capital of the U.S. And there's warm weather almost year-round.

The Southeast region needed a reboot. Revenue and market share were declining. The BOGO programs of 2016 and 2017 didn't help the brand equity of Budweiser, Bud Light, and Ultra in the South. Keystone Light, a MillerCoors value brand, was gaining ground on Busch Light and Natural Light, Anheuser-Busch's historically strong value brands. The rise of hard seltzers, especially in beach areas, was also proving challenging.

There was only one thing to do. My wife and I canceled our July 4th weekend plans and flew to Atlanta to check it out. We wanted to find a place to live because our four-year-old son was headed for pre-school. My wife was also six months pregnant with our third child, so we wanted to move before the birth. We found a house in the Atlanta suburb of Brookhaven that weekend. We moved to Atlanta in August but lived in temporary housing until we closed on our house in Sep-tember. Our son Brooks was born in October. In between all of that, I visited all seven of my new states, met all ~100 wholesalers who worked in every county across the Southeast, and met with more than 150 peo-ple working on my team. I wanted to get their feedback on what was working and not working in their markets. All of that feedback helped inform my plans to LFG, or Lead Future Growth, in the Southeast.

The plan was simple. I wanted Michelob Ultra to be bigger than

Coors Light and Miller Light combined (it was already larger than both of them individually in the Southeast). I wanted Bud Light (which was already bigger than Miller Light and Coors Light combined) to increase its lead. I wanted Stella Artois to be bigger than Heineken. I wanted Anheuser-Busch's seltzer brands to take the number-2 spot from Truly. To get there, we would develop remarkable national and local marketing campaigns, and then the local wholesalers could execute simple programs like making sure Ultra had more space in the beer cooler than Miller Lite and Coors light combined. Stella had as many SKUs in the store as Heineken, etc. Simple things. I unveiled the plan at the end of 2018. Wholesalers and the team seemed to be on board. Common sense and simplicity are always well received in the beer industry.

2019 saw a rebound. The Southeast returned to revenue growth. The U.S. had its best revenue performance in a number of years. Most of the priorities were working. Wholesalers were on board as well. The annual wholesaler engagement score, based on a survey of wholesalers who can comment on Anheuser-Busch programs, improved dramatically. After bottoming at 74 percent in 2017, the score rose to 90 percent when released in 2019. There was a +25 percent improvement on the wholesaler's belief in the "Strategic Direction" of the company. Led by a resurgence in Bud Light marketing, "Marketing efforts" scores rose by 24 percent. One wholesaler commented, "For the first time in a long time I believe we are on the right track to growth and success." Another remarked, "The new direction lined out within planning meetings has me optimistic about our continued relationship."

But a funny thing happened. Just as we seemed to be getting back on track, the global ESG and DEI initiatives started to trickle in. Like many global initiatives, these were originally well-intentioned and backed by seemingly credible scholarship. The first official Diversity, Equity, and Inclusion initiative that I can remember happened during the summer of 2019, at the Leadership, People, and Culture (LPC) meeting. Every summer, Anheuser-Busch held its annual LPC meeting for Partners. Partners were employees who reached a certain position and, as a result, were permitted to reinvest a portion of their bonus back into company stock. The company would then match this reinvested bonus with a multiplier of additional shares. It was this real "equity" in the company that made people "Partners." The LPC meeting was an opportunity to welcome new Partners and update everyone on where the company was headed.

It was also a chance to invite a guest speaker to talk about leadership. Past speakers included military heroes, star athletes, and corporate executives. These people usually spoke about themes like teamwork, overcoming adversity, and winning against all odds.

2019 was different. This year, the leadership talk was given by Frances Frei, a professor of Diversity and Inclusion at Harvard Business School.

I know what you're probably thinking. I'm about to spill the beans on how we were subjected to struggle sessions and forced to repent for the sins of white privilege and given lectures about why we should implement quota systems for more transgendered hires.

But when controversial ideologies first make an appearance, they rarely announce themselves so loudly. Instead, they offer a soft "hello," couching themselves in reasonable suggestions, inviting the listener in.

Remember, this was back in 2019. Before the summer of George Floyd and racial justice came to the fore (more on that later, of course). And so, in truth, Professor Frei's lecture wasn't all that controversial. Frankly, it wasn't controversial at all.

Professor Frei's talk was about trust. In her view, trust has three components: empathy, logic, and authenticity. "When all three of these things are working, we have great trust, but if any one of these gets shaky, if any one of these three *wobbles*, trust is threatened." Each "wobble" had its own fix. Lack of empathy could be fixed by removing distractions, to give colleagues and customers your full attention. Lack of logic could be remedied by clear and direct communication. And authenticity—the seeds of what would become the diversity, equity, and inclusion movement—could be improved by encouraging every worker to bring their whole, authentic self to work.

Some of this, I'm sure, was met with internal eye-rolling. I know this because I personally had to stifle more than one. No, I don't think that people should wear "whatever makes them feel fabulous" (as Professor Frei suggested) to work every day. There are dress codes and acceptable business attire at most firms. But honestly, if talks like this formed the basis of Diversity and Inclusion programs, and defined the limits of what they would become, I doubt I'd be writing this book.

A lot of what she said wasn't even that controversial. It was basically just a "wobbly" repackaging of good business sense. Trust is important. No doubt about that. Nearly two hundred years ago, Ralph Waldo Emerson wrote, "Trust men and they will be true to you; treat them greatly and they will show themselves great." Famed businessman and longtime General Electric CEO Jack Welch was a similar disciple of trust, writing at length about how important trust was for organizations to succeed. "Leadership is the relentless pursuit of truth and ceaseless creation of trust," he once said.

So it wasn't terribly surprising that most of Professor Frei's "trust" talk was relevant to recent events at Anheuser-Busch. Prior to 2018, there was definitely a "logic" problem at the organization. Many of the sales and marketing programs implemented by people foreign to the U.S. didn't make sense. There was a failure to communicate how these programs would improve sales, and in most cases, they didn't.

There was an "empathy" issue, too. Particularly when it came to Anheuser-Busch's wholesaler and retailer partners. Anheuser-Busch seemed to push programs that benefited the corporation and its executives, without clearly conveying how these programs would also improve the business of wholesalers and retailers. This lack of empathy materialized in low wholesaler engagement scores and the loss of key relationships with top retailers like Walmart.

The "authenticity" issue was not as clear. Anheuser-Busch had been authentic to the InBev playbook of managing costs tightly and importing "best practice" playbooks from other countries to the U.S. And it worked for a short while. But now, AB InBev was trying to figure out what "authenticity" meant as it transitioned from merging and cost-cutting to growing brands organically for the first time. Getting authenticity right would be key to connecting with its customers.

But it would prove to be a challenge. AB would not get authenticity right. Neither would many other companies in corporate America after 2019. Paradoxically, ESG and DEI programs that were supposed to improve company performance would actually accelerate their decline. One reason is because "diversity" programs aren't really about "diversity" at all. Not within an organization, and certainly not across organizations. It's not about each company being authentic to itself, to its customers, to its own brands. It's about uniformly adopting ESG orthodoxy. Every company, across every industry, had to adopt the same set of principles. Oil companies, software companies, beer companies, and hospitals all had to play by the same ESG and DEI rules.

Dare to be different—"just be you," if you will—and you'd soon incur the wrath of your major shareholders. Firms like BlackRock, State Street, and Vanguard were already vocally advocating for ESG and DEI. So were the consultants at McKinsey and ESG ranking companies and proxy advisors and all the players in the corporate ecosystem. Anheuser-Busch was encouraged to "bring the best version of itself forward," but only if that version had a full-scale DEI department ready to bend the knee to its ESG-obsessed overlords.

Diversity and Inclusion started in 2019 as a program to help rebuild trust between AB and its partners. What it became would be the axe that severed trust between AB and its customers. "Authenticity," or the lack thereof, would play a major role. AB would become the poster child of what went wrong with corporate DEI programs, but many other companies would also fall victim.

But before the DEI plague fell upon corporate America, a different plague came first: Covid.

Chapter 14

Covid and Stakeholder Capitalism: A Perfect Match

Anheuser-Busch InBev's experiment with ESG as a way to grow the business was off to a slow start. 2019 was one of the worst years for the global business. The 2019 annual report put it bluntly: global company results were "below our expectations, and we are not satisfied with the results."

The U.S. business was in better shape. It was building momentum heading into 2020. "Improved performance in the U.S., our largest market" was highlighted as a "success" in the same 2019 annual report.

Michel's five priorities seemed to be working for the second year in a row. Michelob Ultra continued growing double digits on a bigger base. AB's craft breweries grew double digits as well. New premium beer innovations like Michelob Pure Gold and Patagonia doubled premium beer volumes since 2017. Mainstream beers like Bud Light and Budweiser stabilized their share vs. Coors Light and Miller Light. And finally, Anheuser-Busch grew its hard seltzer and canned cocktail business by double digits. They bought Cutwater Spirits in early 2019, which was the leader in the canned cocktail market, and were gearing up for an even bigger year in 2020 with the planned launch of Bud Light Seltzer.

Michel put many Americans back in charge of key brands and business units. He had clear priorities. There were measurable goals against these priorities. The U.S. business seemed to be heading in a better direction. The events of 2020 changed that trajectory.

The 2020 Super Bowl was in Miami. It was going to turbocharge all five priorities and set Anheuser-Busch up for its best year since the AB/InBev merger. Miami was part of my Southeast territory, so I was in charge of working with our global and U.S. sales and marketing teams to make sure Anheuser-Busch won the Super Bowl. We blew it out. Super Bowl ads for Michelob Ultra featured Jimmy Fallon and John Cena. Bud Light and Bud Light Seltzer shared a joint commercial with Post Malone. After debating which product to buy, Post Malone decides to "get both" because he is "incredibly rich."

Stella Artois activated a "Port de Stella" featuring host Priyanka Chopra Jonas. Consumers could eat gourmet meals and hitch a ride on a fifty-five-foot Stella Artois yacht to South Beach.

Budweiser took over the Nautilus hotel on South Beach for its first-ever BudX experience. It brought in consumers from all over the world to livestream content on their social platforms. Halsey, Diplo, and the Black Eyed Peas performed.

Not to be outdone, Bud Light sponsored its own concert series at Miami's American Airlines Arena. There were three nights of shows featuring Guns N' Roses, Maroon 5, and DJ Khaled. Bud Light also had its own hotel a few miles up the beach from Budweiser. That was one of the few years Tom Brady was not in the Super Bowl, so we had him do a pregame "chalk talk" for many of our wholesaler and retailer guests in attendance. Consumers could also find Anheuser-Busch products and fun at Gronk's beach party (Rob Gronkowski also was not in the Super Bowl that year), Shaq's Funhouse, and the Maxim party.

|||||||||||||||

The Kansas City Chiefs won Super Bowl LIV that year. So did Anheuser-Busch. And then Covid struck.

One month later, I was back in Miami. I was visiting local Anheuser-Busch wholesalers. It was Wednesday, March 11. A strange new disease called "coronavirus" was on everybody's minds. Donald Trump had just announced a thirty-day ban on most visitors from Europe. The next day, I visited the grocery store Publix. It was packed. It was more crowded than any store I had ever been in. I asked the store manager if it was always that crowded. I'll never forget his response— "Only when hurricanes are coming." They were already out of basic supplies. Toilet paper. Cleaning products. Canned food. And the most important emergency supply of all: beer.

I flew back to Atlanta that night. In the airport, travelers huddled watching the news on a muted TV. Most major sports leagues were suspending play. March Madness was canceled. St. Patrick's Day was, too.

I returned home late that evening and I went to work early the next day. It was Friday, March 13. President Trump declared a national emergency. It was the last time that I would be in an office for more than a year. I spent most of the day on the phone, addressing employee and wholesaler concerns. Employees asked if Anheuser-Busch would allow them to work from home. Wholesalers asked what Anheuser-Busch would do with all of the keg beer sitting in their warehouses for sporting events and St. Patrick's Day parades that wouldn't occur. These were all great questions. That Friday, I had no idea.

I did allow employees to leave early that day if they preferred to work from home. I told them I would pass along additional information as soon as I heard it from our corporate office in New York. I also sent an email to wholesalers. Given all the canceled events, I suggested they significantly decrease their keg and bottled beer orders, which are predominantly sold at bars, restaurants, and events. But given what I'd seen at the Florida Publix earlier in the week, I suggested they significantly increase their orders for twenty-four-packs of cans, which are predominantly sold in grocery stores.

It proved to be good advice. Over the weekend, bars began shutting down. Chicago, D.C., and New Orleans were among the first. Soon, Nashville shut down all bars on Broadway, effective immediately. Before long, the entire country went dark. The following week, California issued a "shelter in place" order for the entire state. By the end of March, almost every state had followed suit. The need to "flatten the curve" felt pressing; governments were scrambling to do their part.

I am not here to debate the merits of the shutdowns. If we knew then what we know now, many different decisions would be made. But in March 2020, we didn't know much. We knew there was a new virus. And we knew it was deadly. We saw footage of hospitals overrun in Italy—hardly a third-world country—and harrowing tales of ventilator shortages and rationing supplies. We understood the virus was coming to our shores—had already arrived, in fact—and that we needed to do our part.

The country effectively went into war mode. President Trump said as much. Reporters asked him whether he considered the U.S. to be at war with the virus. "I do, I actually do, I'm looking at it that way," he responded. "I look at it, I view it as, in a sense, a wartime president. I mean, that's what we're fighting."

Amid all this uncertainty, the Covid-19 pandemic fundamentally changed how business was done.

There was a strong sense that everyone was in this together, and that drastic action would be needed to combat the enemy. The line between business and politics, between business and the greater common good, was blurred, and sometimes eliminated altogether.

Nothing made the blurring more obvious than President Trump's early invocation of the Defense Production Act, or DPA. By April, he had compelled General Motors, General Electric, Hill-Rom, Medtronic, ResMed, Royal Philips, Vyaire Medical, and 3M to make ventilators, hospital beds, face masks, and N-95 respirators.[1] And for every company he compelled to act, there were dozens he worked with voluntarily.[2] Most companies were eager to help. The shift to stakeholder capitalism almost demanded it.

Never in recent history had the cooperation between government and private business been so clear. The Trump administration worked with Walmart to set up testing facilities in their parking lots. It worked with Google to set up a website to help people determine if they needed to be tested and sites to access tests.

Airlines were no longer flying commercial travelers around the country. Many pivoted to flying needed medical and food supplies.[3] Delta, United, American, and Southwest all flew their first-ever "cargo only" flights during this time period. Restaurants shut down or moved to carry-out only options, sometimes donating food to overworked hospital workers. Fitness classes started happening outside, with six feet of distance between participants. Mattel Toys created a lineup of essential-worker action figures.[4]

Anheuser-Busch did its part, too. Hand sanitizer was in short supply in the early days of the pandemic.[5] And as anyone who has ever been a rebellious teenager might know (I, personally, plead the Fifth), hand sanitizer is mostly just alcohol. That meant Anheuser-Busch was uniquely positioned to be able to make it quickly, and in large quantities. So they did. They turned both of their large-scale production breweries in Los Angeles and Baldwinsville, New York, and in some of their local craft breweries, into hand sanitizer plants. They produced more than 500,000 bottles, which were distributed via their wholesaler partners and to the American Red Cross.

Anheuser-Busch also changed its marketing to support the war effort. Budweiser released a "One Team" commercial. The ad highlights how Budweiser redirected $5 million of its sports and entertainment marketing spend to the American Red Cross.

The ad juxtaposes sports references with scenes of people battling the epidemic. So, the line "This Bud is for the blues" references blue-scrubs-wearing healthcare workers, not the St. Louis Blues hockey team.[6] And the "reds" is an homage to Red Cross volunteers, not Cincinnati's pro baseball team. The ad was well received. Like its post-9/11 ad, it seemingly hit the right balance of brand authenticity during a national crisis. Budweiser always sponsored "teams." The "blues" and the "reds" were the newest teams, and those in need of greatest support.

It felt like the entire economy mobilized to go to "war" against what Trump called "the invisible enemy."

And in reality, the U.S. won the first battles. The initial aim of all the shutdown measures was to prevent hospitals from being overrun with coronavirus patients. That happened. Healthcare systems, even in New York City, never ran out of beds. Many sports stadiums across the U.S. converted to field hospitals to serve an expected surge in patients, but the surge never arrived.[7]

By late May 2020, all fifty states began easing coronavirus restrictions. Connecticut was the final state that allowed restaurants to serve seated customers and nonessential retail stores to reopen. Of course, many states still had restrictions on the number of people a restaurant could serve or how many feet needed to separate people in a checkout line, but America was getting back to business.

Consumer confidence was returning as well. Major stock indices hit their low points in mid-March. Most had fallen by more than 20 percent, indicating a bear market. By mid-May, stocks had returned to pre-pandemic levels. Some believed a bull market may now be in play.

Consumers and businesses were flush with cash. The Coronavirus Aid, Relief, and Economic Security (CARES) act, had been passed by Congress in late March. It was the largest financial rescue package in U.S. history, authorizing more than $2 trillion in spending to stimulate the economy. Individuals got $1,200 checks, children $500. The act placed a moratorium on mortgage foreclosures and tenant evictions. Student loan payments were suspended. It extended unemployment insurance.

The Paycheck Protection Program, or PPP, was part of the package. Its purpose was to keep small businesses from potentially collapsing. Many of the beer wholesalers I worked with, the independent family businesses, took the PPP loans. Early in the pandemic, they didn't know what to expect. The entire bar and restaurant industry shut down, as did beer sales to that industry. The economic threat was real.

But then the outlook started to improve. Beer wholesalers were quickly deemed essential workers, as they are a key part of the food and beverage supply chain. And as many know, people did not stop drinking during the pandemic. In fact, people started drinking more, just not in bars and restaurants. Zoom happy hours started. Cul-de-sac happy hours started with neighbors sitting six feet apart. Parents no longer shuttled kids from activity to activity, so drinking became more of a regularly scheduled five o'clock activity.

Alcohol sales exploded. Retail alcohol sales were up 34 percent year over year early in the pandemic.[8] Yes, bars and restaurants were closed, but sales at grocery stores and convenience stores more than made up for these losses. Pre-Covid, bars and restaurants sold ~15 percent of beers consumed, and 85 percent of beer was sold in grocery stores, liquor stores, and convenience stores. During Covid, people traded a beer or two at the bar for a twelve-pack from their local grocer, leading to the increase in sales. Beer wholesalers were working overtime to keep products stocked. Many wholesalers used PPP funds to give their rank-and-file employees bonuses, to express their gratitude for their "essential" work during the pandemic.

But just as the U.S. seemed to be weathering one crisis, another was on the horizon. A dark day in America that would change how Americans look at one another and how businesses look at us.

Chapter 15

War Efforts

G oing into Memorial Day weekend of 2020, the U.S. seemed to be pulling out from the depths of the pandemic and looking forward to a much-needed summer. Then a new crisis rocked the nation. A 9-minute, 29-second video of a white police officer kneeling on the neck of a black man, George Floyd, went viral. George Floyd could be heard saying "I can't breathe" in the video before his body went motionless. He ultimately died. The officer, Derek Chauvin, would later be convicted of murder. The effects were far-reaching. Floyd's family grieved. The nation was forced to confront the fact that its justice system wasn't always just. And corporations—Anheuser-Busch among them—were pulled into social activism to an extent that had never been seen before.

In the immediate aftermath of the incident, protests broke out around the U.S. Many people took to the streets. Most were peaceful; some were violent. The newsreels highlighted the most extreme reactions, but most people, of course, didn't fit into that mold. Most people didn't protest, although many were deeply saddened by the murder of Floyd and empathetic to frustrations in the black community. I was one of those people.

I worked with many black people at Anheuser-Busch. The top-performing salesperson on my team was among them. He was based in Atlanta, same as me, and he was responsible for sales in the metro Atlanta area. He did a fantastic job, and his numbers showed it.

He was also a team player, looking for ways to improve the company culture and morale and to help the people who were coming up behind him. To that end, he'd recently presented at a monthly regional coffee chat that I hosted.

Every month, I hosted an optional lunch meeting for regional employees. We'd pack a bunch of people into the conference room in Atlanta and bring our bagged lunches (free pizza, of course, would be a sign of pure corporate excess that would not be countenanced by ZBB); other employees could participate by Zoom. I'd invite different Anheuser-Busch employees to come speak.

One month, we had Rocky Sickmann. Rocky worked at Anheuser-Busch for more than thirty years. Prior to that, he was a Marine. He was one of the Marines charged with protecting the U.S. embassy in Iran in 1979 when it was overrun by Iranian militants. Rocky was held hostage for 444 days in Iran and has an incredible story about overcoming hardship during that time period. (Fortunately for non–Anheuser-Busch insiders, his story is available on YouTube and is well worth the watch.)

Another month, an Anheuser-Busch teammate offered to share his story on being adopted. He never knew his birth parents, but he was recently reunited with his biological family after an Ancestry.com database matched him to a cousin.

During the first month of pandemic lockdowns, Alex Rodriguez and Jennifer Lopez (when they were together) joined via Zoom. Anheuser-Busch had just hired Alex Rodriguez to be the CEO of the Dominican beer brand Presidente, which Anheuser-Busch owned. A-Rod spoke about his transition from baseball to businessman, and J-Lo spoke about her career as an entertainer and 2020 Super Bowl halftime performer.

My top performer's recent coffee chat also touched on his career. He spoke about his successes—and there were a lot of them—and also some challenges. He had faced discrimination from certain customers. He also had a tough time navigating the 2014 Ferguson protests in St. Louis. He mentioned that he didn't feel comfortable sharing his emotions at work and was disappointed that no one really asked him how he was doing. His big takeaway was simple: When difficult racial issues arise, ask black colleagues, "How are you doing?" It's a small gesture that shows you care. In his view, asking how "you" are doing acknowledges that each person's experience is unique. It shows thoughtfulness. And empathy. And empathy, of course, builds trust.

So when the video of George Floyd went viral and protests broke out, I called him. I asked how he was doing. Not well, it turned out. He was actually in the middle of writing me an email. We spoke for a few minutes. He talked about his reaction to recent events. Not just George Floyd, but also the recent killing of Ahmaud Arbery in Georgia (Ahmaud was jogging when he was murdered in a racially motivated hate crime) and the impact of Covid on his community.

He also had some ideas on how Anheuser-Busch could "bring people together" during what was, for him and many others, a difficult time. He had three asks:

1. To host a regional chat on current events
2. To have the CEO issue an acknowledgment of current events
3. To use brand support to "call for unity around our collective humanity," similar to how Budweiser redirected advertising from sports and entertainment to aid the Red Cross during Covid

The lunch chat was an easy yes. For one, I was the person who ran them, so it's not like I needed to pull a bunch of strings or jump through a bunch of hoops to make it happen. And his talk was very thoughtful and insightful the first time around. I had no concerns that this one would be disruptive or disrespectful, particularly since, as always, participation in the lunch would be strictly voluntary.

His second ask was different. I told him the CEO acknowledgment was not up to me.

Personally, I have mixed feelings on CEO acknowledgments of current events. If the current events directly impact a company's mission, then it might make sense for a CEO to acknowledge them. If they don't, then it probably doesn't.

Some of this is common sense: A solar panel company should issue a press release, or tweet, when there is a major environmental conference or news event, just as Intel made a public statement after the passage of the CHIPS Act.[1] But it would be odd at best, and counterproductive at worst, for McDonald's or Staples to do the same.

Other issues present closer calls. Dove might be able to cash in on a story about body positivity because it's built into its long-standing corporate image. And Ben & Jerry's might be able to get away with commenting on just about every social issue under the sun because commenting on just about every social issue *is* its brand. But these are the exceptions.

For big, national news items with no specific tie to a company or its mission, it rarely makes sense to weigh in. That's doubly true if the news is itself divisive. Before the summer of 2020, that was the prevailing view. "It's a divided world that we live in," Raja Rajamannar, the chief marketing officer at Mastercard said in early 2020. "Can you afford to exclude half of your audience?"[2]

The handful of corporations that defied this wisdom often found themselves in hot water.

The ones that tried to weigh in on race relations spectacularly failed. Pepsi, for example, was lambasted for a 2017 commercial where Kendall Jenner tried to solve race relations by handing a soda to a police officer amid a sea of protestors.[3]

Starbucks was similarly derided for a campaign in which baristas were instructed to write "Race Together" on coffee cups to spark informal conversations about race.[4] Within a week, the initiative "was mocked with such vehemence on social media that the company's senior vice president for global communications deleted his Twitter account because . . . he felt 'personally attacked in a cascade of negativity,' " *The New York Times* reported.[5]

Like the ill-fated Bud Light Party ad, these campaigns tried to place the brand as presenting a unifying solution, but ended up alienating both sides.

Other companies attempted to launch ads that piggybacked off of the #MeToo movement. The results were equally poor.

Gillette, for one, attempted to tackle "toxic masculinity." It's pretty much as bad as you think. The nearly two-minute spot features sexist, boorish antics including boys fighting one another and men grabbing women's rear ends. The narrator then disputes the notion that "boys should be boys," and chastises men for "making the same old excuses." Men were offended. Women were, too. Vox called it "a blatant attempt to make money off a painful and ongoing collective action that has not even an indirect relationship to face razors."[6]

Johnnie Walker's efforts were arguably even worse. In 2019, the company slapped a new "Jane Walker" label on its whiskey to celebrate Women's Day. It was not well received. "Female drinkers everywhere will say, 'Finally, a brand that's condescending to me,' " Stephen Colbert quipped. "Truly what the suffragettes fought for."[7]

Most companies stayed far, far away. Indeed, in the pre–George Floyd era, companies were so fearful of appearing to weigh in on controversial issues that they not only shied away from making public statements themselves, but took steps to ensure that their advertising wouldn't accidentally appear *near* a political headline.

The practice is called "blacklisting." When companies buy ad spots, they give publications a list of words they don't want their advertisement near. It allows airlines to avoid running ads next to articles on plane crashes and Disney to avoid running ads next to stories about pedophiles. But in the years leading up to the pandemic, companies increasingly wanted to avoid being near any political headlines at all. Among the most avoided words at the time were "Russia," "impeach," and "Trump."[8]

Affirmatively *choosing* to step into such topics would be unthinkable. "Most companies no longer see an upside in weighing in on politics, even jokingly," *The New York Times* reported in early 2020, just six months before the George Floyd incident.[9] Even then, political corporate activism was no laughing matter.

Suffice it to say that while I understood the request came from a genuine desire to do what he believed was the right thing, and while I appreciated his willingness to share his views with me, I personally held a great deal of skepticism that wading into political controversies would be a business-savvy move.

But the murder of George Floyd ushered in a new era.

Anheuser-Busch's U.S. CEO, Michel Doukeris, did issue a statement acknowledging current events. In June, the company noted that 2020 had been a wake-up call to the pain and impact of long-standing racial inequality and social injustice. Anheuser-Busch pledged to be part of the solution, reconfirming its commitment of bringing people together for a better world—not just for some, but for all. Michel's focus on ESG over LFG was just beginning.

My colleague's last ask, for brand support, was also not up to me. That was up to the brand teams. If brands like Budweiser could authentically do advertising, aligned with their brand identity, that brought people together, and showed "unity" and our "collective humanity," like during 9/11 or the Covid outbreak, then they would do it. If not, it makes more sense to do advertising that advances the core mission of the brand.

We ended the call optimistically. He appreciated that I trusted him to lead another coffee chat. He also understood that I couldn't deliver everything he wanted.

Both of us wanted to see "unity around our collective humanity." We might have different opinions on how to get there, but we shared the same goal.

As it turned out, corporate America's response to the death of George Floyd was anything but unifying. Propelled by its recent success going to war against Covid, corporate America redirected its efforts to fight new, invisible enemies—systemic racism and social injustice.

The force behind this movement wasn't the invisible hand of the market, or even just the whims of liberal-minded executives seeking to make noble use of their privileged perch. It was guided, in large part, by the stakeholder capitalism movement and the moneyed powerhouses behind it.

Wall Street firms soon issued their commands, sometimes directly, sometimes by example.[10]

Citigroup's approach was perhaps the boldest. Days after the murder, its Chief Financial Officer wrote a statement titled "I can't breathe" on the company's website.[11] The first ten sentences of the post read "I can't breathe," echoing Floyd's last moments. Provocative stuff for a company best known to the public for its fixed-rate mortgages and regional ATMs.

The post went on to describe the video of George Floyd's death in excruciating detail. The company stated that "racism continues to be at the root of so much pain and ugliness in our society," as evidenced by "the violence of white supremacists in Charlottesville" among other recent events. The company pledged to "continue to speak up and speak out whenever we witness hatred, racism or injustice" and implored others to do the same.

JPMorgan Chase's CEO also weighed in: "[T]his week's terrible events in Minneapolis, together with too many others occurring around our country, are tragic and heartbreaking." The company, he pledged, was "committed to fighting against racism and discrimination wherever and however it exists." Wells Fargo chimed in, too, committing "to do all we can to support our diverse communities." So did Goldman Sachs and Bank of America, and all the rest.

BlackRock's Larry Fink spoke out, too.[12] He issued a statement lamenting Floyd's murder while using it as a catalyst for change: "[T]hese events are symptoms of a deep and longstanding problem in our society and must be addressed on both a personal and systemic level. This situation also underscores the critical importance of diversity and inclusion within BlackRock and society at large. . . . We must all work together to build a more fair and just society."

For many of us, these empty Wall Street platitudes may seem to be just that: empty. But for companies, the message was quite clear: Do your part to advance racial justice, or you may soon be drawing the ire of your largest investors. And that's something no company wants to do. Wall Street firms wield enormous power. Not just as lenders or dealmakers or bankers, but as shareholders. They hold important stakes in most publicly traded companies. Technically, that means they *own* most of corporate America. That means they can (and do) call up company management and directors to steer the company's strategy; if existing leadership disagrees, investors have the ability to oust board members and handpick their replacements. Company leaders know that their jobs are on the line.

Following the George Floyd incident, the generals had instructed their soldiers on how to march.

And march they did. The outpouring was tremendous. Company after company issued statements lamenting the state of race relations in the U.S. Some were vague, some were more specific. Some took a more formal tone, while others were more impassioned.

Many statements evoked the sadness of the moment. Target's CEO—Brian Cornell, a middle-aged white guy—spoke of the "pent-up pain of years."[13] The CEO of Coach and Kate Spade's parent company typed as his "eyes well[ed] up with tears." McDonald's opted for a video, slowly listing names from Trayvon Martin to George Floyd who had been killed, before closing with a solemn "Black Lives Matter" followed by its logo.[14] More than one CEO had googled a Martin Luther King quote to really drive the point home.

Ben & Jerry's ben-and-jerried. Their moment had arrived. "The murder of George Floyd was the result of inhumane police brutality that is perpetuated by a culture of white supremacy," the ice-cream maker posted on its website, under the company's cheery banner of a cartoon cow grazing under a cloud-kissed sky.[15] Its 700-word manifesto went on to lay out the company's four-step solution to "dismantle white supremacy in all its forms." An ambitious piece from the makers of Cherry Garcia.

I'm sure some of these tributes were sincere and heartfelt; I'm equally sure that others were issued out of a sense of obligation. But one thing was clear: the rules had changed.

Suddenly, everyone felt the need to say something.

As *The Wall Street Journal* reported, it was "a marked change from earlier eras, when executives avoided statements that could be seen as political."[16]

Soon after the initial flood of statements, more than three hundred CEOs, mayors, and government officials gathered over Zoom to discuss racial justice, peer to peer. A number of CEOs on the call acknowledged that their views had changed, and that they now felt an obligation to speak up where they used to fall mum. Johnson & Johnson's CEO opined that CEOs may try to see their role as neutral, but "there are few decisions we make that aren't political—whether it's access to restrooms, whether it's what candidate we might support in a particular stand that we're going to take on an environmental issue— so, frankly, I think that comes with the territory." American Airlines' CEO said his thinking had also changed: "Sometimes we convince ourselves, look it's not really my responsibility as a CEO to opine on this or make a statement on this," he said. "Oftentimes you think, well, it's not going to matter, because who am I to be making comments on this? It does matter."

Just one CEO reportedly advised caution. That was Pepsi's former CEO Indra Nooyi. She "spoke bluntly about the realities involved," including the risks of backlash from speaking out. She spoke from firsthand experience. Four years earlier, Mrs. Nooyi was asked about Donald Trump's then-recent election at *The New York Times'* Deal-Book conference. Her response was fairly measured, but candid. She congratulated the president on his victory, but said "we should mourn for those of us who supported the other side." She also said she "had to answer a lot of questions from my daughters, from my employees, they were all in mourning," before concluding that "we will all come together and unify the country."

The backlash was swift. Republicans rushed to YouTube, Twitter, and Facebook to denounce her views.[17] Three days later, #BoytcottPepsi was trending on Twitter, tweeted more than nineteen thousand times. Pepsi released a statement that Mrs. Nooyi "misspoke."

Now retired, an older and wiser Mrs. Nooyi sat poised on the Zoom call. She recounted her experience to the hundreds of other CEOs. When she took political stances as CEO, she said, a third of employees praised her, a third sent angry emails, and a third remained quiet. "So you could interpret it as two-thirds are on your side, or two-thirds are against you," she said.

That's even truer when it comes to public sentiment. You never really know where the public stands. Much less where the public *will* stand a week, a month, or a year after a statement is made.

And that's the problem with making bold public statements in moments of crisis. In the immediate aftermath of a sudden and unexpected tragedy, there is often unity. Or at least the semblance of it. When Covid hit, we all came together to fight the common enemy. We still trusted one another and our institutions. We rushed to buy masks, and, for the most part, were willing to do our part and stay home.

But such unity is often short-lived. New facts emerge. Things happen. Nuance begins to take shape. Causes and crises that were once so black-and-white—who could possibly support a man who murders his fellow citizen on camera, before our very eyes?—become blurry.

The waters become even muddier once solutions are proposed.

Everyone can agree that disease and war and murder and racism are objectively "bad." We might even all agree that we each have a moral imperative to try to end them. But how we should go about doing it is often hotly contested. There is no easy fix. There are trade-offs and costs and realities that come into play. There are also simple differences of opinion.

It's particularly dangerous to assume the country is unified—and that that unity will hold—when the topic is one that is as historically rife with controversy as race relations.

In this context, Mrs. Nooyi's comment about silence was particularly sage. Most people don't say anything at all. They don't wear MAGA T-shirts or BLM hats to work. They don't announce how they voted at the water cooler. They don't decorate their cubicles with campaign bumper stickers. They just go about their everyday lives. Their

politics may hold private importance to them, but they're not in public
view. It's impossible to know where your employees truly stand, and
the public even less so.

But for a group so eager to talk, no one on that fateful Zoom call
seemed willing to listen. Mrs. Nooyi's warning fell on deaf ears. Silence
was now violence, and no company wanted to be viewed as complicit.

Companies didn't stop at speech alone. Seemingly without fail,
companies would follow up on their statements with a pledge to donate
to the NAACP, the Equal Justice Initiative, Black Lives Matter, or all
of the above. Corporate executives wanted to show they were willing to
put their money—or, more precisely, their company's money—where
their mouth was.

The money piled in. Microsoft pledged $200 million; Nike pledged
$100 million.[18] Apple, Google, and Facebook threw their own cool,
nine-figure donations into the pot.[19] By the end of the first year, Fortune 1000 companies had pledged $200 billion to support racial jus-
tice causes—approximately equivalent to the gross domestic product
of Portugal.[20]

This is staggering. Not only because of the eye-popping amounts
involved, but because of who was giving and how quickly. Corporate
America is in the business of, well, business. They make goods. They
sell things. But more than anything, they're bean counters. They pore
over each expenditure to determine whether the return is worth the
investment. Every budget item is justified, fought for in meetings and
among teams. I should know—I was bean counter in chief at Anheuser-
Busch for many years. I spent months shaving pennies off of aluminum
cans from our suppliers; crunching numbers on spreadsheets to see if
we could make a particular investment work.

Yet in the days following George Floyd's murder, the corporate
pocketbook didn't just burst open, it was turned upside down and
shaken. At nearly every company.

It went about as well as you'd expect. Black Lives Matter touted a $90 million cash haul in 2020.[21] Weeks after donations began pouring in, a cofounder purchased four homes for a total of $3.2 million,[22] in addition to the sprawling $6 million mansion purchased by the organization itself.[23] She also hired her brother's company to provide security services for $700,000. In July 2021, BLM leaders in Canada, aided by the U.S. group, bought another multimillion-dollar mansion in Toronto. By 2023, only 33 percent had been given to charitable foundations.[24]

Participation in this kind of financial mismanagement is unheard-of in corporate America. If ten dollars goes missing from a cash register, Walmart takes action. But when tens of millions of donated dollars vanished, all of corporate America stayed silent. The donations that followed the murder of George Floyd weren't just distractions from corporate business; they were a perversion of it. The frittering away of hard-earned revenues; displays of corporate excess masquerading as do-good measures.

But in some quarters, the problem with these eight- and nine-figure pledges wasn't that they were too large, or given too quickly, with too little oversight, but that they weren't enough. Activists seized on the moment. "These messages of support mean nothing without taking action to support their black employees," a spokesperson for the civil rights group Color of Change said.[25] Others called the donations "pocket change" and shamed corporate giants for not giving more.[26]

Companies were cowed into looking inward. Self-flagellation was the call of the day. Apple pledged to "reexamine our own views and actions in light of a pain that is deeply felt but too often ignored."[27] Coca-Cola acknowledged it had not done enough to put black people in leadership positions, saying "we need to be more effective in making progress."[28]

Facebook fell in line, too, but couldn't avoid the backlash. CEO

Mark Zuckerberg had intoned the right incantations and tithed the appropriate $10 million sum, but these efforts were soon used against him. As violent protests erupted across the United States, President Donald Trump had taken to Facebook. "When the looting starts, the shooting starts," he wrote, borrowing a phrase used by a Miami police chief in the 1960s. Zuckerberg had allowed the post to stand.[29]

Now, employees and the press were calling him out for his alleged hypocrisy.[30] "Instead of throwing money at this, can we take a real stand and change our policies and products to get at the root of the problem?" one employee wrote on an internal message board shared with the press. Dozens of employees participated in a "virtual walkout" that Monday, refusing to sign into work and changing their avatars to a raised-fist icon. Other employees weighed in to support Zuckerberg's move, claiming the "silent majority" agreed with the CEO's free-speech approach.[31]

The media appeared split on the issue. *The Washington Post* wrote a scathing editorial condemning Zuckerberg's refusal to take down the President's post,[32] while outlets like *The New York Post* praised him for "standing up against censorship."[33] Public opinion was also divided: A then-recent National Research Group poll had shown that a slim majority (about 54 percent) of Americans supported Twitter's decision to flag and fact-check President Trump's posts. Presumably, fewer would support deleting the President's posts entirely.[34]

Already, the unity was fraying. If it ever existed at all.

Initial feelings of solidarity as the country came together to mourn a collective loss soon fractured as solutions were posed. Was the solution for social media companies to censor "hate speech," defined purely in the eyes of the supposedly oppressed? Should the government pay reparations to black people to compensate them for historical injustices perpetrated on their ancestors decades or centuries ago, as Snapchat's CEO believed?[35] What about other minorities, like the Japanese, who had been placed in internment camps much more recently than blacks had been enslaved? Where would this money come from? Who should have to pay? Rational minds could differ.

Amid the fray, there was no proposal more divisive than calls to defund the police. Days of riots had led protestors to call for abolishing the police so that community-based services and social workers could rebuild communities instead. The cause was never particularly well defined—how, exactly, a society without a police force would be able to function, and what, precisely, these activists meant—but the general message was to eliminate, or substantially reduce, police forces. And fast. "Yes, we mean literally abolish the police," one *New York Times* headline ran.[36]

Many cities took these calls seriously. In June 2020, nine members of Minneapolis's city council appeared at an event where they pledged to work to dismantle the police. Standing in front of large cut-out letters spelling "Defund Police," they proudly announced their "process of ending the Minneapolis Police Department."[37] Other cities rushed to follow suit.[38]

Companies began echoing these calls. IBM, for example, sent a letter to Congress imploring it to eliminate qualified immunity to hold police accountable for misconduct.[39] Salesforce focused mainly on state-level laws, supporting a choke-hold ban in California and a slate of police reforms in Washington.[40] Microsoft agreed[41] not to sell facial recognition technology to law enforcement—a policy Amazon had already adopted—but refused to cede to activists' most radical demands to stop doing business with police departments altogether.[42]

In addition to defunding the police, companies pledged to fight systemic racism within their own ranks. Companies would first pledge to disclose the racial and gender makeup of their employees. Simple enough. Then they would disclose any "gaps" in how each demographic group was paid. Soon, they would set specific "targets" or "goals" (a quota by any other name) for a certain number of black people, or LGBTQ+, or women in all of the company's ranks. They'd force suppliers, and sometimes even customers, to do the same. They'd appoint a new DEI department to oversee these efforts. And they'd agree to pay their executives based on whether the company was making progress toward these goals, to make sure it all got done.

This new corporate navel-gazing also led to a new cottage industry: DEI training and consulting. June 2020 saw 4.3 times as many job posts for DEI roles as five years prior,[43] and Chief Diversity and Inclusion Officer roles surged 169 percent over the next two years.[44] By March 2021, 53 percent of S&P 500 companies had a chief DEI officer on the company dole.

These new employees soon got to work. The only way to rid themselves of the scourge of racism, companies soon learned, was not to be race-blind, but to be affirmatively anti-racist. Trainings called on employees to recognize their white privilege. A Coca-Cola diversity training urged workers to "be less white," which the presentation helpfully defined as being "less oppressive," "less arrogant," and "less ignorant." A private hospital chain required white healthcare workers to admit they were racist. A similarly mandatory course in Kentucky told nurses that "implicit bias kills," that white privilege is a "covert" form of racism, and explained how nurses may contribute to "modern-day lynchings in the workplace."[45]

Things were quickly getting out of hand.

McDonald's promised that at least 35 percent of its senior director and higher leadership would be held by racial minorities by 2025, and women would make up 45 percent of its top brass.[46] Adidas similarly pledged that 30 percent of new hires would be black or Hispanic.[47] Before you could blink, seventy big companies from Airbnb to Bank of America to GE to McKinsey to TaskRabbit had set specific, numeric quotas for how many racial and gender minorities they would hire by 2025 or 2030.[48]

Companies scrambled to outdo each other. They got creative. Retail shelf space would now be allocated by race, rather than by what sells.[49] Nordstrom, Macy's, Sephora, Ulta, and two dozen other companies rushed to sign on to a pledge to reserve 15 percent of shelf space to black-owned brands. Irish-, Asian-, or Hispanic-owned companies need not apply. Coca-Cola even announced a policy that 30 percent of its outside lawyers had to be minorities, and half of all billable time had to be from black lawyers specifically.

Target was more innovative still. It launched a program with agricultural supplier Cargill to pay black farmers more for cotton, compared to cotton grown by their Hispanic, white, or Asian counterparts, and promised not to ask for discounts if cotton produced by black farmers was of inferior quality.[50] Cargill got hauled in to testify before Congress on that one. But the program appears to be alive and well. You cannot make this stuff up.[51]

None of this helped business. It wasn't designed to. It was lavish, feel-good expenditures made by CEOs, encouraged by Wall Street, and applauded by progressive pension systems in California and New York and endowments at elite colleges like Harvard and Brown to do everything in their power to pursue the extreme race-forward policies of the political left.

But, for a while anyway, it didn't exactly *hurt* business either. The silent majority was still mostly silent. The silence that made companies think these increasingly extremist measures were a good idea also, in a kind of self-fulfilling prophecy, allowed them to continue without significant repercussions. It's hard to organize a boycott, after all, if merely sharing your views in a private forum is going to get you fired.

There was also safety in numbers. When every company is giving a sermon, or updating its social media logo, there's no clear target. Customers may not like it, but there's no credible outlet. Consumers aren't going to start boycotting Walmart and Target and Microsoft and Nabisco and Coca-Cola and everyone else all at once.

And so the movement went unchecked, even as bottled-up frustration continued to build.

Anheuser-Busch, of course, was not spared. In early 2021, it released its first-ever ESG report—a separate document, sixty-six pages long, focused entirely on its "commitment to a better world." It detailed all of the company's efforts in 2020 to help the environment, increase diversity, fight human rights violations, and more.[52]

In the intro, an intensely focused Carlos Brito appears against the backdrop of a World Economic Forum banner. "Sharpening global focus on climate resilience, inclusive recovery, racial equity and public health have further propelled us all to reimagine a brighter future and catalyze transformative change," he wrote. "Our consumers and stakeholders are looking to us to use our scale, capabilities and iconic brands to help drive change." Finally, a beer company that would save the world.

But as grandiose as the report seemed, the devil was in the details. And on closer inspection, Anheuser-Busch's pledges seemed to fall into one of two categories: vague, aspirational pledges cast in lofty but generalized tones and concrete plans to improve society in ways that would also help Budweiser's business and bottom line.

In the first category were things like Anheuser-Busch's pledges to "continue fostering an inclusive workplace so that underrepresented groups across our different markets are not only represented but can succeed in our business." The company also promised to "respect human rights in our operations and across our value chain." Good stuff, sure. But Anheuser-Busch wasn't exactly going out of its way to explain what any of that meant.

The pledges in the second category were much more detailed. There were targets. And metrics. And deadlines. Real business stuff. The section devoted to Anheuser-Busch's Water Stewardship program, for example, spent pages detailing how the company planned to reduce its water use from 2.7 hectoliters of water per hectoliter of beer brewed (a measurement abbreviated as hl/hl) to 2.5 hl/hl by 2025. Sure, there was talk of the UN Global Compact and the necessity of clean drinking water for communities across the world, but at the end of the day, water is a—if not *the*—most critical input to Anheuser-Busch's business. No water, no beer. And driving efficiencies in key resources is just smart business.

In the Brito Era, Anheuser-Busch was willing to play the stakeholder capital game, but only to a point. It would laud ESG goals and shake hands at Davos, but it wasn't going to abandon good business sense. ESG would be a way to sell more beer, to more people, more efficiently. Anheuser-Busch would drink the ESG Kool-Aid responsibly, but it wasn't going to get drunk behind the wheel. Not yet, at least.

Chapter 16

No More Merit

2020 had been particularly challenging for Anheuser-Busch InBev. Whereas the U.S. alcohol business benefited from Covid lockdowns, the international business did not. Countries like Mexico and South Africa banned the sale of alcohol for part of 2020. In China and Brazil, where most of Anheuser-Busch's beer was consumed in bars and restaurants, people did not drink as much at home.

Globally, it was the worst financial year Anheuser-Busch InBev had ever had. Beer volumes decreased by 5.7 percent. Revenue decreased by 3.7 percent. EBITDA decreased by 12.9 percent. As a result, its debt-to-EBITDA ratio increased from 4.0x to 4.8x, worrying investors. If the trend continued, AB might not be able to pay back the debt. The concern sent the stock price plummeting. At the beginning of the year, AB stock was trading around $83/share. When Covid hit, the stock tumbled by more than 50 percent to below $40. It recovered to ~$70 by the year end, but that's still down ~15 percent. Compared to the S&P 500 15 percent gain that year, which hit a record high, the performance was poor.

Throughout 2020, rumors emerged that Carlos Brito, the only CEO the post-merger Anheuser-Busch had ever known, might be stepping down. Global performance was down, sure, but there was more to the story. In truth, there simply wasn't much more for Brito to do. He bought and integrated Anheuser-Busch. He bought Grupo Modelo. He bought SABMiller. He created the world's largest brewer. He had won the beer wars. Yes, he could have potentially bought Coca-Cola or Pepsi (which was always rumored), but not anytime soon. Especially not with AB's debt/EBITDA ratio approaching 5.0x.

Covid provided an opportunity for a fresh start.

When CEO transitions occur, a company board sometimes "leaks" information ahead of time so the market is not completely surprised. It softens the blow. This is what likely happened at AB. In September 2020, the *Financial Times* reported that AB was "seriously considering" candidates. The story cited three sources with knowledge of the search. Brito was helping to pick his successor, with a goal of stepping down next year and transitioning to a board seat. The board was considering one internal candidate—Michel Doukeris, Anheuser-Busch's North American CEO—but was primarily focused externally. Choosing someone from outside the company would bring in a "fresh perspective," one Credit Suisse analyst wrote, which could lead to a "greater focus on diversity across senior management."[1]

Just to be clear, the "focus on diversity" was related to "diversity of thought." Most of the senior management team was still Brazilian. All were masters of ZBB. None had delivered transformative innovations or top-line revenue growth. Bringing someone from the outside could help drive the shift from a growth-through-acquisition mentality to one focused on growth through brand development. It wasn't a bad idea.

But the board ultimately went in a different direction. In May 2021, AB InBev announced Michel Doukeris as its next CEO. The press release read: "Michel Doukeris is uniquely suited to accelerate AB InBev's transformation and lead its next chapter of growth. Throughout his career at AB InBev Michel has consistently delivered strong results while serving in key leadership roles in Brazil, China, and the United

States, three of the company's largest markets. As President of the North America Zone, the U.S. business has delivered consistent topline growth and led the beer industry in innovations for the last two years."

That was all true, if perhaps a bit rosy. Yes, Michel had delivered top-line revenue growth in North America. But not astoundingly so. He inherited a business with revenue that was declining by −1.8 percent. He cut the loss to −0.7 percent in 2018. In 2019, he grew the business 0.2 percent. In 2020, it reached 0.8 percent. Compared to how AB was doing across the globe (in 2020, the global company declined −3.7 percent), Michel's 0.8 percent revenue growth looked good. Compared to other North American companies, an average annual growth rate of +.01 percent over the past three years wasn't exactly great. Competitors like Constellation Brands (which owned Grupo Modelo and Corona) and Sam Adams (owner of Sam Adams Boston Lager, Truly, and Twisted Tea) had been growing revenue double digits over the same time period.

The claim about leading "the beer industry in innovations for the last two years" was similarly questionable. Preliminarily, "innovation" is itself a bit of a euphemism. A term of art. Pasteurized bottles were a beer innovation; refrigerated railcars were an innovation; figuring out how to brew hard seltzer and package it in a Bud Light wrapper is not. "New product launch" would probably be more apt. And even on that front, Anheuser-Busch was hardly on the cutting edge. AB may have led the industry in the *number* of new product launches, true enough, but those launches saw little success.

In 2019, there was Bon & Viv Spiked Seltzer, which was supposed to overtake White Claw and Truly. Bon & Viv never gained traction and was essentially out of the market within a year. Then there was Bud Light Lemon Tea. After sampling it, I remember one wholesaler remarking that it "tastes like Lysol." Consumers agreed. Bud Light Lemon Tea was a lemon.

2020 was not much better. When Bud Light Seltzer made its debut at the Super Bowl, there was a massive distribution push to get the brand in 80 percent of stores nationwide that week. But by the end of 2020, it was clear that Bud Light Seltzer would never seriously challenge Truly for the number-2 spot. Truly maintained well above 20 percent market share while Bud Light Seltzer was consistently below 10 percent. Then there was Social Club Seltzer. And Budweiser Nitro Gold. Doukeris was guided by a "throw it at the wall and see what sticks" mentality. Nothing really stuck.

All of this failed innovation came at a cost. AB InBev was addicted to innovation. Every year, Anheuser-Busch had to bring out more and more innovation to make up for the lost innovation from the prior year. To make up for lost Bon & Viv launch sales, it had to bring out Bud Light Seltzer and Social Club Seltzer. To best Bud Light Lemon Tea, it had to launch Budweiser Nitro Gold. And even recognizing new product launches for what they are—new products, not innovative new technology—AB's launches weren't particularly new. They were essentially knockoffs of the competitors they hoped to overtake. Other companies had a better reading on the beer consumer and what they wanted. AB's leadership team struggled to keep up.

Existing brands suffered. Company resources, focus, and shelf space were redirected from traditional stalwarts like Bud Light, Budweiser, Busch, and Natural to feed the innovation addiction. Budgets for existing brands were slashed, and precious shelf space was given to the unproven brands. Wholesalers were concerned, especially as the new innovation volume and focus on higher-end growth brands like Michelob Ultra and Stella Artois were not offsetting volume losses from Bud and Bud Light. Michel's LFG strategy was supposed to grow the high-end brands AND stabilize core brands. The stabilization wasn't really happening.

Anheuser-Busch's board didn't seem to care. Michel was the safe choice. He'd worked at the company for decades. He operated in its biggest zones. He had a global mindset.

He also committed to taking Anheuser-Busch's half-hearted ESG efforts to the next level, rather than focus on successful product building and brand creation. Other U.S. companies had taken the ESG plunge, so Michel saw little downside.

Michel started making changes immediately. First up was the Anheuser-Busch mission. Anheuser-Busch's mission had been to be "The Best Beer Company, Bringing People Together, for a Better World." Now it was "We Dream Big to Create a Future with More Cheers." "A future with more cheers" is "like an infinite game, where there is always a next step," Michel said about the new mission.[2]

Now, honestly, if you ask me what the difference is between those two corporate missions, I can't say I'm entirely sure. Infinite games are fantastic, of course, but it's not as though anyone at Anheuser-Busch was looking at the prior mission statement and saying, "Best beer company? Check. Bringing people together? Check. For a better world? Check. I guess we can all go home." But if this was Doukeris's only Day One priority, it probably wouldn't have done too much harm.

But of course, it was not. Changing the company's mission statement didn't really matter in substance, it mattered for what it signaled: that Doukeris was now in charge, and he wasn't afraid to make changes. And changes he made. At an investor meeting in late 2021, he outlined three new goals: lead and grow the beer category, digitize the business, and focus on global brands to drive the debt/EBITDA ratio down to 2.0. Typical company stuff. But there was a fourth priority: ESG.

Prior to 2021, ESG had never been a focus of discussions at these investor summits. Summits happened only every two years. And the purpose was to explain how AB was planning to deliver financial returns.

Michel's presentation now devoted an entire section to ESG. Most of the ESG presentation was on cost reduction activities AB had done for years—using less water to brew beer, using less energy, using less packaging material, etc. But now the ESG agenda also included "Diversity and Inclusion" initiatives.

⁙⁙⁙⁙⁙⁙⁙⁙⁙⁙

This would not be an isolated event. Whereas Brito took a more restrained approach to ESG, Michel quickly went all in.

Shortly after leaving Anheuser-Busch, Brito did an interview at Miami's Herbert Business School where he was asked about the role of corporations in society.[3] He allowed that "Companies have to engage—not on every environmental or social topic—but on those where you can have a voice and an impact if you're a business." For AB InBev, that meant water.

"For us, it's very simple: no water, no beer," he said. "Water is something we share with the communities in which we have our brewers; so, we have to work together with our brewers to keep the water sources healthy."

Michel had a more expansive view. In 2022, he appeared on *Fortune*'s *Leadership Next* podcast with Alan Murray.[4] In the beginning, he echoed many of Brito's comments about acting locally, being good community stewards, and ensuring that there is water for beer. He also mentioned that being more efficient with energy usage or barley yields per barrel of beer brewed is good for business. Those are things AB had been doing for decades.

Then Alan asked him about a pin that he was wearing on his jacket. It was a United Nations pin, adorned in seventeen colors, one to rep-

resent each of the UN's sustainable development goals (SDG). Michel
mentioned that AB InBev worked closely with the United Nations on
the company's own development goals, and it was "trying to really understand what is the role that we play in society."

Alan was intrigued. "So a little more on why you do this. I mean,
Milton Friedman said the social responsibility of business is to make
a profit. Why the focus on UN ESG goals, SDG goals, why is that so
important to AB InBev?"

Michel's response was telling: "We understand today that you cannot be insulated. Of course, profit is one of the goals of the company,
and that's why companies exist—to deploy capital and to be able to
compensate the shareholders having returns on the capital that you
deploy. But our role goes far beyond that." He went on to discuss how
ESG is integrated into executive compensation and how "financial
goals, commercial goals, ESG goals, they need to be aligned for us to
deliver on the purpose and overall goals of the company."

Alan followed up. "So you spend a lot of time in the United States.
You have some familiarity with our political system. What do you
think when you hear the governor of Florida or the governor of Texas
basically say that ESG is a dirty word and people embracing it are
woke CEOs? I mean, are you a woke CEO?"

"I don't think so, but it is to be judged," Michel answered.

And judged it would be.

Now, the word *woke* gets thrown around a lot. I don't particularly
like it because it is not well defined and means different things to different people. In the business sense, I define "woke" as a view that
businesses and brands should support liberal causes on politically and
socially contested issues, even when these issues have nothing to do
with the underlying mission of the company. A "woke CEO" would
therefore be one who uses their position to advance a progressive political ideology unrelated to their corporate role. Software CEOs who

called to defund the police, airline CEOs who asked to overturn election integrity laws, and finance CEOs who lamented the overturning of *Roe vs. Wade* would be "woke."

And by that definition, Anheuser-Busch was becoming decidedly more woke. It was becoming more "fancy." The annual ESG reports were growing longer. The principles of the company began to change. Meritocracy was minimized. "Diversity" was maximized. AB changed its principle that stated "We will be judged by the quality of our teams" to be "We will be judged by the quality and diversity of our teams." Nowhere was the shift more obvious than in how employees were promoted.

Every year, Anheuser-Busch conducted an exercise called OPR—Organizational People Review. Every employee was given a rating: Mover, Expected, New, or Underperformer. Managers were expected to grade on a curve, with approximately 20 percent of their team being movers, 70 percent of the team performing as expected (or too new to grade) and 10 percent of the team underperforming. Movers could expect to be promoted in the next year. Underperformers could expect a Performance Improvement Plan (or PIP). If they did not complete the PIP, they'd be fired.

I enjoyed OPR because it was a real meritocracy. Ratings were based on 360 reviews that an employee's direct reports, peers, and managers conducted. Managers then discussed ratings with other managers to align on ratings. The human resources team facilitated OPR to make sure that it was done fairly and consistently across organizations. Feedback was then quickly given to all employees. Stars quickly rose through the organization. Laggards found more suitable opportunities elsewhere.

In 2021, the company introduced "diversity dashboards." These dashboards showed the race and gender makeup of each team. They were supposed to be used for "informational purposes" only, but they were quickly used to judge managers whose teams were not "diverse" enough. And, of course, diversity of thought did not matter. That wasn't even on the dashboard. Diversity meant race and gender.

The practice was troubling, not least because the beer industry is unique. Certain departments were naturally more gender and ethnically diverse than others. Marketing, for example, had an equal balance of men and women, which makes sense since marketing appeals to a lot of people and there are no physical limitations involved. Logistics, on the other hand, heavily skewed male. The logistics operation had to work in cold warehouses, lift heavy cases and kegs of beer, and load them onto trucks. Unsurprisingly, not many women applied for these jobs.

Still, people's careers were impacted. Having a "diverse" team almost became a prerequisite to getting a Mover rating. It wasn't a formal policy, but it was becoming one.

Apart from the dashboards, there was the annual engagement survey. The survey asked a variety of questions about how happy employees were and how satisfied they were with particular initiatives. All fine enough. But under Michel's leadership, there was only one question that really mattered: how happy everyone was with diversity, equity, and inclusion.

Nowadays, people might be unhappy in both directions: some employees might think that the company isn't doing enough, while other employees might think the DEI efforts have gone too far. But back then, that wasn't the concern. It was basically a one-way ratchet. The question was really asking: Are we doing enough to promote the DEI agenda? And Michel desperately wanted the answer to be yes. Some departments, like HR, were even given targets to increase the number of employees who agreed, who were "satisfied" with the company's DEI efforts.

In case you're wondering, this was not an altruistic effort. Anheuser-Busch reported these scores externally in its ESG report so that it could curry favor with its largest Wall Street shareholders—firms like BlackRock, Vanguard, and State Street—which were pushing companies to diversify their ranks, create DEI departments, and achieve DEI goals. If companies achieved these goals, they could be included in ESG funds and more people would buy their stock, theoretically pushing up the price.

In 2021, 87 percent of employees were "satisfied" with the efforts that Anheuser-Busch was doing to support DEI initiatives.[5] Some of these DEI initiatives, like better maternity leave and matching charitable donations, weren't terribly controversial. And, as the 87 percent satisfaction rate reflected, most employees were satisfied with the programs. But it wasn't enough. The score had to not only be high, but increase every year. Progress on this metric started superseding other problematic scores. In the same 2021 employee engagement survey, for example, 50 percent of employees in certain functions said that they planned to leave Anheuser-Busch within the next twelve months. One in two employees! Yes, the Covid pandemic was leading to the Great Resignation, but this was a much higher number than anticipated.

If 50 percent of the company's employees planned to leave, and Anheuser-Busch really believed that "people are our greatest strength," there should have been concerted efforts to retain more people. Instead, the focus remained on what AB InBev could do to increase its DEI score. Some departments placed a two-hour executive meeting placed on the calendar each week to discuss initiatives. Executives from each function reported on what their plans were to push DEI scores into the 90 percent range. And to do so in time for the next survey. Unsurprisingly, many people started to leave the organization. Some by choice. Some not.

When Michel was promoted to CEO, one of the first changes he made was replacing Tony Milikin. The person who recruited me to AB InBev, who gave me a tour of the brick-clad Belgian headquarters, who introduced me to his humble, five-person team, just ten years before. In that time, he'd risen to become the Chief Procurement, Sustainability & Circular Ventures Officer. A C-suite exec. And he deserved it. He probably generated more value at the company than anyone else over the prior fifteen years. His team produced billions of synergies at Grupo Modelo and SABMiller. He also recruited some of the most promising talent in the organization. And I'm not just saying that because he recruited me. Tony was a living testament to AB In-Bev's commitment to radical meritocracy.

But merit was no longer a virtue. Tony didn't fit the "profile" for Diversity, Equity, and Inclusion. He was in his fifties, white, and male. If Michel was going to judge managers by the diversity of their teams, Tony didn't make him look good. So he was replaced. Ezgi Barcenas was appointed the new Chief Sustainability Officer, reporting directly to Michel.

In the press release announcing the move, Michel stated, "The appointment of Ezgi as our fully dedicated Chief Sustainability Officer is a recognition of the importance of sustainability and reflects our commitment to driving business outcomes and delivering value through our ESG agenda. Ezgi has been a leader in sustainability for many years, and I am delighted to welcome her to our Senior Leadership Team."[6]

Ezgi's new position did not have Tony's more expansive procurement responsibility. The procurement function was the one that delivered tangible results and real value over the past decade. It decreased costs. Increased cash flow. Produced real shareholder value. This function was now demoted to be part of the supply chain organization. The more narrowly focused sustainability and ESG role was elevated as a priority reporting directly to the CEO.

After her promotion, *Time* magazine profiled Ezgi as part of its Time 100 Climate series that highlights individuals fighting climate change by creating business value. Ezgi said, "We need to continue bringing focus to the innovations that can help multi-solve for growing global challenges. . . . Understanding interdependencies can help us avoid siloed-thinking and focus on initiatives that will not only deliver environmental benefits but also pay social or economic dividends." This is an ambitious agenda for a beer company.[7]

I have never met Ezgi. I have no idea how she performed in this role. I don't know how she compared to Tony Milikin. But I do know she left Anheuser-Busch two years after her promotion to Chief Sustainability Officer.

Michel made other personnel moves, too. He tapped Brendan Whitworth to replace him as CEO of the North America Business Unit. I was with Brendan the night he received the call. It was the summer of 2021. We were at a bar and chicken wing joint called Mr. Chubby's in Jacksonville, Florida. Brendan had been rumored as Michel's backfill. But now it was confirmed. People were generally happy, mostly because Michel chose an American to be the CEO of North America, the first since the 2008 takeover.

As the personnel shake-ups kept coming, I wasn't particularly worried. True, I didn't fit the "diversity" mold either, but the Southeast region I managed had performed well. It led the country in many of Michel's priorities, including driving Michelob Ultra growth, craft beer growth, and hard seltzers. We also did some pretty innovative and local programs for Bud Light. When the Tampa Bay Lightning won the Stanley Cup in 2020, we produced limited-edition "Bud Lightning" bottles and merchandise for the Tampa Bay market. They sold out immediately. In 2021, we celebrated the return of spring break in Florida with a retro nineties Spring Break Bud Light package. LL Cool J kicked off the campaign, as the light blue and pink pack brought back some of the MTV Spring Break vibes. It was a success. So were the custom Busch Light saltwater fishing packages we did in the South and the retro Natural Light packaging that we brought back in the Carolinas.

A few weeks after Michel promoted Brendan, I got my own phone call. Brendan was on the line. He was promoting me to President of Anheuser-Busch Sales & Distribution Company. This business unit was responsible for Anheuser-Busch's network of wholly owned distributors that stretched from Hawaii to New York City. It employed more than 3,500 people across sales, marketing, logistics, and operational functions and was one of the largest business units in the company. I was grateful for the opportunity and accepted the role. In my own mind, though, I was beginning to think about opportunities outside of Anheuser-Busch. The company I joined ten years prior was changing, and not for the better.

Chapter 17

From SUDS to STRIVE

The cultural revolution happening inside Anheuser-Busch was matched only by the cultural revolution happening outside its doors. Corporate America's war efforts that started with the Covid-19 pandemic and Summer of Reckoning marched on. I witnessed the next battle firsthand.

In 2021, I was still living in Atlanta, Georgia. In March of that year, Georgia's governor, Brian Kemp, signed Georgia Senate Bill 202, otherwise known as the Election Integrity Act of 2021. This bill overhauled the voting process in Georgia with the intent of restoring trust in the electoral process. Some aspects of the bill were seen to restrict voting access, like replacing signature matching requirements on absentee ballots with voter identification requirements, or limiting the use of ballot drop boxes. Other aspects of the bill expanded voting access, like increasing in-person early voting and adding voting stations or staff and equipment where there had been long lines.

The bill generated significant controversy. President Joe Biden labeled the bill "Jim Crow in the 21st century"; the Brookings Institute called it "an assault on our democracy."[1] Georgia governor Brian Kemp called criticism of the bill "disingenuous and completely false," pointing out it differs little from voting laws in other states. In hindsight, the bill had little impact. Early voting surged in the 2022 election cycle, and more than 99 percent of voters did not have a problem voting. A 2021 Department of Justice lawsuit alleging the bill was racially discriminatory was thrown out by a federal judge in 2023. But when the bill was passed, President Biden went to war, and corporate America joined him.

BlackRock was one of the first companies to speak out: "Equal access to voting is the very foundation of American democracy. While BlackRock appreciates the importance of maintaining election integrity and transparency, these should not be used to restrict equal access to the polls," CEO Larry Fink wrote.[2]

Fink's message was a call to action. Other companies took note, soon issuing statements of their own. Companies in Atlanta were particularly quick to chime in. Delta said in a memo to employees that the "final bill is unacceptable and does not match Delta's values," CEO Ed Bastian said.[3] Coca-Cola was similarly disappointed: "As soon as Georgia's legislature convened this year, our company joined with other Georgia businesses to share our core principles: We opposed measures that would seek to diminish or restrict voter access and we advocated for broad access, voter convenience, election integrity and political neutrality," he said.

Commitment to political neutrality, eh? By joining up with other Georgia businesses to fight legislation that has literally zero connection to soft drinks or soda cans? Paint me skeptical.

Skeptical, but not shocked. That came later, when Major League Baseball decided to weigh in. Atlanta was hosting the All-Star game in 2021. It was going to be big—one of the first major sporting events to be held at full capacity post-lockdowns. Anheuser-Busch was a sponsor. Budweiser would be featured prominently throughout the stadium and all across the metro Atlanta area. This was a big deal to me, not just because it was a great promotional opportunity generally, but because the Atlanta Braves were one of the few MLB teams that Anheuser-Busch did not sponsor. Therefore, it was generally difficult to find Budweiser in or around the stadium, or featured in grocery stores around Atlanta during baseball season. The All-Star game, sponsored by Budweiser, was about to change that.

But the All-Star game never came to Atlanta that year. On Friday, April 2, MLB commissioner Robert Manfred declared, "I have decided that the best way to demonstrate our values as a sport is by relocating this year's All-Star Game. . . . Major League Baseball fundamentally supports voting rights for all Americans and opposes restrictions at the ballot box."

I was stunned. What did voting have to do with baseball? Was the MLB commissioner now a voting rights expert? And how was corporate bullying—using the financial heft of a multibillion-dollar enterprise like the MLB—to pressure Georgia to repeal the laws passed by the democratically elected representatives of Georgia supposed to somehow *save* democracy? None of it made any sense.

Making matters worse, MLB moved the game to the worst-possible place for Anheuser-Busch to sell beer—Coors Field. MillerCoors was our largest rival, and Coors Field was based in their hometown of Denver, Colorado. Anheuser-Busch sold essentially zero beer at Coors Field. The fact that Colorado *also* required voters to bring photo ID with them to the polls apparently didn't matter. Ice-cold hypocrisy would be on tap.[4]

People in Atlanta didn't care as much as I did about Coors Field, but they did care a lot about the All-Star game being moved. They also cared a lot about the statements that Atlanta companies like Coca-Cola and Delta made. I knew employees at Coca-Cola who were very upset about the public statement that their CEO made. Many of them had voted for Governor Kemp and the representatives who put the Election Integrity Act into motion. The statement was very divisive, effectively telling half of the company that their beliefs were wrong and unwelcome.

It was also divisive within the Coca-Cola bottling ranks. Similar to the Anheuser-Busch distribution network, Coca-Cola has a system of independent bottlers and distributors across the country. This system was frustrated with Coca-Cola's statement, preferring that the company stay out of the issue.[5] They were frustrated not necessarily because they supported the voter ID law (though some of them undoubtedly did), but because they witnessed retailer and customer losses. In North Carolina, a county banned Coca-Cola vending machines at government offices.[6] Neighbors I knew stopped drinking Coca-Cola. Other neighbors stopped flying Delta Air Lines. Friends and colleagues stopped going to MLB games.

I was watching the country divide itself in real time. Corporate America was losing trust in the process. Customers trusted these companies to provide great products—soda from Coke, safe travel from Delta, home runs from MLB All-Stars. But they did not trust these companies to govern them. To play King. To tell them that the officials they put into office were wrong; that the billionaire CEO in charge of their local multinational food conglomerate knew better. In the words of Professor Frei, it was a big wobble. Customers responded with their wallets and stopped buying products.

Corporate politics seemed bad for our democracy as well. America had thrived over the past +200 years because individual citizens had the ability to vote for the representatives and laws that governed them. With the rise of stakeholder capitalism, and more corporate involvement in politics, it seemed like the country was taking a step backward. If companies like BlackRock and CEOs like Larry Fink could dictate political policies to CEOs like Alfredo Rivera at Coke and Ed Bastian at Delta, and those companies could influence U.S. laws, that looks very *un*democratic.

In late spring 2021, I started discussing these issues with a friend from high school. My friend is Vivek Ramaswamy. Long before he was a presidential candidate, Vivek and I were mock-trial partners. Vivek was the lawyer and I was the defendant in fictional court cases. We practiced our cases for hundreds of hours before competing against other high school teams. After graduation, Vivek and I stayed in contact. He attended Harvard while I was at Yale. Then we switched. He went to Yale Law School while I went to Harvard for my MBA. And during our early professional years, we lived in New York City at the same time. Back then, we spent more time shooting hoops than debating corporate policies, but times had changed.

Vivek was the CEO and founder of a publicly traded biotech company called Roivant Sciences. Roivant's mission was to use technology to discover life-saving medical treatments that were overlooked by other pharmaceutical companies. And it had success doing so, including bringing multiple new FDA-approved drugs to market.

Vivek had experienced corporate America's culture wars firsthand. In the summer of 2020, he had been asked by various employees and board members to comment on Roivant's position on Covid policy and systemic racism in America. He declined. His view was that Roivant's role was to bring new drugs to market. Roivant's view on unrelated political and social issues was irrelevant. Besides, Roivant's employees, board members, and shareholders all had different views on these issues. What they had in common was the desire to see Roivant succeed, so Vivek wanted to focus on that.

Not all board members agreed. Vivek decided that he would step down.

When Vivek and I were chatting in late spring 2021, he was finishing a book called *Woke Inc.*, which warned of the dangers of corporate political activism. The book became a *New York Times* bestseller. Not enough corporate executives read it, though, as businesses' entanglement with politics continued to accelerate.

Vivek was also thinking about next steps. What he could do, beyond the book, to get America back on track. He considered getting into politics. There was an open Senate seat in Ohio in 2022. He also thought about launching a nonprofit dedicated to restoring universal ideals of free speech, meritocracy, and capitalism.

Or he could start a new company. Maybe we could do it together. Many people were already ditching Coke, Delta, and Major League Baseball. There would be market demand for the products and services these now politically tainted companies once offered.

The possibilities were endless. One by one, we could launch new companies. They'd have a clear mission. They would focus on giving customers great products and services. They would hire the best and the brightest employees. These employees would come from all different backgrounds, but be unified in accomplishing the mission of the company, which would create great shareholder value for investors.

We could start with a new alternative to Coca-Cola. I knew beverages, so creating a new "pops without politics" was a natural fit. We could launch a new airline to compete against Delta. We would advertise our airline as having the best and most qualified pilots. Most flyers don't care what their pilot looks like, they care that they can fly the plane (and that the doors don't fall off the plane, although, to be honest, we hadn't even considered that possibility in 2021). We even discussed creating a new baseball league. Our league would simply "play ball." The location of the All-Star game would be based on where the fans demanded it, not on whose election integrity laws most closely aligned with our views.

As you can see, we were thinking big. Probably too big. In the end, we decided that it would take too much money to start a new soda company, a new airline, and a new baseball league. The U.S. probably didn't need two baseball leagues anyway. It would be better if MLB would just get back to playing ball (and Coca-Cola would sell soft drinks and Delta would fly planes).

But how could we do that? How could we get all of those companies back on track?

That's when we decided to look upstream. Who were these companies all taking their marching orders from? BlackRock. We didn't need to be the new Delta or MLB. We needed to be the new Black-Rock. We had been thinking about it all wrong. We'd laid out a battle strategy where we'd attack every colonial governor, every duke, every landed lady across corporate America; it would be much more effective to go after the King.

We settled on a plan. The best way to get business back to business was competing against BlackRock, the leader of the stakeholder capitalism and ESG movement. It wouldn't be easy, but it seemed much more realistic. If we could replicate the same exchange-traded funds BlackRock had—ones that tracked the S&P 500, that tracked the U.S. energy sector, that tracked semiconductors, etc.—people could move their retirement accounts and other investments from Black-Rock's funds to ours. Then we could be investors in all of the publicly traded companies in the United States. That would give us the ability to engage with all corporations and vote on shareholder resolutions at their annual meetings. We would take the reins of power from Black-Rock to refocus corporate America on business alone.

Our goal was to become the most trusted asset manager in the United States. Customers could trust that we were maximizing value for shareholders. Period. No politics. No corporate virtue signaling. Just investing to increase the savings of everyday citizens. That would be better for American capitalism, setting the free markets free from the distorting influence of politics. It would also be better for American democracy, setting our government free from the corrupting influence of corporate money. Everyone would be better off.

Vivek found this mission more compelling, and potentially more impactful, than running for Senate or starting a nonprofit. I found it more important than selling beer for a company that was quickly heading south, fecklessly riding the ESG wave until it inevitably crashed upon the shores of good business sense.

The new company would be called Strive Asset Management. We both liked the ring of it. The high school Vivek and I attended, St. Xavier, had an unofficial motto of "striving for excellence." It seemed fitting. And the ideal it embodied, of "making great efforts to achieve or obtain something."

"Invest in excellence" would be our motto. Asking individual companies to define what excellence meant for them would be better than forcing a uniform ESG agenda on all firms.

I remember exactly where I was when I knew it was time to leave Anheuser-Busch. I was on the corner of 24th Street and 6th Avenue in New York City, right outside of Anheuser-Busch's U.S. commercial office. It was February 2022, right after the meeting I had on Black Rifle Coffee Company. Brendan Whitworth had deferred the decision to Anheuser-Busch's Head of Corporate Affairs, who scuttled the opportunity for Anheuser-Busch to partner with one of the fastest-growing coffee companies in the U.S. A coffee company that was committed to supporting many of the same groups—military, law enforcement, first responders—that Budweiser supports. But in those days, any company that even tacitly supported law enforcement was persona non grata.

I immediately called a good friend of mine from business school—Patrick Cleary. Patrick is a former Marine and runs a company called ETF Architect. His company helps financial startups launch new exchange-traded funds. I mentioned to him that I was planning to leave Anheuser-Busch and start a new firm to compete against Black-Rock. "Hell yeah!" Patrick responded. His firm had a bad experience with BlackRock allegedly trying to get a peek at the proprietary algorithms that trade some of their funds. His firm would become our first partner.

Throughout February, Vivek and I continued to meet and finalize fundraising for our new venture. Our hometown Cincinnati Bengals were in the Super Bowl. We attended the game together in L.A. As February closed, funding came together from folks across the U.S. and across the political spectrum. That was important to us. We wanted to create a broad coalition of investors committed to the ideal of restoring American shareholder capitalism. Republicans like Peter Thiel and Democrats like Bill Ackman were both onboard, along with top venture firms like Founder's Fund, Flex Capital, and Narya.

With funding secured, it was time for me to leave. It was more difficult than I imagined. Although I was frustrated by many of the changes that were made and the direction the company was headed, I had made many friends across Anheuser-Busch and the wholesaler network over the past ten-plus years. The first week of March, I was at the winter wholesaler panel meeting in Florida. This is a meeting where a group of wholesalers and senior Anheuser-Busch executives discuss how the year is starting and what needs to be tweaked ahead of the key summer selling season. I knew that this would be the last time that I would see many of these friends. I was having second thoughts about leaving. Luckily, my wife was very supportive. We discussed the pros and cons throughout the week. Just as she had helped convince me that Anheuser-Busch was the right job after business school, she also helped convince me that if I did not pursue this opportunity now, I would always regret it. She was right. At the end of the meeting, on Friday, March 5, I resigned.

My last day at Anheuser-Busch was two weeks later. I made a nice LinkedIn post. I spoke about the things I most admired about the company—dreaming big, meritocracy, brands like Budweiser that historically united people, the entrepreneurial spirit of the craft beer founders who joined Anheuser-Busch. My new venture was not publicly announced yet, but my goal was to bring these ideals back to corporate America.

I had no idea that one year later my two professional worlds, Anheuser-Busch and Strive, would massively collide.

Chapter 18

The Emperor's New Clothes (Stakeholder Capitalism Exposed)

After leaving Anheuser-Busch, I dedicated 100 percent of my time to building Strive.

We wanted to provide a counterweight. A different place for investors to put their money. Where people could invest with an asset manager who would tell Exxon and Chevron to proudly produce the energy that powers the world today, rather than to stop drilling in fear of a warmer tomorrow that may never come. Where people could invest in the S&P 500 knowing that their asset manager was willing to stand up to Disney CEO Bob Iger and tell him that picking a fight with Governor DeSantis was not going to help the company succeed. And where they could enjoy all the upsides of investing in the market, with an asset manager who would tell companies to focus on business alone.

By the end of 2022, we'd already seen tremendous success. Cracks in stakeholder capitalism movement were beginning to show. Charles Munger, Warren Buffett's number 2 at Berkshire Hathaway, stated in *The Wall Street Journal* that "we have a new bunch of emperors, and they're the people who vote the shares in index funds." He went on to note about Larry Fink that "I'm not sure I want him to be my emperor." Elon Musk went further. He called ESG "the devil" after Tesla received a lower ESG score than cigarette manufacturers.[1] The cigarette companies embraced Diversity, Equity, and Inclusion more than Tesla, you see, which had laid off its LGBTQ+ President and DEI head amid a broader 10 percent layoff. Tesla was eventually removed from the S&P 500 ESG index fund for "a lack of low carbon strategy and codes of business conduct, racial discrimination, poor working conditions, as well as product responsibility." Many people scratched their heads. Tesla is seemingly doing more than any other company on earth to transition the world away from fossil fuels, yet it is removed from an ESG index over "a lack of low carbon strategy."

Something was astray. In 2022, the Securities and Exchange Commission began fining banks for "greenwashing." During the ESG boom, many banks had created specific ESG funds to capitalize on the trend. At a time when mutual funds were losing appeal to many customers, banks looked to ESG funds to fill the void. The banks promised they could deliver better financial returns by selecting companies that performed the best on ESG metrics. That way, investors could see their dollars being put to good use by virtuous companies, while reaping the financial benefits that inevitably flow to companies that behave best. "Doing well by doing good" was the pitch.

But often, ESG funds weren't much different than their vanilla counterparts. After most booms, the inevitable bust was around the corner. In some instances, banks just literally renamed existing non-ESG funds with a better label. If you read the fine print closely enough, you'd see they were promising only to tinker around the edges, but then failed to even tinker. In other instances, fund managers promised to do careful research to select only the best, most ESG-friendly companies for their funds, but then never did. Goldman Sachs paid a $4 million fine to the Securities and Exchange Commission for that one.[2] Bank of New York Mellon paid a $1.5 million fine for the same thing. The only way these ESG funds were different from their non-ESG counterparts, it appeared, was the fee: Since ESG funds were supposedly a premium product, featuring stocks handpicked to deliver both financial and societal benefits, the fees were typically much higher than for index funds. Often 40 percent higher or more.[3]

And the claim that ESG outperformed in financial terms was beginning to be called into doubt. The *Harvard Business Review* had just published a damning article titled "An Inconvenient Truth About ESG Investing."[4] It was one of the first comprehensive reviews in a leading academic forum questioning ESG's promise to improve investment and societal outcomes. The article cited a recent *Journal of Finance* paper, where University of Chicago researchers looked at the ESG ratings of more than twenty thousand mutual funds. The highest-rated funds attracted more capital than the lowest-rated funds, but none of the high sustainability funds outperformed in financial terms.[5] Some investors might be okay trading off investment returns for higher sustainability, but additional research showed "high sustainability" funds don't even deliver on that front.

In another study, researchers at Columbia University and the London School of Economics compared the ESG record of U.S. companies in 147 ESG fund portfolios with that of U.S. companies in 2,428 non-ESG portfolios.[6] Surprisingly, the researchers "found that the companies in the ESG portfolios had worse compliance record for both labor and environmental rules." They also found "that companies added to ESG portfolios did not subsequently improve compliance with labor or environmental regulations."

The *Harvard Business Review* explores this paradox of ESG funds underperforming on both financial and sustainability metrics by noting:

> Part of the explanation may simply be that an express focus on ESG is redundant: in competitive labor markets and product markets, corporate managers trying to maximize long-term

shareholder value should of their own accord pay attention to employee, customer, community, and environmental interests. On this basis, setting ESG targets may actually distort decision-making.

The authors highlighted another, darker possibility as well: companies embracing ESG to mask bad business performance.[7] There was some research to support the idea. Ryan Flugum at the University of Northern Iowa and Matthew Souther at the University of South Carolina published a paper noting that when executives underperformed analyst earning expectations, they publicly speak about their focus on ESG. When they beat earnings expectations, they focus on their revenue and profitability growth, making few, if any, ESG comments. Therefore, if asset managers funnel dollars to companies extolling their ESG commitments, they might actually be overcommitting themselves to financially underperforming businesses.

The article ends with a warning: "funds investing in companies that publicly embrace ESG sacrifice financial returns without gaining much, if anything, in terms of actually furthering ESG interests."

The dramatic downfall of crypto billionaire Sam Bankman-Fried and his company FTX became the personification of the perils of ESG. For years, Sam Bankman-Fried had positioned himself and his company as an ESG darling. He supported government regulation of cryptocurrency. He bowed to the climate gods by promising to make FTX "carbon neutral" and donating to solar energy projects. FTX was rewarded with a higher ESG score on "leadership and governance" than Exxon Mobil. FTX was a progressive darling, demonstrating that good values got good results. Until it all came crashing down.

Sam Bankman-Fried had been swindling his customers all along. FTX went bankrupt. Investors lost billions. SBF now sits in jail. All the ESG talk was just cover, it turns out, for ordinary fraud. Even SBF admits as much. "ESG has been perverted beyond recognition," he told Vox before his indictment dropped. It's a "dumb game we woke westerners play where we say all the right shibboleths and so everyone likes us."

Still, the conventional wisdom at the time was that ESG outperformed in financial terms. For every news article or academic paper engaging in the heresy of ESG skepticism, there were five singing its praises.

Perhaps that's why so many companies kept barreling ahead, unwilling to get off the ESG bandwagon. Anheuser-Busch was one of them. It was doubling down on the corporate fad of touting its ESG credentials. Its stock had been in the tank since Covid hit. It declined from ~$80 a share at the end of 2019 to ~$70 at the end of 2020 to ~$60 at the end of both 2021 and 2022. Its use of ESG buzzwords like sustainability, ESG, stakeholders, gender, and diversity on earnings calls increased dramatically over this time period. Prior to 2018, AB averaged fewer than ten of these buzzwords per year on analyst calls reviewing its business plan and financials. From 2018 through 2022, it averaged more than thirty mentions per year.

AB's annual ESG reports ballooned in size as well. The first report, issued for the year 2020, was sixty-six pages. By 2022, its annual ESG report was more than one hundred pages long. It reviews AB's eight ESG priorities, from climate to ethics to sustainable agriculture to DEI and more. Some of the sections were mostly updates from prior years. The water stewardship section, for example, continued to report on the company's efforts to improve water availability, including how it was faring toward its 2025 goals.

But some sections trumpeted more significant changes, particularly when it came to growing its ever-expanding diversity initiatives. In 2022, the company "created a new leadership position to grow our DEI strategy"—a Vice President of DEI, who would report directly to the C-suite. All managers would now receive unconscious bias trainings each year. And more than three thousand employees had "annual performance targets linked to delivering our ESG strategy." The diversity dashboards announced in 2020 seemed less and less like they were informational only; now, up to 20 percent of some employees' bonuses were tied to their ability to meet their "ESG-related target." Whether the official targets were related to diversity or climate change or something else isn't quite clear, but given that DEI was a "global priority" for senior leadership, the pressure was unquestionably on.[8]

There was another change as well, one buried in the back half of the report. For the first time in the company's 150-year history, it would offer "inclusive benefits such as gender-affirming medical support" for U.S. and Canadian employees.

Companies, of course, are free to offer whatever benefits they deem prudent to attract the best talent. That might mean paying for gender-affirming care for transgender individuals, travel reimbursement for women seeking abortions, in vitro fertilization for couples trying to have a baby, or egg freezing for women who seek to delay childbearing. These internal policies might be controversial for those who oppose such procedures, but they are just that: internal policies. Jehovah's Witnesses oppose blood transfusions on religious grounds, after all, but that doesn't mean that insurance doesn't cover it.

The situation is different, however, when a company publicly touts its internal policies in order to take a political stance. That's the case when these policies are broadcast in ESG reports or used to score points with activist groups that push companies to offer them and shame companies that decline.

When it comes to LGBTQ+ issues, there is no group more active than the Human Rights Campaign. In 2002, the group launched the Corporate Equality Index, which rates companies on how LGBTQ+

friendly they are. Back then, the criteria were relatively tame.[9] Companies had to have written nondiscrimination policies and engage in "respectful and appropriate marketing" to the LGBT community. You couldn't hire only straight folks and couldn't air commercials making fun of gays. Fair enough. But even these weak requirements were rarely met. The year it launched, just thirteen businesses received perfect scores.

Over time, the Human Rights Campaign toughened its scoring. If corporate America could go to war against Covid, systemic racism, and voter integrity laws, it could go to war for the LGBTQ+ community also. By 2022, HRC required making at least three "public commitments to the LGBTQ+ community," including legislative lobbying, donating to LGBTQ+ charities, and creating supplier set-asides reserved only for companies owned by people who identified as LBGTQ+.[10] It also required "transgender inclusive healthcare," including "mandatory services and treatment options." Businesses rose to the challenge. In 2022, more than 840 companies received perfect scores. Anheuser-Busch, with its newly unveiled healthcare policies, was among them.[11] An ESG report almost seemed incomplete without the HRC stamp of approval.

The impact of the Human Rights Campaign can hardly be understated. Transgender issues were just beginning to come to the political fore. The political fight moved from acceptance, tolerance, and non-discrimination (topics on which most of America was rightly onboard) to the more controversial. Bathroom bills were making headlines, as states like North Carolina sought to preserve separate spaces for members of each biological sex. So were drag queen story hours, where public libraries would host men in drag to read books to kids.

And then there was Lia Thomas, the transgender woman breaking collegiate swimming records while competing in the women's division. Many people reasonably questioned whether Lia, who was born male, had an unfair biological advantage. But those who did so publicly often found themselves labeled transphobes, bigots, or worse. An Oberlin coach who did so was reprimanded by the college, subjected to questioning, and, in her words, "burned at the stake."

But corporate America was undeterred. One by one, corporate America supported the LGBTQ+ agenda, however radical or controversial it may have become. Adidas praised trans women competing against biological women in its "Impossible" ad.[12] McKinsey wrote white papers on "being transgender at work."[13] Pantene launched a video series featuring transgendered people talking about going home for the holidays.[14] Gillette debuted an ad depicting a father teaching his transgendered son how to shave.[15] Tampon companies started using phrases like "people who menstruate"[16]; Tampax tweeted "not all people with periods are women."[17] Nickelodeon produced children's content featuring transgendered characters.[18] Disney did, too.[19] No one dared to oppose the agenda. If you did, your Corporate Equality Index score would surely drop.

The other organization now prominently touted in Anheuser-Busch's annual reports was Cannes Lions. Cannes Lions is an advertising festival in the South of France that debuted in 1954. Recently, it has evolved into one of the marketing industry's most prestigious annual gatherings. It calls itself a "Creativity Festival," since "convention for ad agencies" probably sounds too crass. But the marketing by the marketing awards folks has worked: Ad agencies and companies highlight the number of Cannes Lions awards that they win each year to brag about their marketing prowess.

Historically, winning the *USA Today* Super Bowl Ad Meter was the pinnacle of marketing success in the U.S. The Cannes was a hoity-toity European thing; the ad meter measured what consumers actually liked. No longer for Anheuser-Busch, which hadn't won the *USA*

Today Ad Meter in more than a decade. It won the Cannes Marketing of the Year award in 2021 and 2022, though, and at least nowadays, companies cannot simply submit the ad they like the best. To win, entries must have "diversity, equality and inclusion as part of its core values." As the Cannes website ominously explains, "We will not move forward with any content submission that does not live up to these values." If that's not clear enough, it ends by demanding, "Just ask yourself before submitting, does my cast of characters represent society at large? If not, please continue to work on your content idea and lineup before submitting." Ouch.

The Cannes is also the birthplace of the Global Alliance for Responsible Media,[20] which describes itself as a cross-industry initiative created to establish safe advertising guidelines—to ensure, for instance, that a brand's online ad doesn't wind up on a website depicting child pornography or teaching terrorists how to build pipe bombs. In fact, however, the group goes much further. It uses its collective muscle to force social media companies to take down "misinformation" and "hate speech," including things like "misgendering." Otherwise, advertisers will threaten to pull their revenue. AB InBev is proudly listed among the group's members.

Before 2020, Cannes awards were not mentioned in AB's annual reports. By 2022, they were highlighted eight times. Page after page tout ad campaigns featuring organic farmers or angler fishermen cleaning up plastic waste. In one award-winning ad, a gender-ambiguous minority is seen cheering at a rock concert powered by renewable energy provided by Budweiser; in another, a group of diverse friends are enjoying no-alcohol Corona on the beach to support responsible drinking. In 2022, Anheuser-Busch won more Cannes Lions—fifty of them—than any other company. The ads seemed to promote a lot of things—the environment, diversity, sobriety—but Anheuser-Busch's core brands were rarely among them, and never the true focus. The brands seemed lost. Not sure who their customer was or what need the brand filled in their life.

All of these awards amounted to little. A reckoning was coming. Anheuser-Busch's 2022 ESG report—released in March of 2023—would be its last.

Chapter 19

Mulvaney Madness

B y early 2023, Anheuser-Busch InBev was desperate for new ideas. The stock had been stagnant for years. The company's emerging markets were taking longer than expected to recover from Covid declines. ZBB had long run its course. There was no more fat to trim. The largest brand in the U.S., Bud Light, had stagnated. Despite being Anheuser-Busch's longtime breadwinner, the top brass hadn't made it a priority for years. Hundreds of millions of marketing dollars had been pulled from Bud Light to reinvest in other brands and innovation. AB InBev sought a more exciting path forward, with "sexier" international brands, new products, and new initiatives. It moved to New York to turn over a new leaf, to freshen the company up, to finally leave its St. Louis roots behind.

DEI was that new leaf.

And one of its chief proponents—at least when it came to gender diversity—was its new VP of Marketing, Alissa Heinerscheid. Heiner-scheid replaced Andy Goeler, who retired at the end of 2022 after a forty-year career with Anheuser-Busch. His last gift was resurrecting Bud Light with the Dilly Dilly campaign, but meager budgets made the momentum hard to sustain. The marketing genius with a long and storied history was gone.

Heinerscheid was an interesting choice to lead Bud Light. The

California native had attended boarding school in Massachusetts, before attending Harvard and, eventually, University of Pennsylvania's Wharton Business School. Her friends found it "slightly hilarious" that she worked at Anheuser-Busch; one described her as "one of the last people I think of when I think of 'beer.'"[1] She was in her late thirties, married with three kids, well-connected among the coastal elite. She'd joined Anheuser-Busch in 2014 after stints at Johnson & Johnson, where she was in charge of Listerine, and General Mills, where she worked on branding for Cheerios. From the beginning, she was hired to work in New York, rarely stepping foot on Anheuser-Busch's St. Louis grounds.

I worked with Alissa on numerous projects during her time at Anheuser-Busch. Early in her career, she led sports and music events for Bud Light. We partnered on a dive bar tour in Colorado when I was based there. She wasn't the most creative marketer I'd worked with, and definitely not the typical Bud Light drinker, but dependable when managing budgets and executing events.

The pandemic had hit her hard. At that point, she was VP of direct-to-consumer marketing at Anheuser-Busch. It was her dream job, but she was listless—particularly working remotely from the long-term Airbnb she rented in San Diego to escape Manhattan. She wanted to do something more meaningful, to help women in particular. She debated whether to start a female-oriented group within Anheuser-Busch, but eventually decided to launch an initiative called "One Hundred Women in One Hundred Days," where she chatted with similarly situated female professionals about how to solve racial justice and fight climate change.

Her lifestyle and politics were public—the One Hundred Women in One Hundred Days initiative earned her a 2021 profile in the *New Yorker*. But despite (or perhaps because of) her public-facing progressive outlook, she was promoted to lead marketing for Bud Light—the world's largest beer brand at the time. Article after article touted her as the "first woman" to lead the brand, and so did her own LinkedIn profile.[2] It was the dawn of a new era; impossible to miss.

The changes came rapidly. In June 2022, Anheuser-Busch gave up its exclusive rights to advertise alcohol during the Super Bowl—rights it had held for thirty-three years.[3] Competitors pounced on the opportunity; Heinerscheid defended the move as part of a broader "rebalancing" of the company's ad spend. But where Bud Light lacked the money for Super Bowl exclusivity, it found money to fund a new partnership with the National LGBT Chamber of Commerce, donating $200,000 to its Communities of Color Initiative.[4]

2022 also marked the fortieth birthday of Bud Light. One might say Bud Light was having a bit of a midlife crisis as it transitioned leadership. When people have midlife crises, they tend to do things that remind them of their youth and past greatness. Buy fast cars. Go on adventurous trips. Meet up with old friends. Other people get lost trying to figure out who they are and what they want to be. Bud Light would quickly become lost.

In March 2023, Heinerscheid appeared on the *Make Yourself at Home* podcast. On the podcast, Alissa mentioned that she was tasked with turning around Bud Light:

> I had a really clear job to do when I took over Bud Light. . . . This brand is in decline. It has been in decline for a very long time. And if we do not attract young drinkers to come and drink this brand, there will be no future for Bud Light.
>
> "So I had this super clear mandate; we need to evolve and elevate this incredibly iconic brand. . . . What does evolve and elevate mean? It means inclusivity. It means shifting the tone.

Had Bud Light been in decline? Yes. That was true. A lot of the decline was self-imposed. Belgian marketing execs and Brazilian sales leaders had implemented programs that didn't resonate with the American population. Michel's goal for Bud Light was to maintain its share of the core beer category (vs. Miller and Coors). Bud Light's TV ad spend declined by 38 percent from 2019 to 2023, while Modelo eclipsed Bud Light as the largest TV beer advertiser during this time. Covid did not help Bud Light either. Bud Light sold best in convenience stores and bars. When those channels shut down during Covid, and people moved their buying to grocery stores, Bud Light suffered. Hard seltzer brands like White Claw, Truly, and High Noon won.

But that didn't mean that Bud Light needed a radical makeover. Andy Goeler showed that the brand could be turned around with great, funny, authentically Bud Light marketing. He did it with the Dilly Dilly campaign, before Michel pulled resources out from under the brand. It could be done again. It would be hard. But it could be done.

Anheuser-Busch and Alissa Heinerscheid took the easy path. Later in the *Make Yourself at Home* podcast, Alissa mentioned that "Bud Light had been kind of a brand of fratty, kind of out-of-touch humor and it was really important that we had another approach." The "inclusive" approach. But who, one must ask, was the one who was truly out of touch with Bud Light's core customer base? Fraternity brothers, or a New York marketing executive who was "known for planning her schedule in twenty-minute increments, not shotgunning cold ones."[5]

In the end, AB felt it was safer for Bud Light to ditch its authentic self and try to appear more supportive of ESG and DEI causes in the name of "inclusivity." Even if this approach didn't turn around the brand, Anheuser-Busch could at least publish in annual ESG reports what it was doing to be more Diverse, Equitable, and Inclusive. It could highlight its top scores in Bloomberg's Gender Equality Index and Human Rights Coalition Corporate Equality Index. It could talk about its "public commitments to the LGBTQ+" community. It could win Cannes Lions. When it missed analyst earnings forecasts, it could wax and wane about all of the inclusive marketing it was doing. It could therefore still get included in ESG stock funds.

This approach would have been unheard of under the Busch family. The Busch family would have demanded better marketing to grow sales and share. Period. The approach would have been similarly dead on arrival when I first joined Anheuser-Busch InBev. Under Carlos Brito and 3G Capital, the company was fanatical about shareholder value. They weren't great at building brands, but they held individuals responsible for missing financial targets.

Anheuser-Busch's awkward transition from a company focused on shareholder results to one that adopted stakeholder capitalism to try to grow the business was shortly on display for the whole world to see. The missteps were a culmination of the InBev execs never understanding the American consumer, the move from St. Louis to NYC, the adoption of stakeholder capitalism, and the focus on ESG and DEI over financial results.

On April 1, 2023, the ESG bubble popped. And Anheuser-Busch was caught holding the pin.

On April Fool's Day, Anheuser-Busch partnered with the controversial transgender actor Dylan Mulvaney to promote a March Madness "easy carry" sweepstakes. But this was no prank. Consumers could win $15,000 by uploading a video of them carrying as many Bud Lights as possible. Dressed in an Audrey Hepburn outfit, Dylan talks about March Madness and says, "Just found out this had to do with sports and not just saying this is a crazy month." Dylan also mentions that "Bud Light sent me possibly the best gift ever, a can with my face on it." Bud Light sent the can as a "gift" to celebrate a personal milestone. The milestone was Dylan's 365-day journey of transitioning from a biological male to a female.

Over the previous year, Dylan Mulvaney had amassed millions of followers on social media documenting the transition in a daily series of videos titled "Days of Girlhood." Dylan attracted a lot of controversy along the way.

First, Dylan advocated for normalizing "women having bulges." At the time, Dylan still had male genitalia and said this led to unusual stares from people in public when wearing tight clothes. Mulvaney said in a video, "I forgot that my crotch doesn't look like other women's crotches sometimes because mine doesn't look like a little Barbie pocket." The video ends with Mulvaney singing, "Normalize the bulge. We are normalizing the bulge. Women can have bulges and that's okay."

Controversy continued in October 2022. Dylan met with President Joe Biden to discuss transgender issues. The meeting was organized by the online news outlet NowThisNews, an organization known for liberal politics. Dylan asked President Biden about recent Republican-led legislation regulating gender-based medical interventions for children. Biden called the legislation "outrageous" and "immoral."

Conservatives were predictably furious. U.S. Senator Marsha Blackburn from Tennessee shared the video on Twitter, with a caption reading "Dylan Mulvaney, Joe Biden, and radical left-wing lunatics want to make this absurdity normal." Caitlyn Jenner, who is a conservative transgender woman, agreed with Blackburn's remarks via Twitter and said, "this is absurdity."

It was a hot topic. And a divisive one. Did most Americans care how people dressed or identified? No. But sex-change surgeries for kids were a different matter. Sixteen states had recently passed laws regulating the practice. Another twenty-five had banned biological males from competing against biological women in K–12 sports. Twenty-five out of fifty states. The country was divided precisely in half.

The week leading up to April 1 had transgender issues especially in the national spotlight. On March 27, 2023, a mass shooting occurred at a private Christian school in Nashville, Tennessee. Twenty-eight-year-old Aiden Hale (born Audrey Elizabeth Hale) killed three nine-year-old students and three staff members. It was the deadliest school shooting in Tennessee history.

The day before Dylan Mulvaney's Bud Light post, NBC news reported, "The gender identity of the suspect in this week's Nashville school shooting has become one of the central storylines in a horrific tragedy that left six people dead." NBC went on to note: "Some on the far right rushed to blame the shooting on the suspect's gender identity,[6] while some on the left pointed to an already combustible political environment in which transgender people have become a frequent target of right-wing lawmakers and pundits."[7] Put differently, both the right and the left agreed transgenderism was to blame: the right blamed the transgendered person pulling the trigger, while the left blamed the transphobic society that pushed them to pull it.

Bud Light's partnership with Dylan Mulvaney could not have come at a worse time.

The reaction was explosive. The post went viral. Customers called for boycotts. Celebrities chimed in. Kid Rock was among the first to do so, posting a video of himself shooting a stack of Bud Lights with a semiautomatic rifle. "Fuck Bud Light and Fuck Anheuser-Busch," he eloquently concludes. Country singer Travis Tritt tweeted quickly after, "I will be deleting all Anheuser-Busch products from my tour hospitality rider. I know many other artists who are doing the same." Some artists took a different view. Zach Bryan, another country singer, tweeted: "I just think insulting transgender people is completely wrong because we live in a country where we can all just be who we want to be. It's a great day to be alive I thought." Within a few days, Howard Stern shared that he was "dumbfounded by why someone would care so much" about a trans person representing the beer brand.

Bud Light had become embroiled in the national debate over transgender issues, and everyone seemed to be discussing it.

Initially, Bud Light defended the partnership, releasing a statement to CNN on April 6 saying, "Anheuser-Busch works with hundreds of influencers across our brands as one of many ways to authentically connect with audiences across various demographics. From time to time we produce unique commemorative cans for fans and for brand influencers, like Dylan Mulvaney. This commemorative can was a gift to celebrate a personal milestone and is not for sale to the general public."[8]

Anheuser-Busch hoped the comment would douse the debate; instead, it threw gasoline on the political fire.

On April 10, national news outlets began reporting on Bud Light's VP, Alissa Heinersheid. Reporters had found the podcast. Her comments that Bud Light was too "fratty" and "out of touch" appeared in a new light.

Many loyal customers felt personally insulted. The boycotts gained traction. The week before the partnership with Mulvaney, Bud Light sales declined by 1.6 percent compared to the prior year. For the week ending April 8, sales were down 11 percent. By April 15, sales were down 21 percent.

Anheuser-Busch needed to stop the bleeding. Bud Light was the number-1 beer in America.

Anheuser-Busch had a choice to make. Bud Light is a brand. Brand messaging is curated to appeal to certain consumers. Anheuser-Busch could let the American population know that Bud Light's new "super clear mandate" meant that Bud Light would get involved in more political and social issues moving forward, as the DEI movement demands.

It wouldn't be the first. Brands like Ben & Jerry's have a clear mission and mandate to do just that. Ben & Jerry's website clearly states that "We believe that ice cream can change the world." There is an "Activism" tab on their website that proclaims "Our Progressive

Values." Consumers can clearly see that Ben & Jerry's is "Leading with progressive values across our business we seek to meet human needs and eliminate injustices in our local, national, and international communities." They then highlight issues that the company advocates for, including Rights of Refugees, Climate Justice, Fighting Election Integrity Laws, Defunding the Police, etc. Ben & Jerry's has been advocating such change since two Vermont hippies founded the company in 1978.

When they sold the business to multinational conglomerate Unilever in 2000, they maintained an independent board to make decisions on the company's social mission. Their customers expect this activism and buy such ice-cream flavors as "Save Our Swirled" and "Empower Mint" to support social causes. Some customers want that. Some don't. Ben & Jerry's happily serves the ones who do. Maybe Bud Light wanted to head in this direction and serve a progressive consumer.

The other choice Bud Light had was to admit its mistake. To apologize. To acknowledge that the Mulvaney campaign was not aligned with Bud Light's brand mission to be "easy to drink, easy to enjoy."

This would have also been a reasonable choice. Bud Light had become the number-1 beer brand in the U.S. because it was remarkably apolitical. It was already the most inclusive beer brand in the country. Studies showed that it was enjoyed by Democrats and Republicans equally. That is because it steered clear of political and controversial issues. Past campaigns that had dabbled in politics, even neutrally, were widely regarded as failures. Instead, it traditionally focused on things that brought people together, like sports, music, humor, and backyard BBQs. That made it easy to drink. That made it easy to enjoy. That allowed it to authentically connect with millions of customers across various demographics.

It also had a history of acknowledging when it made a mistake, and people were forgiving. When it released the label "The perfect beer for removing 'No' from your vocabulary for the night" as part of the "Up for Whatever" campaign, it quickly acknowledged its mistake and apologized. People moved on and the issue immediately died.

Anheuser-Busch didn't choose either of those paths.

Instead, the weekend of April 15, many people across the country were introduced to Anheuser-Busch's North American CEO, Brendan Whitworth. Michel Doukeris, Anheuser-Busch's Global CEO, apparently wanted nothing to do with it. The issue landed on Brendan's desk. Brendan was paralyzed. How could he balance Michel's commitment to ESG and DEI when sales were plummeting? He couldn't. So he released a generic and widely criticized statement titled "Our Responsibility to America." He highlighted Bud Light's "proud history supporting our communities, military, first responders, sports fans, and hard-working Americans" and said, "We never intended to be part of a discussion that divides people. We are in the business of bringing people together over a beer" without mentioning the specific controversy. This angered both conservatives who wanted an apology and liberals who wanted a defense.

Comically, he simultaneously released a seemingly patronizing video of Clydesdale horses running across America. At one point, the ad shows two people raising an American flag, with one placing a hand over her heart. He hoped this ad would make people forget about Bud Light's ad with Dylan. They obviously didn't.

Bud Light then tried to make light of the situation by making its first social media post since the controversy erupted. That Friday, it released a simple "TGIF?" on its social media accounts. On most days, Bud Light was lucky to get a few hundred comments on social media when it posted a sweepstakes or a new commercial. But that Friday was not most days. The post got more than thirty-two thousand comments. More than 99 percent of them were negative.

Liberal consumers quickly joined the boycott. Prominent gay bars across the country stopped selling Anheuser-Busch products. By the end of April, Bud Light sales were down 30 percent year over year.

It wasn't just Bud Light that was hit. Anheuser-Busch's entire portfolio of brands suffered. Budweiser declined by 15 percent. Brands like Michelob Ultra and Busch Light that had been growing before the controversy were now in decline.

Brendan decided to walk through the middle of a corporate cultural war, and Anheuser-Busch was now getting fired at from both sides. There is a quote attributed to Teddy Roosevelt: "In any moment of decision, the best thing you can do is the right thing, the next best thing is the wrong thing, and the worst thing you can do is nothing." When stakeholder capitalism demands you be everything to everyone, you become nothing to anyone.

Chapter 20

"Would you do this partnership again?"

The vague non-comments continued. Anheuser-Busch placed Alissa Heinerscheid and her boss, Daniel Blake, on "administrative leave." Neither firing them for a campaign that caused massive sales losses nor standing by them for adhering to a "clear mandate" obviously given by top brass. This added to the drama and storyline.

In May, things went from bad to worse. CNBC estimated that Anheuser-Busch's total U.S. sales declined by 18 percent. Its stock price entered bear territory, declining by 20 percent since the Mulvaney partnership. More than $20 billion of shareholder value had been destroyed.

Then the Human Rights Campaign launched an attack. It suspended Anheuser-Busch's 100 percent rating, pending further review. And its execs started giving media interviews slamming the company. The organization had initially been pleased to see Anheuser-Busch work with Mulvaney, but now it felt betrayed. HRC was now "disturbed" by "the company's reaction once the backlash started happening," one of HRC's Senior Vice Presidents told CNN. He finished by telling reporters, "Anheuser-Busch's actions demonstrate a profound lack of fortitude in upholding its values of diversity, equity, and inclusion."

That's the thing with these ESG and stakeholder activist groups.

They've got the carrot and the stick. To get companies on board, it's all sunshine and rainbows and positivity and promises of good press and little badges that say "BEST places to work." But if you fail to adhere to their dogma for even a moment, the knives come out.

The losses continued to pile on. Bud Light lost its crown as the number-1-selling beer brand in America. Modelo Especial, the Mexican brand that Anheuser-Busch fumbled the purchase of in 2013, took its spot. At the start of 2023, Bud Light held a 10.3 percent share of the U.S. beer market. Modelo Especial held 7.5 percent. By May 2023, they'd swapped places. Bud Light's share plummeted to 7.3 percent while Modelo's rose to 8.4 percent. It was the first time in twenty-two years that Bud Light did not hold the top spot in the U.S. beer market.

Michel Doukeris, Brendan Whitworth, and Anheuser-Busch were alarmed. They'd thought the controversy would quickly blow over. Consumer boycotts are rarely sustained. This time was different.

There're a number of reasons why.

One key factor in the success of any boycott is, intuitively, whether consumers believe they have the power to impact the company's bottom line. If a boycott would be futile, there's no point. Bud Light's customers were witnessing success in real time. That's unusual. Most companies report sales figures quarterly or annually, well after the fact. Bud Light sales are released each week. And there's not much Anheuser-Busch can do about it: The figures are reported by a trade publication, based on surveys sent to liquor stores, convenience stores, and supermarkets. Anheuser-Busch could not force the media storm to die down by starving it of data.

Evidence on social media confirmed the sales decline. Baseball fans posted videos of long concession lines for Coors Light while the Bud Light line was empty. Same went for store shelves. Coors Light and Miller Lite were empty on the shelf while Bud Light remained fully stocked.

A boycott is also more likely to succeed if it's easy to switch to another product.[1] If there is a competitor that is offering basically the same product for basically the same price in basically the same locations, boycotts are a lot easier to sustain.

Real-life examples bear this out. One of the most-cited examples of a successful boycott is the 1995 Shell boycott, where consumers protested the company's plans to sink an oil platform into the Atlantic Ocean. A critical factor was that the boycott was virtually costless to consumers: gas is gas, and there's almost always another station across the street.[2]

Sometimes switching is not so easy. Take the calls to boycott the NFL after San Francisco 49ers quarterback Colin Kaepernick kneeled during the national anthem. Offended fans flocked to Twitter to vow they'd never watch football again. But they did. There is no real alternative to the NFL. The 2023 Super Bowl pitting the Chiefs against the 49ers was the most watched of all time.[3]

Bud Light is more like Shell gasoline. It's not particularly unique. Pour a Bud Light into an unmarked Solo cup, and most people can't distinguish it from a Coors Light or a Miller Lite. Nor do consumers have strong preferences based on taste alone.

In a sense, Bud Light's easygoing, generic, inoffensive appeal *was* the appeal. That appeal was now gone. But other brands have retained their inoffensive status. That's likely why as Bud Light's sales fell, Coors and Miller enjoyed +20 percent sales boosts in April and May 2023. It might be easy to drive to a different gas station, but it's *really* easy to reach for something else from 7-Eleven's beer fridge.

There's another reason why Bud Light's sales continued to fall, one that seemed to elude most commentators: the Bud Light boycotts weren't driven exclusively, or even primarily, by radical extremists.

Certainly, the most politically devout patrons were the most dissatisfied with Bud Light's recent brand strategy.[4] And the noisiest. But for every Kid Rock shooting bullets into Bud Light cans on TikTok or gay bar loudly dumping the brand for not being LGBT-friendly enough, there were millions of Americans who just didn't want their choice in beer to be political—not pro-trans, not anti-trans, not any-trans.[5] Michel Doukeris alluded to this in the company's Q1 2023 earnings call that happened in May: "The beer itself should not be the focus of the debate."

Most Americans agreed. A Stagwell poll conducted in early 2023 showed that 68 percent of Americans think that companies that speak out on social issues do it as a marketing ploy. The same study noted that 60 percent of Americans said that if a company does speak on social issues, it better be living the same values. And a 2023 Pew Research Study shows that Americans are much more likely to distrust institutions they view as politicized—even when they take political positions that align with their views.

Trust was exactly what Bud Light was lacking.

Authenticity, logic, empathy. Those three concepts from Frances Frei's talk, silly as they may sound, played over and over in my head as I watched the Bud Light controversy unfold.

Bud Light is Bud Light. It's easy to drink. Easy to enjoy. It wins Super Bowl ad meter awards—six since inception, topped only by its father, Budweiser, which has won eight. It's funny. It likes sports. It's mainstream.

Mulvaney was none of those things. Choosing Dylan as a brand ambassador was inauthentic to the brand. Dylan was controversial. It's not a Dylan thing. It would have been equally weird if Bud Light had decided to send cans to "celebrate a personal milestone" of Joe Biden or Donald Trump. And to make matters worse, Dylan was sponsoring a March Madness competition with apparently no knowledge of what March Madness actually is. Authenticity was lacking. So was logic.

I say this not to fault Dylan. I'm certain there are many brands for which Dylan would be a fantastic brand ambassador. But don't take my word for it. Dylan's got a long list of brand sponsorships. At a glance it looks like most of them are very, for lack of a better phrase, "girly brands." Kate Spade. Rent the Runway. Ulta Beauty. They sell handbags, fashion, and makeup, mostly to women. That's their core customer base: feminine women. Dylan has gone to great lengths to count among them. Dylan's public image is authentic to those brands. The partnership fits. As a result, none of those companies, or their customers, seemed to be complaining. But Bud Light does not fall into that category.

I'm not sure when it became controversial to say that not every spokesperson is the right fit for every brand. But that has to be true. It would be odd and somewhat off-putting to have the Rock sing the praises of a tampon brand, or to have Taylor Swift hawk jock itch cream. Meryl Streep wouldn't be caught dead hawking Burger King, and Kid Rock isn't going to be selling caviar from the back of his pickup truck. Audrey Hepburn, it should be noted, never even drank beer. Nothing about the Mulvaney partnership made sense.

Anheuser-Busch clearly lacked empathy for its loyal customer base as well. When Alissa Heinerscheid called Bud Light's marketing "fratty" and "out of touch," she insulted a large portion of Bud Light's consumer base. Frat boys still exist, after all. And they drink a lot of beer. Former frat boys do, too. And the attack simply didn't ring true. How could the most popular beer brand in the U.S. get there with "out of touch" marketing? "Dilly Dilly" was a cultural phenomenon. Bud Light was not "out of touch" with consumers. Its executives were.

In June, the madness reached a fever pitch. At that point, Anheuser-Busch had lost more than $20 billion in shareholder value. Bud Light sales continued to be down around 30 percent each week. It was clear the boycott was not going to pass as quickly as Michel Doukeris and Brendan Whitworth had hoped.

But in their minds, the solution to their vagary was more vagary.

On June 15, Brendan Whitworth released a second statement.[6] This one was titled "Anheuser-Busch announces support for frontline employees and wholesaler partners."

In it, Brendan says to customers "we hear you" but once again fails to even mention the partnership with Mulvaney, much less acknowledge its mistakes. "We recognize that over the last two months, the discussion surrounding our company and Bud Light has moved away from beer, and this has impacted our consumers, our business partners, and our employees."

Whitworth planned "three important actions" to move the company forward, including "investing to protect the jobs of our frontline employees" and "providing financial assistance to our independent wholesalers to help them support their employees.

"Third, to all our valued consumers, we hear you. Our summer advertising launches next week, and you can look forward to Bud Light reinforcing what you've always loved about our brand—that it's easy to drink and easy to enjoy," Whitworth added.

Brendan assured: "As we move forward, we will focus on what we do best—brewing great beer and earning our place in moments that matter to you."

The bland statement was again widely criticized. It created another cycle of negative news for the company. It didn't help that the next big "moment" for beer consumption was right around the corner.

July 4th is the largest beer consumption occasion of the year. More beer gets purchased and consumed the week of July 4th than any other week of the year. On Wednesday, June 28, which led into the July 4th weekend, Brendan tried for a third time to address the controversy and move the company forward. On his third attempt, he struck out.

He made his first public appearance since the debacle. He did it on *CBS Mornings*. Some pleasantries were exchanged. The hosts seemed sympathetic. They thanked him for coming when most CEOs would be "running for the hills." Brendan repeated his position that there was only one can produced, and it was a gift to Mulvaney. It was uncomfortable to watch; I can only assume it would have been more uncomfortable to be in Brendan's chair.

Then came the money question: "Knowing what you know now, if you could go back, would you send this one can to this one person again?"

Brendan launched into his prepared remarks: "There's a big social conversation taking place right now and big brands are right in the middle. And it's not just our industry or Bud Light. It's happening in retail. It's happening in fast food. And so, for what we need to understand, deeply understand and appreciate, is the consumer. What they want, what they care about, and what they expect from big brands."

Perhaps he hadn't heard the question. The host wasn't asking if there was a big social conversation taking place. He wasn't asking about what was happening in the fast-food industry. He asked whether Bud Light would send the can again. It was a yes-or-no question.

Brendan hadn't answered.

So the host tried again: "So this is part of why you are getting it from all sides. I asked you 'would you do it again' and people on the trans rights side who support that community want you to say 'of course' we want that fortitude. And people on the right would criticize you for saying yes. So where are you on the issue? Was this a mistake?"

This question could not have come as a surprise. If he was going to give a canned answer, it should have been a canned answer that at least answered the question asked.

Instead, it was more word salad. Brendan said things that were true, maybe, and sounded good, sure, but he never said whether he felt the can was a mistake. Judge for yourself:

Yeah, so, Bud Light has supported LGBTQ since 1998, so that's twenty-five years, and as we've said from the beginning we will continue to support the communities and organizations that we've supported for decades. But as we move forward, you know, we want to focus on what we do best. Which is brewing great beer for everyone, listening to our consumers, being humble in listening to them, do right by our employees, and take care and support our partners and ultimately make an impact in the communities that we serve.

The word *yes* or *no* does not appear.

Now, it's easy to second-guess these things when you have all kinds of time to think about it. But Brendan absolutely did! The hosts didn't bring out his high school girlfriend to confront him on why they broke up in eleventh grade. This wasn't some shocking, unexpected question. Gayle King voiced over a whole video montage before the interview started, showing Mulvaney and the cans and the controversy. He should have known.

So here's a shot: "Of course it was a mistake. No, we wouldn't send the can again. We have lost millions of consumers and billions of dollars of shareholder value by involving Bud Light in a political agenda item where Bud Light doesn't belong. Bud Light has never been involved in political issues. And it won't be again. It will be dedicated to sports, music, humor, and fun. That makes it easy to drink and easy to enjoy. That's what consumers want and that's what we are going to give them. That will make us the number-1 beer in the country once again. Bud Light's great American comeback starts now!"

Look, I'm not saying it's perfect. But it's a lot better than what Brendan threw out.

But Brendan could never say anything like that. He just couldn't. Stakeholder capitalism, ESG, and DEI would not allow it. Michel

Doukeris wouldn't allow it. Anheuser-Busch's Corporate Affairs department wouldn't allow it. The Human Rights Campaign wouldn't allow it. The Cannes Lions Awards wouldn't allow it. The marketing agencies Anheuser-Busch employed wouldn't allow it. The NYC elites, sitting in Anheuser-Busch's tastefully adorned Manhattan offices wouldn't allow it. Brendan was a corporate monkey put into a scripted cage; all he could do was perform.

Funny enough, Dylan Mulvaney had the balls to say what Brendan didn't. And Dylan said it the very next day. On Thursday, June 29, Dylan said in an Instagram post, "For a company to hire a trans person and then not publicly stand by them is worse than not hiring a trans person at all." Mulvaney blasted the company for their failure to "reach out to her" in the aftermath of their ill-advised campaign.

In other words, the campaign was a mistake.

Chapter 21

The Human Cost

On July 1, I penned a letter asking Brendan Whitworth to step down as CEO of North America. I was a shareholder at Anheuser-Busch. It was clear to me that Brendan was not carrying out his fiduciary duty to act in the best interests of shareholders. He was accountable to the U.S. business unit, and the U.S. business unit was failing. Sales were plummeting. Conservative and liberal consumers abandoned the brand. Brendan could not answer a simple question about the merits of the Mulvaney campaign.

The inability to answer is at the core of the shareholder capitalism vs. stakeholder capitalism debate. When companies are accountable to shareholders, people can trust that the company is acting in its own interest to generate more profits by delivering great products. These profits can be used to hire more people. These people can create more products and drive more innovation. This leads to more profits, the ability to hire more employees, a company paying more taxes to local, state, and federal officials and a pathway to further growth. Anheuser-Busch historically delivered for its shareholders by building great brands. InBev historically delivered by implementing ZBB.

When companies are beholden to stakeholders, they answer to no one. They succumb to endless wars with endless combatants. It is hard for consumers to trust a company's motives. Is it to create shareholder value? Is it to appease government officials? Is it to get high scores from LGBTQ+ groups that it can highlight in annual reports? Is it to defund the police? Is it to get recognition from conservative groups on political donations to Republican officials? Is it to appease the World Economic Forum climate initiatives?

Incredibly, the same week that Brendan gave his widely criticized CBS interview, Larry Fink stopped using the term ESG. At the Aspen Ideas Festival, he said "I don't use the ESG any more, because it's been entirely weaponized . . . by the far left and weaponized by the far right. . . . I'm ashamed of being part of this conversation."[1] BlackRock would go on to officially ditch ESG as an investment strategy pushed on clients. It adopted the term *transition investing* instead. It focused on investment opportunities related to the transition from fossil fuels to clean energy. "Transition investing is specific and concrete. Clients know what we're talking about," said Mark Wiedman, who is head of the global client business at BlackRock and a potential replacement for Fink. "ESG as a category is a vague grab bag for many clients."[2]

Vague indeed. And now the consequences of that vagueness were on full display at Anheuser-Busch. Not focusing on shareholders would lead to pain for all of Anheuser-Busch's many stakeholders—employees, wholesalers, suppliers, and many other people in the Anheuser-Busch ecosystem.

That pain came quickly. On July 2, the Ardagh Group, which manufactures glass bottles for Anheuser-Busch, announced that it was laying off 645 people. It shuttered two production facilities in North Carolina and Louisiana. An internal memo from Ardagh executives made clear that the layoffs were "due to slow sales with Anheuser-InBev."[3]

Later that month, on July 26, Anheuser-Busch announced that it was laying off 350 people. "Today we took the very difficult but necessary decision to eliminate a number of positions across our corporate organization," Brendan Whitworth reported. "While we never take these decisions lightly, we want to ensure that our organization continues to be set for future long-term success."

Brendan's note said the layoffs did not include frontline staff members such as "brewery and warehouse staff, drivers, and field sales, among others." It was only a matter of time before these people would also be affected.

A week later, Anheuser-Busch InBev reported its Q2 2023 earnings. This was the first time the company itself would be reporting on the impact of the boycott. The decline in the U.S. was staggering. Total volume of all beer sold from April through June declined by 14 percent vs. 2022. EBITDA declined by 24 percent, or almost $400 million. Profits declined faster than volumes as the U.S. business lost brewing productivity and logistics synergies while increasing sales and marketing spend. At this rate, the U.S. business unit would lose $1.6 billion of profits on annualized basis versus the prior year. This would greatly impact the global company's ability to pay down the ~$70 billion of debt still outstanding from the SABMiller transaction. It would delay future acquisitions the company wished to make. Less funds would be available to grow brands in the U.S. and abroad over the long term.

Even though Anheuser-Busch was temporarily protecting some of its frontline employees, its independent wholesalers could not. The more than five hundred family-owned wholesalers, who delivered beer to every grocery store, convenience store, and bar across the United States, did not have international operations to offset the losses in the U.S. They were hit hard by the 14 percent volume decline, and probably suffered similar profit losses as fewer cases of beer were being delivered from the same warehouses and trucks that needed to be paid for. I spoke with many of them that had to let employees go to pay their rent and protect the remaining staff.

For wholesalers, there was one silver lining. After fifteen years, the

Brazilian executives in charge of Anheuser-Busch might have finally understood what Bud Light is about. On the Q2 earnings call, Michel Doukeris said they commissioned a study of seventeen thousand Bud Light drinkers to understand what they want from Bud Light. Michel reported, "One, they want to enjoy their beer without a debate. Two, they want Bud Light to focus on beer. Three, they want Bud Light to concentrate on the platforms that all consumers love, such as NFL, Folds of Honor, and Music."

It took the Brazilians fifteen years, a flawed partnership with Dylan Mulvaney, the loss of millions of customers, and then a seventeen-thousand-person survey to understand that Bud Light beer drinkers just want cold beer and good times.

Now Anheuser-Busch wanted to make things right. And for the first time in a while, it seemed like it was genuinely committed to trying. After slashing Bud Light's marketing budget for years, and real-locating those funds to many failed innovations and smaller brands, Anheuser-Busch committed to spending 3x what it originally intended to spend on Bud Light marketing over the summer of 2023. It announced a "Back Yard" concert series, where consumers could win seats to see rock and country bands like Bush, Midland, and Zach Bryan in intimate concert settings. For the 2023 NFL season, it hired NFL greats Peyton Manning and Emmitt Smith to star in its commercials. It signed a reported $100 million deal to sponsor the Ultimate Fighting Championship, six years after it dropped the sponsorship to go in a "different direction."

This last decision proved somewhat controversial, at least for the UFC. Their fans were skeptical of a Bud Light partnership. In a press release announcing the deal, UFC CEO Dana White said, "Anheuser-Busch and Bud Light were UFC's original beer sponsors more than fifteen years ago. I'm proud to announce we are back in business together. There are many reasons why I chose to go with Anheuser-Busch and

Bud Light, most importantly because I feel we are very aligned when it comes to our core values and what the UFC brand stands for. I'm looking forward to all of the incredible things we will do in the years ahead."

Dana White then went on the talk show circuit to defend the partnership, especially after facing criticism from many fans. He went on Fox News and Sean Hannity's show to list a number of things Anheuser-Busch and Bud Light do for the country. He fired off a number of talking points highlighted on Anheuser-Busch promotional material and seemingly fed to him by Anheuser-Busch.[4] "They employ 65,000 Americans. They have thousands of vets that work for them. They spend $700 million a year with U.S. farmers, using their crops to make their products and many, many other great things that Anheuser-Busch has done in this country. And those are the things that I'm focused on." He went on to say, "I'm very big into law enforcement and military, and over the last I don't know how many years, they've spent like $45 million taking care of these servicemen and first responders who have died, taking care of their families, scholarships for their kids and things like that."

Those sound like similar talking points that a certain Black Rifle Coffee Company uses. . . .

Suddenly, even President Donald Trump was parroting the same talking points. In early February 2024, Donald Trump wrote on Truth Social that "The Bud Light ad will go down as the WORST ad in history. In a matter of minutes, 30 billion worth of market cap simply disappeared from the face of the earth. Will they ever get it back? Who knows, but what a mess!!!" After this tweet, Dana White personally reached out to Trump to encourage more positive commentary about the company. A few days later, during the week leading up to the Super Bowl, Trump released a new post on Truth Social asking his supporters to give Anheuser-Busch a "second chance." His post said

"Anheuser-Busch spends $700 million a year with our GREAT farmers, employ 65 thousand Americans, of which 1,500 are Veterans, and is a Founding Corporate Partner of Folds of Honor, which provides Scholarships for families of fallen Servicemen & Women. They've raised over $30,000,000 and given 44,000 Scholarships." These were the same talking points Dana White highlighted. It didn't hurt that an Anheuser-Busch lobbyist was throwing a political fundraiser for Trump in March where attendance cost upward of $10,000.[5]

Bud Light's 2024 Super Bowl ad featured many of the people who it had hired to revive the brand over the past six months. It featured a Bud Light Genie who grants wishes to friends during a night out. Some of those wishes included hanging out with Peyton Manning and attending a UFC fight with Dana White. Bud Light spent hundreds of millions of dollars buying a lot of friends over the previous six months. It was hoping the Super Bowl ad would buy back its loyal customers as well.

It didn't.

For the two weeks after Super Bowl, Bud Light sales remained down 30 percent year over year. Modelo remained the number-1-selling beer in America.

Then Bud Light got an unlikely endorsement from someone they couldn't buy—Kid Rock. On February 22, Kid Rock joined Joe Rogan's podcast. Joe opened the main topic of the podcast by saying "So what's it like being the dude who took out Bud Light?"

And Kid Rock replied, "I was just having fun. To be honest with you, I was pissed. . . . I was just kind of like, what the fuck are they doing?"

Joe and Kid Rock then discussed the whole Bud Light machine-gun episode and how Kid Rock became the "straw that broke the camel's back" and "the face of the boycott."

Kid Rock then surprisingly discusses how he developed a relationship with CEO Brendan Whitworth over the past few months. He originally met him at a UFC fight. Kid Rock was with Donald Trump in Dana White's green room. Kid states, "I go, Trump? I go, see that dude behind me? I go, that's the CEO of Bud Light or Anheuser-Busch. And Trump's like, you want to go talk to him? Which in my mind, Trump said, you want to go fuck with him? And I'm like, yes, absolutely. So we go over there, we're talking to him. We actually had a great conversation."

After the conversation, Kid Rock invited Brendan and his top executives to hang out with him in Nashville. They came. They spoke about opportunities to potentially work together, but Kid Rock "threw out some ideas that scared the living fuck out of them." He also let them know "At the end of the day . . . I don't feel right taking your money. . . . I don't want any corporate deals. I don't feel right. There's not a penny on earth that could make me change who I am or have people look at me in a different way."

Kid Rock did "break bread" with Brendan and Anheuser-Busch, though. Kid Rock mentioned "one of the things I told him [Brendan], as a friend, somebody who doesn't want to see this brand destroyed anymore. . . . 'You got smacked . . . a pretty hard spanking, and I don't want to hold your head underwater, drown this company and put people out of work . . . you got the message."

Kid Rock was moving on from his boycott, but many people weren't. Rock told Brendan why and gave him sage advice: "People are angry because you didn't apologize."

He even gave him the way to apologize. "Have something that shows light of the situation, but do it in that fun fucking Anheuser-Busch old school, funny fucking way. We're like, we get it. We fucked up."

He then tore into Brendan's disastrous CBS interview. "I was like, whoever coached you on that CBS morning show? I was like, you were coached, right? He [Brendan] was like, I was . . . Gayle King [the CBS interviewer] set it up. She goes, would you send that can back to that influencer? And he goes into this, well, Anheuser-Busch has been supporting the LGBT ABCD. I'm like, what the fuck, man? All you had to do was say, like, look, no, we would not. While we want everyone to enjoy our beer, we understand that we shouldn't be sticking our noses into polarizing conversations. And we understand who our market is. And at the end of the day, we're in business to sell beer, keep people employed . . . [give] shareholders back a return. Fucking end of it."

Amazing. The singer of "American Badass" and "Bawitdaba" was starting to sound more like a disciple of Warren Buffett.

Anheuser-Busch had spent hundreds of millions of dollars trying to repair its image over the past nine months. They bought back the loyalty of NFL stars and the UFC. They apparently even bought the loyalty of Donald Trump. But that is not what their consumers wanted. They didn't want Anheuser-Busch being a political football blowing in the wind. They wanted one thing—an apology.

It seemed like Kid Rock got an apology, or at least an explanation of why Anheuser-Busch made its mistakes and why Brendan could not say anything meaningful on CBS. But everyday Americans who drink Bud Light still have not. This is why Kid Rock moved on but Bud Light sales remain down. Americans love great comeback and redemption stories. But the path to redemption goes through forgiveness.

For customers to forgive Bud Light, there has to be an admission of a mistake. To this day, that hasn't happened. There is a way to do this. A way that is authentically Anheuser-Busch and Bud Light. If they do it right, they could immediately regain trust with consumers. They could also lead the way in ending the corporate culture wars.

Chapter 22

End the War: The Path Forward

A merica has always been reluctant to enter wars. They were late to enter World War I and World War II. Politicians in the U.S. know that wars are unpopular with the American population. Especially foreign wars with unclear aims and hard-to-identify enemies. Vietnam and the "war on terror" are other clear examples.

The corporate culture wars are no different. American corporations were dragged into European stakeholder capitalism after resisting for decades. Covid then lit the fuse for corporate America to battle a litany of political enemies—systemic racism, election integrity, police, transgenderism, the Israeli-Palestinian conflict, and colonialism. Americans are tiring of the corporate culture wars. They are becoming increasingly unpopular. Trust in large corporations has been lost. But there is hope.

According to Pew Research, the most trusted institutions in America in 2024 are small businesses.[1] Small businesses beat the military, churches, the government, and big business. The race isn't even close. Eighty-six percent of Americans say small businesses have a positive impact on the way things are going in the country. This is up from 80 percent in 2023. This broad support is across party lines, with 88 percent of Democrats and 87 percent of Republicans agreeing. According to the same poll, large corporations are now one of the least trusted institutions in America. Only 29 percent of people trust large corporations, trailing banks and other financial institutions (37 percent) and colleges and universities (53 percent). Once again, Democrats and Republicans both agree that large corporations can't be trusted. Only 26 percent of Democrats and 32 percent of Republicans say large corporations have a positive impact on the country.

There is a clear reason small businesses can be trusted—they are the most motivated by profits. If small businesses don't focus on their customers and giving them great products and services, they can't make payroll. They can't pay rent. The owner can't pay his or her mortgage. Small businesses act in a manner that people can trust. They don't have the luxury of spending money on superfluous political activities or risking alienating half of their customer base by taking political stances unrelated to their business.

Large businesses can learn from smaller businesses. Some already are. In September 2020, the cryptocurrency exchange Coinbase was one of the first companies to proclaim that they are a "mission-driven" company. Their CEO, Brian Armstrong, wrote a letter to employees saying that his company would "focus on being the best company we can be, and making progress toward our mission, as compared to broader societal issues." This was in response to a virtual walkout by some employees after Coinbase did not release a statement supporting Black Lives Matter. Instead, Brian asked his employees to play as a "Championship Team," which meant:

- **Be company first:** We act as #OneCoinbase, putting the company's goals ahead of any particular team or individual goals.
- **Act in service of the greater mission:** We have united as a team to try and accomplish something that none of us could have done on our own.
- **Default to trust:** We assume positive intent among our teammates, and assume ignorance over malice. We have each other's backs.

- **Focus on what unites us, not what divides us:** We help create a sense of cohesion and unity, by focusing on what we have in common, not where we disagree, especially when it's unrelated to our work.

- **Sustained high performance:** As compared to a family, where everyone is included regardless of performance, a championship team makes a concerted effort to raise the bar on talent, including changing out team members when needed.

If people were unhappy with this policy, Brian allowed them to take a severance package. Sixty people, or 5 percent of Coinbase's workforce, did. Interestingly, thousands of people subsequently applied to be part of Coinbase's "apolitical" culture. And after a rough couple of years for the crypto industry that saw people like Sam Bankman-Fried thrown into prison and Changpeng Zhao, the CEO of Binance, resign, Brian Armstrong and Coinbase emerged as the undisputed U.S. leader, with 75 percent share of U.S. crypto exchange volume. They won the crypto race by sticking to their mission and not diverting attention to divisive causes. Shareholders were rewarded with a company worth tens of billions of dollars.

Netflix is another company that has weathered the culture wars and emerged victorious. Netflix's mission is to "Entertain the World." In 2022, Netflix updated its famous "Culture Document" to remain focused on that mission. The "Culture Document" was originally produced in 2009 by CEO Reed Hastings. The original document was a 125-slide presentation that has been viewed more than 21 million times on YouTube. The core principles of Netflix Culture include requiring candid feedback, empowering employee decision-making, and terminating staffers who aren't up to "dream team" status. It was updated in 2017, and Reed wrote a book on the culture in 2020 called *No Rules Rules: Netflix and the Culture of Reinvention.*

This is not to say that Netflix hasn't been tested. It has. In late 2021, Netflix aired a Dave Chappelle comedy special called *The Closer*. In it, Chappelle makes jokes about the LGBTQ+ community. Some employees were offended. A few LGBTQ+ groups were, too. They demanded Netflix stop airing the special.

Did Netflix cave to these demands? No. It doubled down on its commitment to entertain the world. To do so, Netflix updated its culture document with a new section: "Netflix Culture—Seeking Excellence." They added specific commentary on "Artistic Expression." Netflix explained that they will not "censor specific artists or voices" even if employees consider the content "harmful."

The section explains: "Entertaining the world is an amazing opportunity and also a challenge because viewers have very different tastes and points of view. So we offer a wide variety of TV shows and movies, some of which can be provocative. . . . To help members make informed choices about what to watch, we offer ratings, content warnings and easy to use parental controls.

"Not everyone will like—or agree with—everything on our service," the Artistic Expression section continues. "While every title is different, we approach them based on the same set of principles: we support the artistic expression of the creators we choose to work with; we program for a diversity of audiences and tastes; and we let viewers decide what's appropriate for them, versus having Netflix censor specific artists or voices."

The section ends, "As employees we support the principle that Netflix offers a diversity of stories, even if we find some titles counter to our own personal values. Depending on your role, you may need to work on titles you perceive to be harmful. If you'd find it hard to support our content breadth, Netflix may not be the best place for you."

Simple. Netflix is going to put out a lot of content. Some of the content might be more liberal. Some might be conservative. What is funny to one person might be offensive to another. Netflix is not going to police this, though. People can police it for themselves. This is a customer-centric view as the customer ultimately decides what gets watched, not Netflix employees. Netflix subscriber numbers surged over the next two years. More than 30 million more consumers signed up for their services. Netflix's stock tripled in the twenty-four months after the "Seeking Excellence" document was released.

So let me ask you this: If a tech company based in San Francisco, and a media company based in L.A. can issue statements that keep them out of political issues, why can't a beer company headquartered in St. Louis (or even NYC) do the same? It can. And it should.

Many companies already have. In the summer of 2024, Tractor Supply, John Deere, Ford, Harley Davidson, and Lowe's all backed off their DEI policies. So did Jack Daniel's and even AB InBev's archrival Molson-Coors. They've promised to stop submitting data to LGBTQ+ groups like the Human Rights Campaign. They're no longer using supplier set-asides to favor diverse business owners over those who are not. They're dropping hiring targets based on race, gender, and sexual orientation. Instead, they're focused on their business.

Incredibly, the backlash has been minimal. Indeed, one poll showed 78 percent of Tractor Supply's customers cheered the move—a group that included a roughly equal number of Republicans and Democrats. Most people, regardless of political affiliation, understand that businesses exist to conduct business.

Sure, AB InBev could keep digging its heels in. InBev doesn't need Bud Light. It's a global company with many brands in many countries. Its Central American region has surpassed the North American region in both revenue and profitability anyway. Michelob Ultra has surpassed Bud Light as Anheuser-Busch's largest brand by revenue in the U.S. (but Ultra is still number 2 to Modelo). Short term, Anheuser-Busch InBev can continue to find ways to cut marketing costs, pay down its debt, and eventually acquire another large company. It doesn't need Bud Light to do this.

But that kind of thinking is shortsighted. Bud Light is an American icon. It was the crown jewel of Anheuser-Busch and the cornerstone of AB InBev's portfolio. Tossing Bud Light aside at the first sign of turbulence not only puts its longtime cash cow out to pasture, but undermines the very foundation of the company. If AB InBev does not learn from its mistakes, if it does not learn to respect the brands that it has now inherited and the customers who consume them, its entire suite of brands is at risk.

And Bud Light needs Anheuser-Busch InBev, too. So do the hundreds of other owned brands (and future acquired brands), thousands of wholesalers around the world, and millions (probably billions) of consumers. This is a company that owns brands that are synonymous with great times and good people. But brands don't last forever unless companies focus on making them excellent and irreplaceable. This leads to volume growth. Revenue growth. Employment growth. Profitability growth. Cost-cutting becomes secondary. This is the only way to sustainably grow a consumer company in the long run. This is the real "infinite game" that Anheuser-Busch InBev needs to be playing. And they need to have the right players to compete.

Bud Light has become the poster child of everything that has gone wrong with the stakeholder capitalism movement and large corporations going to war against perceived social injustices. The company lost millions of customers, shed billions of dollars of shareholder value, laid off thousands of employees across the Anheuser-Busch ecosystem, damaged its reputation, and exacerbated a contested political issue in the U.S. Almost every Anheuser-Busch stakeholder lost trust in the company. Now it is time to restore trust in Anheuser-Busch and American shareholder capitalism. They can do it in a much larger way than companies like Coinbase, Netflix, John Deere, or Harley Davidson can since those companies never experienced the intense public debate surrounding their choices. They can even do it as a Brazilian-led, European-headquartered, and NYC-centered organization, because the company historically looked to the U.S. for direction and best practices. Here's how Anheuser-Busch can do it.

First, they need to be crystal clear about the mission of Anheuser-Busch. Like Coinbase, which declared that it is a "Mission Driven" organization, Anheuser-Busch needs to do the same. If its mission is to "Dream Big to Create a Future with More Cheers," great. That seems like a fine mission. I want to live in a world where there are "more cheers." I bet many other Anheuser-Busch customers do as well.

Then, like Netflix, they need to be crystal clear how they are going to achieve this mission. Netflix did it with their "Netflix Culture—Seeking Excellence" document. They clearly state how they are going to serve ALL customers. Here is how Anheuser-Busch could adopt almost the same language that Netflix has for its "Artistic Expression" section for its beers. It could be called "Beer Me." It could be serious, but also light-hearted like many of the beers Anheuser-Busch brands. It could look something like this:

"Creating a future with more cheers is an amazing opportunity and also a challenge because drinkers have very different tastes and points of view. So we offer a wide variety of beers, wines, spirits, and non-alcoholic beverages, some of which can be provocative, some of which might be fratty and out of touch. To help customers make informed choices about what to drink, our marketing teams create content that is authentic to each brand and remarkable in the minds of our consumers.

"Not everyone will like—or agree with—everything our products sponsor or promote," the "Beer Me" section could continue. "While every beer is different, we approach them based on the same set of principles: we support the authentic nature of each beer we choose to brew; we brew for a diversity of audiences and tastes; and we let drinkers decide what's appropriate for them. Brands like Busch Light are for hunters, fishermen, and farmers who want to 'crack a cold one.' Michelob Ultra is for athletes who understand 'it's only worth it if you enjoy it.' Bud Light is going to be 'easy to drink, easy to enjoy,' which means it will stick to platforms like sports and music and do it in a hopefully funny, but unapologetic manner. Anheuser-Busch–owned craft brands like Elysian and Goose Island will brew more progressive beers like 'Sounds Queer I'm In Wheat Ale [which is a real beer brewed by Goose Island, highly rated and apparently quite good].' Why? Because those brands have always had a more progressive and urban customer base. Anheuser-Busch will work to ensure these brands remain authentic and innovate to reach additional consumers. We hope at least one of our brands appeals to you, the consumer."

In this announcement, maybe they highlight that they have just signed a new distribution partnership with Black Rifle Coffee Company to serve customers who don't drink alcohol. There are more and more people limiting their alcohol intake, so this could be a new growth avenue. They can announce that they are bringing a brand that "serves coffee and culture to people who love America" to more stores nationwide. If people want to support veterans, law enforcement, and first responders, buy Black Rifle coffee. If not, don't. Anheuser-Busch also had a relationship with Starbucks to brew and distribute Teavana teas. AB InBev lets the consumer decide.

They should throw in the final Netflix paragraph for good measure: "As employees we support the principle that Anheuser-Busch offers a diversity of beers, even if we find some beers counter to our own personal values. Depending on your role, you may need to work on brands you perceive to be harmful. If you'd find it hard to support our portfolio breadth, Anheuser-Busch may not be the best place for you."

This seems reasonable. It worked for Netflix. It should work for Anheuser-Busch. People can trust that Anheuser-Busch is going to brew a ton of beers for every different consumer. This allows them to be true to who they are and push back against stakeholders who demand that all brands be everything to everyone.

And there will still be times when the company screws up marketing. Brand teams don't hit the mark 100 percent of the time with their campaigns. When they don't, they can find an authentic way to admit mistakes.

Bud Light recently hired comedian Shane Gillis as a spokesperson. Shane is probably the perfect spokesperson for Bud Light. Not only is he one of the most popular comedians in the world, but he had a "Bud Light" moment not too long ago. In 2019, Shane was hired as a cast member for *Saturday Night Live*. His tenure lasted only a few days after a clip of him using an anti-Asian slur on his podcast went viral. He was subsequently fired and then received more backlash as other clips of him using offensive language surfaced.

Shane apologized. "I'm a comedian who pushes boundaries," he said in a written statement. "I sometimes miss. If you go through my 10 years of comedy, most of it bad, you're going to find a lot of bad misses. I'm happy to apologize to anyone who's actually offended by anything I've said. . . . My intention is never to hurt anyone but I am trying to be the best comedian I can be and sometimes that requires risks." He pokes fun at the situation at the end by saying, "I was always an *In Living Color* fan anyways," referencing SNL's one-time sketch comedy competitor.

Shane bounced back in a big way. He released a stand-up special on YouTube in 2021 that has more than 23 million views. He landed a Netflix comedy special in 2023 called *Beautiful Dogs*. And he returned to host *Saturday Night Live* in 2024. He is once again one of the most popular comedians in the world. That is quite the comeback.

What can Bud Light learn from its newest spokesman? First, it could issue a simple apology to "anyone who's actually offended" by comments former Bud Light VP of Marketing Alissa Heinerscheid said referring to Bud Light as a "fratty" and "out of touch" brand.

But it could also state that it will continue to take "risks" with some of the funny and edgy marketing it has always been known for. Heck, in the 1990s, Bud Light probably had the first "transgender" commercial of any major brand. They had a series of commercials called "Ladies Night." In these popular and memorable commercials, a group of men dressed up as "ladies" so they could get "Ladies Night" beer specials at the bar. They even competed in sports like "pool" to win free Bud Light. It was funny. It was edgy. It was fratty. It was authentically Bud Light. Customers loved it. Sales skyrocketed.

And then when the company misses in marketing, like it did with the "Up for Whatever" campaign or the Dylan Mulvaney campaign, it can admit that also and move on. And hopefully it can find a way to leverage Shane Gillis to "do it in that fun fucking Anheuser-Busch old school, funny fucking way" that Kid Rock and loyal Bud Light fans across the political spectrum are craving. Wouldn't that be an amazing way to end the corporate cultural wars and reassert Anheuser-Busch as the leader of American culture and trust? I suspect many more companies would follow their lead and commit to staying true to their mission. American shareholder capitalism would flourish. Politics would once again be left to politicians and the electoral process. Customers, shareholders, and I could cheer a cold Bud Light to that.

Acknowledgments

Making, distributing, and selling beer is a team sport. I had no idea that writing a book would equally be a team sport. There are endless people to thank.

I want to first thank God for the countless blessings I have had in life, including my time at AB InBev. I had no idea that my time at AB InBev would result in this book and an opportunity to share the merits of American free market shareholder capitalism with a broader audience, but that was part of God's plan all along.

I want to thank my mom and dad for their never-ending support. I am incredibly lucky to have a mom who is a teacher and a dad who is an entrepreneur. My mom instilled a strong sense of learning and curiosity, and my dad taught me a strong work ethic. Both were necessary to write over 80,000 words while building a business and juggling a family. Also, thank you for looking the other way when I turned my high school bedroom into a bar with all the neon beer signs.

I want to thank my brothers, Chris and Brad, and sister-in-law Jacque for being lifelong friends and being part of so many fun memories—many of which were included in this book—throughout high school, college, and the present day.

I want to thank all of my high school, college, and business school friends who have shared more beers and good times with me than most. I especially want to thank Hank Davis, Jordan Weidner, and Michael Heekin for dreaming up the Bud Lightning campaign after a few beers in Montana. I still owe you a few drinks.

I want to thank many of the great people I worked with at Anheuser-Busch. I spoke with a number of you while writing this book, and you reminded me of the fun we had working for "The Best Beer Company, Bringing People Together, for a Better World." I hope Anheuser-Busch brings people together again.

I want to thank all of the independent beer wholesalers I partnered with during my time at Anheuser-Busch. No system embodies the "Making Friends Is Our Business" mantra like you. I hope that this book helps revive sales and sets up your businesses for generations of future growth.

I want to thank my Strive co-founder, Vivek Ramaswamy, for helping me rediscover my passion for writing and for his advice on how to write a compelling narrative.

I want to thank my book agent, Keith Urbahn, and the entire team at Javelin for encouraging me to submit a book outline and a sample chapter to see if anyone might be interested in publishing this story.

I want to thank Simon & Schuster—and especially my editor, Paul Choix, and publicist, Jill Siegel—for taking a chance on a first-time author. I could not have asked for a better publishing team as they provided great feedback and support throughout the process.

I want to thank my editor and researcher, Stephanie Solomon, for getting the book into acceptable shape for Simon & Schuster. Stephanie has been a dream to work with since we partnered on numerous pieces at Strive. There is no one better to write on the issues of stakeholder capitalism, and I suspect there is now no one better to write about the history of Anheuser-Busch and beer.

I want to thank the numerous people who provided feedback on various drafts of the book. To my brother-in-law Adam: you spent more time than anyone. I tried my best to edit out as many of Kid Rock's "f-bombs" as I could. Hopefully you like the final product. To Craig Baum, my business school classmate, who knocked out my two front teeth in the racquetball game before my AB InBev interview: we are now even! To Griffin Schroeder: rearranging the opening chapters was the right call. To Cameron Fine: hopefully my voice came through in the stories and the final draft makes you laugh. And finally, to Professor Robert Eccles: thanks for the great discussions and keeping me honest about the merits of American free market shareholder capitalism!

I want to thank my wonderful kids, Graham, Eden, and Brooks. I predominantly wrote this book early in the morning, before they were awake. Nothing was better than hearing them come into my office after they woke up and ask me, "How's the book going?" I hope they read this book when they grow up and are inspired to bring out their best selves. I also hope they get to work in a meritocratic world where they are judged by their results and character.

Finally, I want to thank my incredible wife, Tori. Without her, this book never would have happened. She agreed to move to Belgium the day after we got married so I could work at AB InBev. She moved us five times—in the midst of having three kids—over the next ten years. She affirmed my decision to leave AB InBev and start an entrepreneurial journey at Strive. She endured my 5:00 a.m. alarm clock every day for months when I got out of bed to write this book. She has been my chief editor, my motivational coach, my spiritual director, and my biggest supporter, both with this book and in life. Cheers to you, Babes, and thank you for being on this wild, unpredictable, crazy life journey with me. I love you.

Endnotes

Chapter 3: "Making Friends Is Our Business": The Rise of Anheuser-Busch

1   William Knoedelseder, *Bitter Brew: The Rise and Fall of Anheuser-Busch and America's Kings of Beer*. New York: Harper Business, 2012.

2   Timothy J. Holian, "Adolphus Busch," *Immigrant Entrepreneurship*, April 30, 2013, https://www.immigrantentrepreneurship.org/entries/adolphus-busch/.

3   Peter Hernon and Terry Ganey, *Under the Influence: The Unauthorized Story of the Anheuser-Busch Dynasty*. New York: Simon & Schuster, 1991.

4   Christopher Klein, "How America's Iconic Brewers Survived Prohibition," *HISTORY*, January 29, 2019, https://www.history.com/news/brewers-under-prohibition-miller-coors-busch-yuengling-pabst.

5   Emily Standlee, "A brewery without booze: how Anheuser-Busch pivoted to survive Prohibition," *Feast Magazine*, May 31, 2023, https://www.feastmagazine.com/bars/a-brewery-without-booze-how-anheuser-busch-pivoted-to-survive-prohibition/article_00cfc35e-fef2-11ed-9dd7-03c38231f703.html.

6   Mary Beth Skylis, "How the Budweiser Clydesdales Became a Commercial Success," *Mental Floss*, February 6, 2023, https://www.mentalfloss.com/posts/budweiser-clydesdales-history.

7   "History," Budweiser.com, Anheuser-Busch, https://us.budweiser.com/history.

8   Jeannette Cooperman, "Royal Tease: Bill Knoedelseder Finds the Busch Family Story No One's Told," *St. Louis Magazine*, November 29, 2012, https://www.stlmag.com/dining/Royal-Tease-Bill-Knoedelseder-Finds-the-Busch-Family-Story-No-Ones-Told.

9   Patricia Sellers and Barbara C. Loos, "How Busch Wins in a Doggy Market," *Fortune Magazine*, June 22, 1987, https://money.cnn.com/magazines/fortune/fortune_archive/1987/06/22/69168/index.htm.

10 "Taplines: How the Light Beer Wars Began," *Vinepair*, podcast audio, April 19, 2023, https://vinepair.com/taplines-podcast/light-beer-wars.

11 Tom Szaroleta and Gary T. Mills, "A history of Budweiser Clydesdales Super Bowl commercials," *Florida Times-Union*, January 24, 2017, www.jacksonville.com/story /entertainment/local/2017/01/24/history-budweiser-clydesdales-super-bowl -commercials/15740003007.

12 Alan Siegel, " 'Bud-weis-er': the origin story of the Super Bowl–famous Budweiser Frogs," *USA Today*, January 13, 2015, https://admeter.usatoday.com/2015/01/13 /budweiser-frogs-super-bowl-commercial.

13 "Looking back at historic Bud Light sports sponsorships," *Sports Business Journal*, June 11, 2007, https://www.sportsbusinessjournal.com/Journal/Issues/2007 /06/11/SBJ-In-Depth/Looking-Back-At-Historic-Bud-Light-Sports-Sponsor ships.aspx.

14 Bruce Weber, "Party Cove: Wild in the Ozarks," *The New York Times*, July 22, 2005, https://www.nytimes.com/2005/07/22/travel/escapes/party-cove-wild-in-the-ozarks .html.

15 Susan Berfield, "The fall of the House of Busch," NBC News, July 17, 2011, https:// www.nbcnews.com/id/wbna43704785.

Chapter 4: The Birth of AB InBev

1 Alex Cuadros, "The Brazilian Billionaire Who Controls Your Beer, Your Condiments, and Your Whopper," *Bloomberg*, August 29, 2013, https://www .bloomberg.com/bw/articles/2013-08-29/the-brazilian-billionaire-who-controls-your -beer-your-condiments-and-your-whopper.

2 Luciana Magalhaes, "How Brazil's Richest Man Does Business," *The Wall Street Journal*, February 26, 2013, https://www.wsj.com/articles/BL-234B-989.

3 Alex Cuadros, "Jorge Lemann: He Is . . . the World's Most Interesting Billionaire," *Bloomberg*, August 30, 2013, https://www.bloomberg.com/news/articles/2013-08-29 /jorge-lemann-he-is-dot-the-worlds-most-interesting-billionaire.

4 "Lojas Americanas S.A.," Reference for Business, https://www.referenceforbusiness .com/history2/57/Lojas-Americanas-S-A.html.

5 Simon Bowers, "Jorge Paulo Lemann: A brewing, banking Brazilian billionaire," *Guardian*, July 14, 2008, https://www.theguardian.com/business/2008/jul/15 /fooddrinks.mergersandacquisitions1?source=content_type%3Areact%7Cfirst_level _url%3Aarticle%7Csection%3Amain_content%7Cbutton%3Abody_link.

6 "Company News: Anheuser-Busch Buys Stake in Brazilian Beer Maker," *Reuters*, February 2, 1995, https://www.nytimes.com/1995/02/23/business/company-news -anheuser-busch-buys-stake-in-brazilian-beer-maker.html.

7 Steve de Bonvoisin and John W. Miller, "Interbrew, AmBev Get Nod To Merge From Shareholders," *The Wall Street Journal*, August 30, 2004, https://www.wsj.com /articles/SB109360028317902890.

8   Thomas Buckley, "Brewing Giant's Strategy: Sell More Beer," *Erie Times-News*, March 3, 2019, https://www.goerie.com/story/business/2019/03/03/brewing-giant-s-strategy-sell/53213433007.

9   Susan Berfield, "The fall of the House of Busch," NBC News, July 17, 2011, https://www.nbcnews.com/id/wbna43704785.

10   "InBev Makes $65 a Share Bid for Anheuser-Busch," CNBC, June 11, 2008, https://www.cnbc.com/2008/06/11/inbev-makes-65-a-share-bid-for-anheuserbusch.html.

11   Neil Hume, "InBev targets takeover of Anheuser-Busch," *Financial Times*, May 23, 2008, www.ft.com/content/2ce956be-52ef-3390-9d8c-96588d6b61ce.

12   Jeremiah McWilliams, "Drastic changes, no apologies," *St. Louis Post-Dispatch*, November 15, 2009, https://www.stltoday.com/news/drastic-changes-no-apologies-the-new-anheuser-busch-has-emerged-as-a-leaner-and-meaner/article_e3fe351c-bb6f-5d4f-85fb-dbbbd9f310ce.htm.

13   Vinod Sreeharsha, "When Warren Met Jorge Paulo: Buffett and Lemann Recall Their First Deal," *New York Times*, April 10, 2017, https://www.nytimes.com/2017/04/10/business/dealbook/warren-buffett-jorge-paulo-lemann-brazil-conference.html.

14   Quelch Former and Julio Frenk, "Jorge Paulo Lemann on Why People Should Take Risks, and His Differences with Warren Buffet," Miami Herbert Business School, August 31, 2020, YouTube video, https://www.youtube.com/watch?v=T5OVGQ-P6Wk.

15   David Kesmodel, "Brazil's Brito Aims to Revive Bud in the U.S.," *Wall Street Journal*, June 27, 2010, https://www.wsj.com/articles/SB10001424052748704853404575322873079776934.

16   Matthew Dalton, "AB InBev Leans on Cost-Cut Efforts," *The Wall Street Journal*, November 13, 2009, https://www.wsj.com/articles/SB100014240527487045762045745530890633506588.

17   "Anheuser-Busch InBev SA/NV," *Yahoo! Finance*, https://finance.yahoo.com/quote/ABI.BR.

Chapter 5: Welcome to Belgium

1   James Kanter, "Anheuser-Busch InBev Aims Its Tax-Trimming Skills at SABMiller," *New York Times*, October 19, 2015, https://www.nytimes.com/2015/10/20/business/international/anheuser-busch-a-b-inbev-sabmiller.html.

2   David Streitfeld, "Housing Crash Is Hitting Cities Once Thought to Be Stable," *New York Times*, February 14, 2011, https://www.cnbc.com/id/41574051.

3   Ron Miller, "BlackBerry phones once ruled the world, then the world changed," *TechCrunch*, January 3, 2022, https://techcrunch.com/2022/01/03/blackberry-phones-once-ruled-the-world-then-the-world-changed.

4   Ingrid Lunden, "Groupon, which has lost 99.4% of its value since its IPO, names a new CEO . . . based in Czech Republic," *TechCrunch*, March 31, 2023, https://

techcrunch.com/2023/03/31/groupon-which-has-lost-99-4-of-its-value-since-its-ipo
-names-a-new-ceo-based-in-czech-republic.

Chapter 6: Beat the Monkey

1 Carlos Brito, "Barclays Capital Back-to-School Consumer Conference," PowerPoint
  presentation, September 7, 2011, Boston, https://www.ab-inbev.com/content/dam
  /universaltemplate/ab-inbev/investors/presentations-pdf-archive/presentations/2011
  /Barclays_consumer_conf_070911.pdf.

2 Anheuser-Busch InBev, *2011 Financial Report*, https://cdn.builder.io/o/assets%2F
  2e5c7fb020194c1a8ee80f743d0b923e%2F5f25b98395af49d89a551c2c62d66012?
  alt=media&token=a779a50e-0dd4-4b70-87e6.

3 Anheuser-Busch InBev, *Commercial Part 2011*, https://cdn.builder.io/o/assets%2
  F2e5c7fb020194c1a8ee80f743d0b923e%2Ff1490353ee7344f1a2b4ffc9af53df7
  5?alt=media&token=a5651b9f-4e9a-4cef-9fe1-afa974deeb90&apiKey=2e5c7fb0
  20194c1a8ee80f743d0b923e.

4 Anheuser-Busch InBev, *2011 Annual Report*, https://cdn.builder.io/o/assets%2
  F2e5c7fb020194c1a8ee80f743d0b923e%2F29f91f55b2f9431ebb31d2ae603e9e87
  ?alt=media&token=b216a547-182d-4ee2-8399-6b3e24914870&apiKey=2e5c7fb0
  20194c1a8ee80f743d0b923e.

Chapter 7: Modelo-poly

1 Anheuser-Busch InBev, Investor Presentation, November 11, 2015, https://www
  .ab-inbev.com/content/dam/universaltemplate/ab-inbev/investors/reports-and-filings/
  quaterly-reports/2015/AB%20InBev_FY14%20Investor%20Presentation.pdf.

2 *United States of America v. Anheuser Busch InBEV SA/NV and Grupo Modelo S.A.B. de
  C.V.*, Civil Action No. 13-127 (RWR), filed January 31, 2013, https://www.justice
  .gov/d9/atr/case-documents/attachments/2013/01/31/292100.pdf.

Chapter 8: There Isn't Even Uber There

1 Luiz Edmond, "Introduction," PowerPoint Presentation, Investor Seminar,
  New York, November 14, 2013, https://www.ab-inbev.com/content/dam
  /universaltemplate/ab-inbev/investors/presentations-pdf-archive/01_Luiz_final-r.pdf.

2 Erin Strecker, "Super Bowl: What was the worst commercial?" *Entertainment Weekly*,
  February 4, 2013, https://ew.com/article/2013/02/04/worst-commercial-super-bowl
  -godaddy.

3 Stuart Elliott, "Ideas & Trends; Proud to Be Your Bud, But It Wasn't Working Out,"
  New York Times, November 20, 1994, https://www.nytimes.com/1994/11/20
  /weekinreview/ideas-trends-proud-to-be-your-bud-but-it-wasn-t-working-out.html.

4 Stephanie Strom, "Bud Light Withdraws Slogan After It Draws Ire Online," *New
  York Times*, April 28, 2015, https://www.nytimes.com/2015/04/29/business/bud
  -light-withdraws-slogan-after-it-draws-ire-online.html.

Chapter 10: Fuel the Future

1 "Wieden+Kennedy Decides to be Good(er)," Wieden+Kennedy, April 19th, 2023, https://www.wk.com/news/wieden-kennedy-decides-to-be-good-er.

2 Carolyn Heneghan, "Bud Light debuts ad supporting gender pay equality," *Food Dive*, June 28, 2016, https://www.fooddive.com/news/bud-light-debuts-ad -supporting-gender-pay-equality/421671/.

3 Reid Nakamura, "Amy Schumer, Seth Rogen Bud Light Campaign Pulled Early," *The Wrap*, October 31, 2016, https://www.thewrap.com/amy-schumer-seth-rogen-bud -light-campaign-pulled-early.

4 Jessica Infante, "Beer Marketer's Insights' 50 Years in Beer: Volume Flattens, Suppliers Grow, Brands Shrink," *Brewbound*, November 24, 2021, https://www .brewbound.com/news/beer-marketers-insights-50-years-in-beer-volume-flattens -suppliers-grow-brands-shrink.

5 Tara Nurin, "Latest Earnings Hint That Bud and Bud Light Might Not Ever Get Their Groove Back," *Forbes*, October 27, 2017, https://www.forbes.com/sites /taranurin/2017/10/27/latest-earnings-hint-that-bud-and-bud-light-wont-ever-get -their-groove-back/.

6 Richard Morgan, "Drinkers don't care about Anheuser-Busch anymore," *New York Post*, October 26, 2017, https://nypost.com/2017/10/26/drinkers-dont-care-about -anheuser-busch-anymore/.

7 Nathaniel Meyersohn, "America is falling out of love with Budweiser," CNN, November 13, 2017, https://money.cnn.com/2017/11/13/news/companies/budweiser -sales/index.html.

Chapter 11: Scared Dinosaurs

1 Geraldo Samor, "Jorge Paulo Lemann is a 'terrified dinosaur.' But he is not lying down," *Brazil Journal*, May 1, 2018, https://braziljournal.com/jorge-paulo-lemann-is -a-terrified-dinosaur-but-he-is-not-lying-down.

Chapter 12: Stakeholder Capitalism and ESG Adoption

1 Milton Friedman, "A Friedman doctrine—The Social Responsibility of Business Is to Increase Its Profits," *New York Times*, September 13, 1970, https://www.nytimes .com/1970/09/13/archives/a-friedman-doctrine-the-social-responsibility-of-business -is-to.html.

2 Susan R. Holmberg, "Workers on Corporate Boards? Germany's Had Them for Decades," *New York Times*, January 6, 2019, https://www.nytimes.com/2019/01/06 /opinion/warren-workers-boards.html.

3 Nyahne Bergeron and Collin Blinder, "How many Americans own a smartphone? 2024," *Consumer Affairs*, November 1, 2023, https://www.consumeraffairs.com /cell_phones/how-many-americans-own-a-smartphone.html.

4 Richard Socarides, "Corporate America's Evolution on L.G.B.T. Rights," *New Yorker*,

April 27, 2015, https://www.newyorker.com/business/currency/corporate-americas
-evolution-on-l-g-b-t-rights.

5 Tim Bontemps, "Michael Jordan stands firm on 'Republicans buy sneakers, too'
   quote, says it was made in jest," ESPN, May 4, 2020, https://www.espn.com/nba
   /story/_/id/29130478/michael-jordan-stands-firm-republicans-buy-sneakers-too
   -quote-says-was-made-jest.

6 Paul Argenti, "Crisis Communications: Lessons from 9/11," *Harvard Business
   Review*, December 1, 2022, https://hbr.org/2002/12/crisis-communication-lessons
   -from-911.

7 "9/11: Mapping our response," Verizon, https://www.verizon.com/story/stories/9-11
   -mapping-our-response.

8 Katie Deighton, "Why Advertising Directors Are Dying to Work With the
   Budweiser Clydesdales," *The Wall Street Journal*, February 10, 2024, https://www.wsj
   .com/business/media/super-bowl-2024-commercials-budweiser-clydesdale
   -advertising-9d0ea096.

9 Michael Greenstone and Adam Looney, "Unemployment and Earnings Losses:
   A Look at Long-Term Impacts of the Great Recession on American Workers,"
   Brookings, November 4, 2011, https://www.brookings.edu/articles/unemployment
   -and-earnings-losses-a-look-at-long-term-impacts-of-the-great-recession-on
   -american-workers.

10 Jan Fichtner, Eelke M. Heemskerk, and Javier Garcia-Bernardo, "Hidden power of
   the Big Three? Passive index funds, re-concentration of corporate ownership, and new
   financial risk," Cambridge University Press, April 25, 2017, https://www.cambridge
   .org/core/journals/business-and-politics/article/hidden-power-of-the-big-three
   -passive-index-funds-reconcentration-of-corporate-ownership-and-new-financial
   -risk/30AD689509AAD62F5B677E916C28C4B6.

11 "Largest U.S. Retirement Plans 2023," *Pensions & Investments*, https://www
   .pionline.com/largest-us-retirement-plans/2023.

12 Sharo M. Atmeh, "State Street Global Advisors Announces New Gender Diversity
   Guidance," Harvard Law School Forum on Corporate Governance, March 9, 2017,
   https://corpgov.law.harvard.edu/2017/03/09/state-street-global-advisors-announces
   -new-gender-diversity-guidance.

13 State Street Corporation, *Form 10-k 2017*. Boston, MA: State Street Corporation,
   March 27, 2017, https://www.sec.gov/Archives/edgar/data/93751/000009375118
   000308/stt-20171231_10k.htm.

14 White House, "Fact Sheet: White House Announces Commitments to the American
   Business Act on Climate Pledge," October 19, 2015, https://www.presidency.ucsb
   .edu/documents/fact-sheet-white-house-announces-commitments-the-american
   -business-act-climate-pledge.

15 Sarah Todd, "Is McKinsey wrong about the financial benefits of diversity," *Quartz*,

July 29, 2021, https://qz.com/work/2038103/is-mckinsey-wrong-about-the-financial
-benefits-of-diversity.

16 Larry Fink, "A Sense of Purpose," *Annual Report 2018*, BlackRock, https://aips.online
/wp-content/uploads/2018/04/Larry-Fink-letter-to-CEOs-2018-BlackRock.pdf.

17 Andrew Ross Sorkin, "BlackRock's Message: Contribute to Society or Risk Losing
Our Support," *New York Times*, January 15, 2018, https://www.nytimes
.com/2018/01/15/business/dealbook/blackrock-laurence-fink-letter.html.

18 Arash Massoudi and Leila Abboud, "How deal for SABMiller left AB InBev with
lasting hangover," *Financial Times*, July 23, 2019, https://www.ft.com/content
/bb048b10-ad66-11e9-8030-530adfa879c2.

19 Ibid.

20 "Bloomberg Live," https://www.bloomberglive.com/agenda-pdf-2.

Chapter 14: Covid and Stakeholder Capitalism: A Perfect Match

1 Yelena Dzhanova, "Trump compelled these companies to make critical supplies,
but most of them were already doing it," CNBC, April 3, 2020, https://www.cnbc
.com/2020/04/03/coronavirus-trump-used-defense-production-act-on-these
-companies-so-far.html.

2 "Google, Walmart join U.S. effort to speed up coronavirus testing," *Reuters*, March
13, 2020, https://www.reuters.com/article/idUSKBN21036R/.

3 Thomas Pallini, "Inside the massive effort by US airliners to transport medical
supplies and mail on cargo-only flights using passenger jets," *Business Insider*, April 4,
2020, https://www.businessinsider.com/coronavirus-airlines-flying-cargo-only
-planes-for-medical-supplies-mail-2020-4.

4 Blake Morgan, "10 Examples Of How COVID-19 Forced Business Transformation,"
Forbes, May 1, 2020, https://www.forbes.com/sites/blakemorgan/2020/05/01/10
-examples-of-how-covid-19-forced-business-transformation/?sh=1a4fce101be3.

5 "Anheuser-Busch Delivering More Than 500,000 Bottles Of Hand Sanitizer For
COVID-19 Relief Efforts," Anheuser-Busch, April 15, 2020, https://www.anheuser
-busch.com/newsroom/anheuser-busch-delivering-hand-sanitizer-for-covid-19-relief-eff.

6 E. J. Schultz and Jeanine Poggi, "Behind Budweiser's 'One Team' Coronavirus
Response: Ad Age Remotely," *Ad Age*, March 27, 2020, https://adage.com/article
/video/behind-budweisers-one-team-coronavirus-response-ad-age-remotely/2246781.

7 Caitlin Owens, "Why the U.S. didn't run out of hospital beds for coronavirus
patients," *Axios*, June 16, 2020, https://www.axios.com/2020/06/16/coronavirus-why
-was-there-no-hospital-bed-shortage.

8 Leon S. Moskatel and David J. G. Slusky, "The impact of COVID-19 on alcohol
sales and consumption in the United States: A retrospective, observational analysis,"
Alcohol, September 2023; 111: pp. 25–31, https://www.ncbi.nlm.nih.gov/pmc/articles
/PMC10202895.

Chapter 15: War Efforts

1 "Intel Statement on Passage of CHIPS Act Funding," Intel, July 28, 2022, https://www.intel.com/content/www/us/en/newsroom/news/us-chips-act-response.html.

2 Tiffany Hsu, "With Impeachment in the News, Ads Are Staying Away from Politics," *New York Times*, January 20, 2020, https://www.nytimes.com/2020/01/20/business/media/politics-trump-advertising-2020.html.

3 Jennifer Maloney, "Pepsi Pulls Ad Featuring Police, Protesters and Kendall Jenner," *Wall Street Journal*, April 5, 2017, https://www.wsj.com/articles/pepsi-pulls-ad-featuring-police-protesters-and-kendall-jenner-1491414509?mod=article_inline.

4 Jenée Desmond-Harris, "Starbucks' push to make baristas talk about race sounds like it could be disastrous," *Vox*, March 17, 2015, https://www.vox.com/2015/3/17/8230723/starbucks-race-conversations.

5 Ravi Somaiya, "Starbucks Ends Conversation Starters on Race," *New York Times*, March 23, 2015, https://www.nytimes.com/2015/03/23/business/media/starbucks-ends-tempestuous-initiative-on-race.html.

6 Kaitlyn Tiffany, "Why Gillette's toxic masculinity ad is annoying both sexists and feminists," *Vox*, January 15, 2019, https://www.vox.com/the-goods/2019/1/15/18184072/gillette-toxic-masculinity-ad-super-bowl-feminism.

7 Tiffany Hsu, "#MeToo Clashes with 'Bro Culture' at Ad Agencies," *New York Times*, December 22, 2019, https://www.nytimes.com/2019/12/22/business/media/ad-industry-sexism.html.

8 Tiffany Hsu and Marc Tracey, "News Outlets Want More Advertisers to Act Like Burger King," *New York Times*, May 5, 2020, https://www.nytimes.com/2020/05/07/business/media/advertising-coronavirus-news.html.

9 Tiffany Hsu, "With Impeachment in the News, Ads Are Staying Away from Politics," *New York Times*, January 20, 2020, https://www.nytimes.com/2020/01/20/business/media/politics-trump-advertising-2020.html.

10 Michelle F. Davis, "JPMorgan, Citi CEOs Condemn Racism After George Floyd Death," *Bloomberg*, May 29, 2020, https://www.bloomberg.com/news/articles/2020-05-29/dimon-asks-jpmorgan-staff-to-help-fight-racism-after-floyd-death.

11 Mark Mason, "I can't breathe," Citi Perspectives, May 29, 2020, https://www.citigroup.com/global/news/perspective/2020/i-cant-breathe.

12 Larry Fink, "Recent Events of Racial Injustice," LinkedIn, May 30, 2020, www.linkedin.com/pulse/recent-events-racial-injustice-larry-fink/.

13 Alexandra Sternlicht, " 'We Must Do More'—What CEOs Like Tim Cook, Jamie Dimon, Larry Fink Say About Racial Inequality Protests," *Forbes*, June 1, 2020, https://www.forbes.com/sites/alexandrasternlicht/2020/06/01/we-must-do-more-what-ceos-like-tim-cook-jamie-dimon-larry-fink-say-about-racial-inequality-protests.

14 "How Brands and Agencies Responded to Racial Injustice in the First Month

Following George Floyd's Death," *Ad Age*, June 30, 2020, https://adage.com/article/cmo-strategy/how-brands-and-agencies-responded-racial-injustice-first-month-following-george-floyds-death/2265626.

15 "Silence is NOT an Option," Ben & Jerry's, https://www.benjerry.com/about-us/media-center/dismantle-white-supremacy.

16 Kathryn Dill, "A Conclave of America's Top CEOs Talks Race and Making Change," *The Wall Street Journal*, June 5, 2020, https://www.wsj.com/articles/a-conclave-of-americas-top-ceos-talks-race-and-making-change-11591349402.

17 Jena McGregor, "Why some Donald Trump supporters are taking aim at Pepsi," *Washington Post*, November 15, 2016, https://www.chicagotribune.com/2016/11/16/why-some-donald-trump-supporters-are-taking-aim-at-pepsi/.

18 Sahil Patel, "Brands Follow Antiracist Statements With Donations. What's Next?" *The Wall Street Journal*, June 6, 2020, https://www.wsj.com/articles/brands-follow-anti-racist-statements-with-donations-whats-next-11591437600.

19 Jay Peters, "Big Tech pledged a billion to racial justice, but it was pocket change," *The Verge*, August 13, 2020, https://www.theverge.com/21362540/racial-justice-tech-companies-donations-apple-amazon-facebook-google-microsoft.

20 Earl Fitzhugh, JP Julien, Nick Noel, and Shelley Stewart, "It's time for a new approach to racial equity," McKinsey, December 2, 2020, https://www.mckinsey.com/bem/our-insights/its-time-for-a-new-approach-to-racial-equity.

21 Zoe Cristen Jones, "Black Lives Matter foundation raised $90 million in 2020," CBS News, February 24, 2021, https://www.cbsnews.com/news/black-lives-matter-raises-90-million-2020.

22 Jason L. Riley, "BLM's Anti-Police Racket Is Coming Undone," *Wall Street Journal*, April 19, 2022, https://www.wsj.com/articles/blm-antipolice-racket-black-lives-matter-mansion-purchase-donations-corruption-police-brutality-shooting-floyd-systemic-racism-antiracist-equity-racial-justice-11650404503.

23 Isabel Vincent and Joshua Rhett Miller, "Inside the $6M Mansion BLM Reportedly Bought with Donated Funds," *New York Post*, updated April 11, 2022, https://nypost.com/2022/04/05/the-6-million-mansion-blm-reportedly-bought-with-donated-funds/.

24 Isabel Vincent, "Only 33% of BLM's $90M in Donations Helped Charitable Foundations," *New York Post*, May 27, 2023, https://nypost.com/2023/05/27/only-33-of-blms-90m-in-donations-helped-charity-foundations/w.

25 Sahil Patel, "Brands Follow Antiracist Statements with Donations. What's Next?" *The Wall Street Journal*, June 6, 2020, https://www.wsj.com/articles/brands-follow-anti-racist-statements-with-donations-whats-next-11591437600.

26 Jay Peters, "Big Tech Pledged a Billion to Racial Justice, but It Was Pocket Change," *The Verge*, April 13, 2020, https://www.theverge.com/21362540/racial-justice-tech-companies-donations-apple-amazon-facebook-google-microsoft.

27 Annie Palmer, "Read the Email Tim Cook Sent to Apple Employees about George

Floyd," CNBC, May 31, 2020, https://www.cnbc.com/2020/05/31/apple-ceo-tim -cook-email-to-employees-about-george-floyd.html.

28 "How Brands and Agencies Responded to Racial Injustice in the First Month Following George Floyd's Death," *Ad Age*, July 7, 2020, https://adage.com/article /cmo-strategy/how-brands-and-agencies-responded-racial-injustice-first-month -following-george-floyds-death/2265626.

29 Sam Shead, "Facebook Staff Angry with Zuckerberg for Leaving Up Trump's 'Looting . . . Shooting' Post," CNBC, June 1, 2020, https://www.cnbc .com/2020/06/01/facebook-staff-angry—zuckerberg.html.

30 Shirin Ghaffary, "Many Facebook Employees Think the Company Needs to Stand Up to Trump Now More Than Ever," *Vox*, June 1, 2020, https://www.vox.com /recode/2020/6/1/21277108/facebook-employees-protest-mark-zuckerberg-trump -looting-shooting-george-floyd-fact-check.

31 Sheera Frenkel, Mike Isaac, Cecilia Kang, and Gabriel J. X. Dance, "Facebook Employees Stage Virtual Walkout to Protest Trump Posts," *New York Times*, June 1, 2020, https://www.nytimes.com/2020/06/01/technology/facebook-employee-protest -trump.html.

32 Editorial Board, "When Trump Posted a Threat on Facebook, Zuckerberg Didn't Remove It. He Called to Help," *Washington Post*, July 2, 2020, https://www .washingtonpost.com/opinions/facebooks-rules-should-apply-to-everyone-so-why -did-zuckerberg-help-trump-skirt-them/2020/07/02/26fc25ea-ba3a-11ea-8cf5 -9c1b8d7f84c6_story.html.

33 *Post* Editorial Board, "Mark Zuckerberg Stands Up against Censorship," *New York Post*, June 4, 2020, https://nypost.com/2020/06/04/mark-zuckerberg-stands-up -against-censorship/.

34 Ina Fried, "Exclusive: Most Favor Twitter Flagging Trump Tweet," *Axios*, June 1, 2020, https://www.axios.com/2020/06/01/exclusive-most-favor-twitter-flagging -trump-tweet.

35 Alex Heath, "Snap CEO Spiegel Calls for Reparations Commission, Taxes to Address Racial Injustice," Information, May 31, 2020, https://www.theinformation .com/articles/snap-ceo-spiegel-calls-for-reparations-commission-taxes-to-address -racial-injustice.

36 Mariame Kaba, "Yes, We Mean Literally Abolish the Police," *New York Times*, June 12, 2020, https://www.nytimes.com/2020/06/12/opinion/sunday/floyd-abolish -defund-police.html.

37 Gregory Krieg, Omar Jimenez, and Peter Mickeas, "Minneapolis Rejects Policing Overhaul, CNN Projects," CNN, November 3, 2021, https://www.cnn .com/2021/11/02/politics/minneapolis-defund-police-results/index.html.

38 Zusha Elinson, Dan Frosch, and Joshua Jamerson, "Cities Reverse Defunding the Police amid Rising Crime," *The Wall Street Journal*, May 26, 2021, https://www.wsj .com/articles/cities-reverse-defunding-the-police-amid-rising-crime-11622066307.

39 "IBM on the George Floyd Justice in Policing Act of 2021," IBM, March 1, 2021, https://www.ibm.com/policy/police-reform-bill/.

40 "Salesforce Pushes for Voting Rights, Police Reform and Criminal Justice Reform; Donates $1.5 for Voting Access," Salesforce, May 13, 2021, https://www.salesforce.com/news/stories/salesforce-pushes-for-voting-rights-police-reform-and-criminal-justice-reform-donates-1-5m-for-voting-access/.

41 Rebecca Heilweill, "Big Tech Companies Back Away from Selling Facial Recognition to Police. That's Progress," *Vox*, June 11, 2020, https://www.vox.com/recode/2020/6/10/21287194/amazon-microsoft-ibm-facial-recognition-moratorium-police.

42 Ashley Stewart, "More than 250 Microsoft Employees Sign a Letter Asking the Company to End Police Department Contracts," *Business Insider*, June 9, 2020, https://www.businessinsider.com/more-than-250-microsoft-employees-sign-letter-end-police-contracts-2020-6.

43 Drew Goldstein, Manveer Grewal, Ruth Imose, and Monne Williams, "Unlocking the Potential of Chief Diversity Officers," McKinsey, November 18, 2022, https://www.mckinsey.com/capabilities/people-and-organizational-performance/our-insights/unlocking-the-potential-of-chief-diversity-officers.

44 Ella Ceron and Lindsey Rupp, "Hiring for Diversity Officers Stalls 2 Years After Big Promises," *Bloomberg*, February 2, 2023, https://www.bloomberg.com/news/articles/2023-02-02/chief-diversity-officer-roles-stall-why-are-dei-efforts-failing.

45 Laura L. Morgan, " 'Implicit Bias' Training Cost Me My Nursing Job," *The Wall Street Journal*, September 30, 2022, https://www.wsj.com/articles/fired-from-my-nursing-job-for-refusing-to-say-im-racist-kentucky-michigan-implicit-bias-training-healthcare-fairness-11664551932.

46 Amelia Lucas, "McDonald's Sets Targets to Diversify Its Leadership, Seeks Gender Parity by 2030," CNBC, February 18, 2021, https://www.cnbc.com/2021/02/18/mcdonalds-sets-targets-to-diversify-its-leadership-seeks-gender-parity-by-2030.html.

47 "Companies Touting Black Lives Matter Face Own Workforce Scrutiny," CNBC, June 11, 2020, https://www.cbsnews.com/news/companies-black-lives-matter-workforce-scrutiny-amazon-microsoft-nike-adidas/.

48 Alexandra Kalev and Frank Dobbin, "How Companies Should Set—and Report—DEI Goals," *Harvard Business Review*, September 29, 2022, https://hbr.org/2022/09/how-companies-should-set-and-report-dei-goals.

49 Brandon Gomez, "Major Retailers Bring $14 Billion in Revenue to Black-Owned Brands," CNBC, August 11, 2023, https://www.cnbc.com/2023/08/11/black-owned-brands-get-boost-from-retailers-like-nordstrom-macys.html.

50 U.S. Congress, House of Representatives, Agriculture Committee, "Hearing on Cattle Market Prices," C-SPAN, April 27, 2022, https://www.c-span.org/video/?519767-1/house-agriculture-committee-hearing-cattle-market-prices.

51 "From Dirt to Shirt—Go Behind the Scenes with the Farmers Who Made Our Black History Month Collection Possible," Target, February 24, 2023, https://corporate .target.com/news-features/article/2023/02/expanded-partnership-black-owned-farms.

52 Anheuser-Busch InBev, *2021 Environmental, Social & Governance Report*, https:// www.ab-inbev.com/assets/pdfs/ABINBEV_ESG_2021_Final.pdf.

Chapter 16: No More Merit

1 Justin Kendall, "Report: Anheuser-Busch Begins Search to Replace Carlos Brito," *Brewbound*, September 8, 2020, https://www.brewbound.com/news/report-anheuser -busch-begins-search-to-replace-carlos-brito.

2 Andrew Edgecliffe-Johnson, "AB InBev's Michel Doukeris: 'We Will Do Things That Will Last,' " *Financial Times*, April 24, 2023, https://www.ft.com/content /ec437651-7b2b-4a46-a1e4-d7f0a6f7722e.

3 Michael Malone, "Former Anheuser-Busch CEO Addresses Leadership, Team Culture," *News@TheU*, September 10, 2021, https://news.miami.edu/stories/2021 /09/former-anheuser-busch-ceo-addresses-leadership,-team-culture.html.

4 *Fortune* Editors, "Anheuser-Busch InBev CEO on Why Global Companies Also Need to Think Locally," *Fortune*, October 5, 2022, https://finance.yahoo.com/news /anheuser-busch-inbev-ceo-why-223000817.html.

5 "2021 Environmental, Social & Governance Report," AB InBev, 2021, https://www .ab-inbev.com/assets/pdfs/ABINBEV_ESG_2021_Final.pdf.

6 "Anheuser-Busch InBev Announces the Appointment of Ezgi Barcenas to Its Senior Leadership Team as Chief Sustainability Officer," AB InBev, June 28, 2021, https:// www.ab-inbev.com/content/dam/abinbev/news-media/press-releases/2021/06 /ABI_%20SLTAnnouncement_062821_EN_final.pdf.

7 "Ezgi Barcenas," *Time*, November 16, 2023, https://time.com/collection/time100 -climate/6333046/ezgi-barcenas/.

Chapter 17: From SUDS to STRIVE

1 Andre M. Perry and Anthony Barr, "Georgia's Voter Suppression Bill Is an Assault on Our Democracy," Brookings, April 19, 2021, https://www.brookings.edu/articles /georgias-voter-suppression-bill-is-an-assault-on-our-democracy.

2 Jessica Bursztynsky and Kevin Stankiewicz, "Major U.S. Companies Take Aim at Georgia's New Voting Restrictions," CNBC, March 31, 2021, https://www.cnbc .com/2021/03/31/major-us-companies-take-aim-at-georgias-new-voting-restrictions .html.

3 Ed Bastian, "Your Right to Vote," Delta, March 31, 2020, https://news.delta.com/ed -bastian-memo-your-right-vote.

4 Ronn Blitzer, "Colorado Voting Laws Are Similar to Georgia's Despite Decision to Move Major League All-Star Game," Fox News, April 6, 2021, https://www.foxnews .com/politics/colorado-voting-rules-georgia-major-league-baseball-all-star-game.

5 "Customer Backlash over Coke Position on Voting Access Concerns Bottlers," *Beverage Digest*, April 20, 2021, https://www.beverage-digest.com/articles/448 -customer-backlash-over-coke-position-on-voting-access-concerns-bottlers?v =preview.

6 "North Carolina County Bans Coca-Cola Machines after Company Criticizes Georgia Voting Law," WSLS, June 6, 2021, https://www.wsls.com/news /local/2021/06/06/north-carolina-county-bans-coca-cola-machines-after-company -criticizes-georgia-voting-law/.

Chapter 18: The Emperor's New Clothes (Stakeholder Capitalism Exposed)

1 "Tesla's Removal from S&P 500's ESG Index Causes Debate on ESG Ratings," Seneca ESG, November 16, 2023, https://senecaesg.com/insights/insights-teslas -removal-from-sp-500s-esg-index-causes-debate-on-esg-ratings/.

2 Paul Mulholland, "Goldman Sachs Agrees to Pay $4 Million to SEC for ESG Violations," Chief Investment Officer, December 6, 2022, https://www.ai-cio.com /news/goldman-sachs-agrees-to-pay-4-million-to-sec-for-esg-violations.

3 Kenneth P. Pucker and Andrew King, "ESG Investing Isn't Designed to Save the Planet," *Harvard Business Review*, August 1, 2022, https://hbr.org/2022/08/esg -investing-isnt-designed-to-save-the-planet.

4 Sanjai Bhagat, "An Inconvenient Truth About ESG Investing," *Harvard Business Review*, March 31, 2022, https://hbr.org/2022/03/an-inconvenient-truth-about-esg -investing.

5 Samuel M. Hartzmark and Abigail B. Sussman, "Do Investors Value Sustainability? A Natural Experiment Examining Ranking and Fund Flows," *Journal of Finance* 74, no. 6 (August 9, 2019): https://onlinelibrary.wiley.com/doi/abs/10.1111/jofi.12841.

6 Aneesh Raghunandan and Shivaram Rajgopal, "Do ESG Funds Make Stakeholder-Friendly Investments?" SSRN, April 19, 2021, https://papers.ssrn.com/sol3/papers .cfm?abstract_id=3826357.

7 Sanjai Bhagat, "An Inconvenient Truth About ESG Investing," *Harvard Business Review*, March 31, 2022, https://hbr.org/2022/03/an-inconvenient-truth-about-esg -investing.

8 "2022 Environmental, Social, and Governance Report," AB InBev, 2022, https:// www.ab-inbev.com/assets/pdfs/shareholder-meetings/2023/2022%20ESG%20 Report_FINAL_EN.pdf.

9 "Corporate Equality Index 2002," Human Rights Campaign Foundation, https:// assets2.hrc.org/files/assets/resources/CorporateEqualityIndex_2002.pdf.

10 "Corporate Equality Index 2022," Human Rights Campaign Foundation, https:// reports.hrc.org/corporate-equality-index-2022.

11 "Corporate Equality Index 2022, Appendix G," Human Rights Campaign Foundation, https://hrc-prod-requests.s3-us-west-2.amazonaws.com/CEI-2022 -Appendices-G.pdf.

12 Victor Morton, Adidas Praises Trans Women Competing against Biological Females with 'Impossible' Ad," *Washington Times*, March 13, 2022, https://www .washingtontimes.com/news/2022/mar/13/adidas-praises-trans-women-competing -impossible-n.

13 David Baboolall, Sarah Greenberg, Maurice Obeid, and Jill Zucker, "Being Transgender at Work," *McKinsey Quarterly*, November 10, 2021, https://www .mckinsey.com/featured-insights/diversity-and-inclusion/being-transgender-at-work.

14 Elizabeth Wolfe, "In Pantene's New Video Series, Transgender People Talk about What It's Like to Go Home for the Holidays," CNN, December 8, 2019, https:// www.cnn.com/2019/12/08/entertainment/pantene-trangender-holiday-video-series -trnd/index.html.

15 Gwen Aviles, "Dad Shows Transgender Son How to Shave in Viral Gillette Ad," NBC, May 28, 2019, https://www.nbcnews.com/feature/nbc-out/dad-shows -transgender-son-how-shave-viral-gillette-ad-n1010891.

16 Amanda Woods, "Tampax Sparks Firestorm for Tweet That 'Not All People with Periods Are Women,'" *New York Post*, October 26, 2020, https://nypost .com/2020/10/26/tampax-under-fire-after-tweeting-not-all-people-with-periods-are -women.

17 "Women Slam Tampax over Tweet Celebrating the 'Diversity of All People' Who Bleed' Amid Calls for Boycott," *Daily Mail*, January 26, 2023, https://www .dailymail.co.uk/news/article-8877425/Tampax-slammed-tweet-celebrating -diversity-people-bleed-amid-calls-boycott.html.

18 Madeline Fry Schultz, "Remember When *Blue's Clues* Celebrated a Beaver Transgender Surgery Scars?" *Washington Examiner*, May 17, 2023, https://www .washingtonexaminer.com/opinion/beltway-confidential/2743435/remember-when -blues-clues-celebrated-a-beaver-with-transgender-surgery-scars.

19 James Factora, "Disney Channel Introduces Its First Trans Character, on Show 'Raven's Home,'" *Teen Vogue*, July 13, 2022, https://www.teenvogue.com/story /disney-channel-first-live-action-trans-character.

20 "Statement on the Global Alliance for Responsible Media (GARM)," World Federation of Advertisers, August 9, 2024, https://wfanet.org/leadership/garm /about-garm.

Chapter 19: Mulvaney Madness

1 Lizzie Widdicombe, "The Rise of the COVID Midlife Crisis," *New Yorker*, August 14, 2021, https://www.newyorker.com/culture/dept-of-returns/the-rise-of-the-covid -midlife-crisis.

2 Jeanette Hurt, "Bud Light Signals New Era in Marketing," *Forbes*, February 2, 2023, https://www.forbes.com/sites/jeanettehurt/2023/02/02/bud-light-signals-new-era -in-marketing/?sh=4e17c6d433b1.

3 Lora Kelley, "Floodgates Open for Beer Ads during Super Bowl," *New York Times*,

February 10, 2023, https://www.nytimes.com/2023/02/10/business/media/beer-ads
-super-bowl.html.

4   "Bud Light Rainbow Aluminum Bottles Return," *Beverage Industry*, June 2, 2022,
    https://www.bevindustry.com/articles/95056-bud-light-rainbow-aluminum-bottles
    -return.

5   Widdicombe, "The Rise of the COVID Midlife Crisis."

6   Alex Seitz-Wald and Mike Hixenbaugh, "Some on the Right Blame Gender
    Identity and Not Guns for Nashville Shooting," NBC News, March 28, 2023,
    https://www.nbcnews.com/news/us-news/right-blame-gender-identity-not-guns
    -nashville-shooting-rcna76969.

7   Matt Lavietes and Jo Yurcaba, "Fear Pervades Tennessee's Trans Community amid
    Focus on Nashville Shooter's Gender Identity," NBC News, March 28, 2023, https://
    www.nbcnews.com/nbc-out/out-news/fear-pervades-tennessees-trans-community
    -focus-nashville-shooters-gend-rcna77066.

8   Danielle Wiener-Bronner, "Anheuser-Busch Facilities Face Threats after Bud Light
    Backlash," CNN, April 20, 2023, https://www.cnn.com/2023/04/20/business/bud
    -light-threats/index.html.

Chapter 20: "Would you do this partnership again?"

1   Gabriel Hays, "Former Anheuser-Busch Executive Slams 'Inauthentic' Bud Light
    for Having 'Lost Track of the Consumer,' " Fox News, April 26, 2023, https://www
    .foxnews.com/media/former-anheuser-busch-executive-slams-company-having-lost
    -track-consumer.

2   Philippe Delacote, "Are Consumer Boycotts Effective?" Research Gate, January
    2006, https://www.researchgate.net/profile/Philippe-Delacote/publication/228930
    946_Are_consumer_boycotts_effective/links/02bfe51091cd1ecd59000000/Are
    -consumer-boycotts-effective.pdf.

3   Chris Bumbaca, "Super Bowl 57 Is Now Most-Watched Ever after Numbers Updated
    by Nielsen," *USA Today*, May 2, 2023, https://www.usatoday.com/story/sports
    /nfl/2023/05/02/super-bowl-57-updated-nielsen-ratings-make-it-most-watched
    -ever/70174195007/.

4   Adam Sabes, "Bud Light Parent Company's Stock Downgraded by HSBC amid
    Branding 'Crisis,' Huge Sales Drop," Fox Business, May 10, 2023, https://www
    .foxbusiness.com/markets/bud-light-parent-company-stock-downgraded-hsbc
    -branding-crisis-sales-drop.

5   Ariel Zilber, "Bud Light 'Will Be Extinct in a Few Years' for Disavowing
    Dylan Mulvaney, Activist Says," *New York Post*, May 5, 2023, https:/nypost
    .com/2023/05/05/bud-light-will-be-extinct-in-a-few-years-for-disavowing-dylan
    -mulvaney-activist/.

6   Greg Norman, "Bud Light Maker CEO Tells Customers, 'We Hear You,' but Doesn't
    Apologize as Sales Tank," Fox Business, June 16, 2023, https://www.foxbusiness

.com/economy/bud-light-maker-ceo-tells-customers-we-hear-you-doesnt-apologize
-sales-tank.

Chapter 21: The Human Cost

1 Isla Binnie, "BlackRock's Fink Says He's Stopped Using 'Weaponised' Term ESG," *Reuters*, June 26, 2023, https://www.reuters.com/business/environment/blackrocks -fink-says-hes-stopped-using-weaponised-term-esg-2023-06-26/.

2 Jack Pitcher and Amrith Ramkumar, "Step Aside, ESG, BlackRock Is Doing 'Transition Investing' Now," *The Wall Street Journal*, March 3, 2024, https://www.wsj .com/finance/investing/step-aside-esg-blackrock-is-doing-transition-investing-now -59df3908/t.

3 Yael Halon, "Glass Bottling Plants Forced to Shut Down, Leaving 600 Employees Jobless amid Bud Light Controversy," *New York Post*, July 2, 2023, https://nypost .com/2023/07/02/glass-bottling-plants-forced-to-shut-down-leaving-600-employees -jobless-amid-bud-light-controversy/.

4 Ryan Smith, "Dana White Defends UFC Bud Light Deal as Anger Grows," *Newsweek*, October 26, 2023, https://www.newsweek.com/dana-white-defends-ufc -bud-light-deal-anger-grows-1838075.

5 Joseph Konig, "Trump Defends Bud Light Ahead of Fundraiser Hosted by Anheuser-Busch Lobbyist," *Spectrum News*, February 7, 2024, https://ny1.com/nyc /all-boroughs/news/2024/02/07/trump-bud-light-anheuser-busch-fundraiser.

Chapter 22: End the War: The Path Forward

1 Ali Donaldson, "Americans Trust Small Businesses More Than Any Other Institution," *Inc.*, February 5, 2024, https://www.inc.com/ali-donaldson/americans -trust-small-businesses-more-than-any-other-institution.html.